Revolutions and the Revolutionary Tradition

Revolutions and the Revolutionary Tradition presents eight European case studies including the English revolution of 1649, the French Revolution and the recent revolutions within the Soviet Union and Eastern Europe (1989–1991) and examines them not only in their specific political, economic and social contexts but also as part of the wider European revolutionary tradition. A chapter on the American Revolution is also included as a revolution which grew out of European expansion and European political culture.

Revolutions and the Revolutionary Tradition brings together a prestigious group of leading historians, who make a major contribution to the controversial debate on the role of revolution in the development of European history. *Revolutions and the Revolutionary Tradition* is a truly comparative book which includes discussion on each of the following key themes:

- the causes of revolution, including the importance of political, social and economic factors
- the effects of political and philosophical ideas or ideology on revolution
- the form and process of a revolution, including the importance of violence and popular support
- the outcome of revolution, both short-term and long-term
- the way revolution is viewed in history particularly since the collapse of Communism in Europe

As well as providing new historical perspectives on the concept of revolution, this book also provides a comparative survey of all the major revolutions in the West over the past 400 years. *Revolutions and the Revolutionary Tradition* will be essential reading for students and scholars alike.

David Parker is Senior Lecturer in Modern History at the University of Leeds.

Contributors: Colin Bonwick, John Breuilly, Robert V. Daniels, Dick Geary, Roger Griffin, Ann Hughes, Gwynne Lewis, Maureen Perrie, W.A. Speck, Marjolein 't Hart, C. J. Wrigley.

Revolutions and the Revolutionary Tradition
In the West 1560–1991

Edited by David Parker

London and New York

First published 2000
by Routledge
11 New Fetter Lane, London EC4P 4EE

Simultaneously published in the USA and Canada
by Routledge
29 West 35th Street, New York, NY 10001

Routledge is an imprint of the Taylor & Francis Group

Typeset in Baskerville by
Florence Production Ltd, Stoodleigh, Devon
Printed and bound in Great Britain by
TJ International Ltd, Padstow, Cornwall

British Library Cataloguing in Publication Data
A catalogue record for this book is available
from the British Library

Library of Congress Cataloguing in Publication Data
A catalog record for this book has been requested

ISBN 0–415–17294–2 (hbk)
ISBN 0–415–17295–0 (pbk)

Contents

Maps

Notes on contributors

Colin Bonwick is Professor of American History at Keele University and Teaching Fellow at the Institute of United States Studies, London University.

John Breuilly is Professor of Modern History at the University of Birmingham.

Robert V. Daniels is Professor Emeritus of History, University of Vermont (USA) and a past president of the American Association for the Advancement of Slavic Studies.

Dick Geary is Professor of Modern History at the University of Nottingham, a Fellow of the Alexander von Humboldt Foundation and a Research Associate of the Institute of European Labour History at the Ruhr University (Bochum).

Roger Griffin is Professor in the History of Ideas at Oxford Brookes University.

Marjolein 't Hart teaches economic and social history at the University of Amsterdam.

Ann Hughes is Professor of Early Modern History at the University of Keele.

Gwynne Lewis is Emeritus Professor of Warwick University, and currently Honorary Research Professor at Southampton University.

Maureen Perrie is Professor of Russian History in the Centre for Russian and East European Studies, University of Birmingham.

W.A. Speck is Emeritus Professor of Modern History at Leeds University and President of the Historical Association.

C.J. Wrigley is Professor of Modern British History at Nottingham University and past president of the Historical Association (1996–99).

Preface

This book was conceived as a result of developing and teaching a first-year undergraduate course on revolutions. Although the students concentrated on only three of the major European revolutions the expectation was that they would range widely and comparatively, an intellectual challenge compounded by the need to assimilate much new information.

At first it seemed surprising, given the immense amount that has been written on revolutions by sociologists and political theorists as well as historians, that there was no single volume that could be recommended by way of an introduction. On reflection, however, it is not at all surprising; for individual academic specialists do not have the range and depth of knowledge required to accomplish such a task. The most impressive and stimulating comparative studies of revolution have inevitably been selective in their range. These include notably Brinton's *Anatomy of Revolution* which covered the English, American, French and Russian revolutions, Skocpol's *States and Social Revolutions* (1979) with its heavy emphasis on the Russian and Chinese experience of revolution, and Arendt's *On Revolution* with its powerful contrasting of the different nature of revolution in France and North America. John Dunn's study of *Modern Revolutions* has wide geographical scope but is limited to recent times. Tilly's recent *European Revolutions 1492–1992*, which employs a very wide definition of revolution and contains comprehensive lists of 'revolutionary situations', is in some ways an exception but it covers large swathes of Dutch, British, French and Russian history in limited space while 1688, for instance, is dealt with in a few allusive words. (For full bibliographical details see p. 14.)

It became apparent that the production of a volume which combined both range and depth would have to be a collective effort. It was nonetheless vital that it was more than a mere compilation of disconnected specialist studies. My own assumptions are therefore reflected in the structure of the book and in the themes which contributors were asked to consider. To some extent my preferences may also be seen in the choice of contributors, although their acknowledged expertise alone would have justified this; on the other hand there would have been little point in seeking out revisionist historians who come close to denying the reality of particular revolutions or postmodernists who represent revolutionary processes in terms of changing intellectual discourse. A brainstorming session was held with all but three of the contributors in June 1998 in order to generate ideas and a degree of cohesion. Once the writing was underway the structure and emphasis of particular chapters was a matter of individual judgement.

Although all the contributors defend the applicability of the term *revolution* to the events in which they specialise, disagreements may be discerned between them and are sometimes explicit. I hope our readers will appreciate as much as I do the efforts of my colleagues to be both informative and suggestive without being prescriptive. My introduction, though drawing on the ideas and material offered in the following chapters makes no effort to be comprehensive. It offers some preliminary thoughts about some key issues without trying to tidy everything up. My collaborators, of course, bear no responsibility for any gloss I may have put on their words. The absence of a concluding chapter is an invitation to readers to write their own if they feel that one is needed. The intention of this book, above all, is that it should provide an informed and stimulating point of departure for the further exploration of particular revolutions and for wider reflection on the nature of revolution in general.

Acknowledgements

Thanks are due to my students for making me think about this book and to my contributors for agreeing to write it. They have been wonderfully responsive throughout. My editor, Heather McCullum is leaving Routledge just as this book is completed, bringing to an end several years of an excellent working relationship. I am indebted to her and to her colleagues for the enthusiastic and efficient way in which they have helped bring this volume to completion.

David Parker
30 September 1999

1   Introduction

Approaches to revolution

David Parker

This book is about the major revolutions which have punctuated the history of Western society from the sixteenth century to recent times. Western society in this context is essentially European society with the significant addition of America, where revolution grew out of European expansion and a European political culture. The establishment and subsequent evolution of the United States is instructive both for the similarities to and divergences from the European experience as well as the way they have been intertwined. Since the collapse of the Communist regimes in 1989–90 pressures on Western Europe to adopt a more American model of social and economic organisation have increased. No doubt it would have been possible to have extended the range of revolutions to others with a European aspect to them; but 'the West' as conceived here makes historical sense, as does the view that it was the source of particular revolutionary traditions; such a focus also lends itself to a book which is manageable and coherent.

A similar pragmatism has governed the selection of the revolutions for each of the following chapters. In all but two instances they were chosen simply because they have been commonly regarded as revolutions by a substantial part of historical opinion. The remaining two – the fascist revolutions in Germany and Italy and the demise of the Soviet Union – have not yet perhaps been as fully incorporated into the conventional historiography of European revolutions, but nowadays no serious consideration of this subject could ignore them. Overall the list of revolutions selected is highly disparate. It embraces national revolutions against foreign domination, the upper-class revolution which installed William of Orange as King of England in 1688, the so-called 'failed' revolutions of 1848, revolutions of the Left and the Right as well as the 'top-down' revolution in Eastern Europe in 1989–91.

Given the varied nature of the revolutions under consideration and the individual interpretations of the writers, there is no uniform pattern to the following chapters. But, with differing degrees of emphasis, they address a number of key themes in order to illustrate and assess the causes, processes and outcomes of revolutionary movements. Placing each revolution in its particular political and social context, the authors discuss the importance of economic developments and conditions, the role of ideas or ideology and the impact of 'external' pressures. The process of revolution is examined from a variety of angles with suggestions about what turns a rebellion into a revolution, the relationship between upper and lower orders and some estimation of both short-term and longer term results. Two rather different chapters – one on the revolutionary tradition in the nineteenth and early twentieth centuries and a second assessing the reasons for the failure of a left-wing revolution to materialise in Western Europe in the years after 1917 – reflect on longer term developments which shaped and then limited revolutionary aspirations.

Revolutionary ruptures

None of the authors represented here disavows the revolutionary character of the events under consideration. Although Robert Daniels draws attention to the limited amount of violence associated with the demise of the Communist regimes and the non-revolutionary way in which their critics worked through existing institutions, the net effect was the political destruction of the old order and a revolutionary shift in the locus of power. There is a certain parallel here with Bill Speck's view that although the rejection of James II in 1688 was a largely peaceful affair, conducted by relatively few people, it also involved a revolutionary shift of power – in this case from King to Parliament. His presentation provides cause for thought for those who think that violence is an essential characteristic of revolutions or that they must have a significant popular dimension or result in major transformations of the social structure. Both Marjolein 't Hart and Colin Bonwick are also firm in their views that the revolts of the Dutch in the 1560s and the North Americans 200 years later cannot be classified as merely national rebellions against foreign domination, although this is how they began. They too were characterised by a profound rupture in the body politic, a transfer of sovereignty and a restructuring of the state apparatus itself. Indeed, these national revolutions generated a more stable and enduring political transformation than that achieved by the Bolsheviks or even by the French revolutionaries who bequeathed to France decades of restless searching for a stable form of government. Most short-lived were the political changes wrought by the extraordinarily rapid collapse of Europe's principal monarchical regimes in a few weeks in 1848. A rapid conservative reaction left authoritarian regimes more deeply entrenched than before – a fact that has given rise to the somewhat paradoxical concept of a 'failed revolution' discussed by John Breuilly.

Yet, as he shows, the 1848 upheavals, despite their brevity, exemplify the way in which the weakening of the old order created space for competing centres of power and brought new actors on to the revolutionary stage for the first time. This process was writ large in those countries where newly empowered representative institutions – the English Parliament in the 1640s, the new French Legislative assembly in 1792, the Russian Duma in 1905 and again in 1917 – were then confronted by rival power bases in the form of the New Model Army, the Paris Commune, and workers' councils (Soviets) respectively. These examples are only the most obvious of those which can be found in the following chapters to illustrate the way in which power exercised by crumbling regimes was dispersed and gathered up by a multiplicity of rival institutions or movements.

The resulting instability may help to explain why revolutions could end up by restoring order through the creation of state structures, which although very different from the old ones, might be just as repressive. However, as will be seen, this was far from an invariable outcome. A number of revolutions produced less authoritarian, less centralised and more representative regimes even if democracy remained a distant prospect. What defines a revolution as such is not the precise form of state which emerges from the battle for power but the rupturing and restructuring of the state and the purposes for which it is used. Put in such terms this may seem to be a very obvious statement. However, it is worth making given the frequently encountered assumption that revolutions are really about bringing power to the people and that those which simply replaced one band of robbers by another, to borrow Babeuf's colourful phrase, had either failed or were not revolutions at all (see pp. 102–3, 135). Once this issue is grasped it becomes possible to describe Nazism, which as Roger Griffin stresses consciously aimed at the creation of a totalitarian state, as revolutionary.

Revolutions and the idea of progress

These reflections bring us to a deeper problem embedded in the historiography of revolutions: the notion that revolutions have been essentially progressive and liberating. Two major, if partially conflicting, schools of thought have been largely responsible for this. One may be broadly described as liberal and the other as Marxist, although these are umbrella labels and inadequately convey the variety of interpretations which have sheltered under each.

The former has some of its roots in Whig convictions that 1688 was one of the major landmarks in the recovery of lost liberties, a view later incorporated into supremely complacent accounts of the rise of freedom and democracy in England. In the aftermath of the French Revolution, despite the doubts of many intellectuals, a sort of French Whiggism also emerged in which the revolution was seen as carrying through the process begun by absolute monarchy of replacing feudal privilege by a rational and meritocratic system. The assumption that the early modern revolutions were essentially about the rise of liberalism and democracy lends itself even more readily to the American experience. In 1959 the American historian R.R. Palmer published the first volume of his *Age of Democratic*

Revolution, a synthesis binding together the English, American and French revolutions within the perspective suggested by his chosen title. A few years later Hannah Arendt (a refugee from Hitler's Germany who had settled in America in 1941) challenged Palmer's interpretation in a brilliant and provocative study in which she argued that the French Revolution had been tragically side-tracked by the 'attempt to liberate mankind from poverty by political means'. However, Arendt acknowledged that it was 'precisely' in the attempt to recover ancient liberties that the French and American revolutions 'had their most conspicuous similarities'.[1]

Arendt also remarked that in the eighteenth century, defence of freedom was synonymous with defence of property, a view articulated by John Locke with great clarity in the 1680s. It is an assumption, one might add, which still pervades much liberal thought today even though traditional Whig history has been under sustained attack for several decades. Indeed the notion that the natural end-point of the revolutionary process is a liberal capitalist democracy has been given encouragement by the collapse of the Communist regimes, a view most famously, if not most convincingly, propounded by Francis Fukuyama.[2] Robert Daniels offers a more measured analysis of the uncertainties of the post-revolutionary situation in Russia; he nonetheless suggests that what occurred in 1989 was a return to more moderate revolutionary principles, the culmination of a long revolutionary process for which he finds analogies in both France (1830) and England (1688).

Marxist historians have long been critical of the Whiggish tendency to gut revolutions of their social content by detaching high politics and constitutional issues from questions of class and economics. For Marx, the English and French revolutions were not just political revolutions but social and economic ones which brought the bourgeoisie to power. As Dick Geary points out, Marx concluded that freedom would not come without a further transformation of economic and social relationships. Nonetheless, Whig and Marxist history are in some ways closer than is often imagined. Marx did not doubt that in global terms the bourgeois revolutions constituted progress. The principle of equality before the law and parliamentary rule espoused by the new ruling class might not bring universal emancipation but they nonetheless represented an advance over a system based on feudal privilege. More importantly, the revolutions achieved the final liberation of capitalism from the constraints of feudalism and made possible a colossal increase in productive capacity which if used aright could benefit all.

Marxists, of course, have never accepted John Locke's view that defence of liberty and property are not only synonymous but ought to be the prime function of government. But they have had no difficulty in accepting Locke as a historical source whose thought was an embodiment of bourgeois ideology. Defence of property rights was central to the early modern revolutions. On that much liberals and Marxists could agree, even if for the latter the historical process would not end with the establishment of capitalist regimes. These in turn would be overthrown by the proletariat which capitalism had brought into being. The poor would inherit the earth, classes would be abolished and the state apparatus, liberal or otherwise, which was required to maintain class rule, would wither away.

The collapse of Soviet style communism, even if it had long degenerated, as Robert Daniels suggests, into a 'post-revolutionary, imperialist dictatorship' (see p. 202), has taken socialism off the political agenda. In retrospect it is clear that the anticipated progress of revolutionary socialism in Europe had long been problematic. As Christopher Wrigley explains in his discussion of the interwar period, Lenin's expectation that other European powers would follow Russia in revolution failed to materialise. Reaction, counter-revolution and fascism prevailed.

Of course it does not follow from any of this that those who believe revolutions have been the result of class struggle are necessarily mistaken. However, well before the events of 1989 threw many left-wing intellectuals into a state of shock, the notion of bourgeois revolution had been subjected to sustained criticism by conservative and revisionist historians. It is now generally accepted, even by those who continue to think that the Dutch, English and French revolutions did advance the progress of capitalism, that this was more a result of these upheavals than a cause. The difficulty of identifying a consciously revolutionary capitalist class prior to these revolutions, despite the evident progress of ideas of economic liberalism by the mid-eighteenth century, has proved difficult. Moreover, as the contributions to this volume show, if the bourgeoisie played a part in precipitating the early modern revolutions so did nobles, gentry, artisans and peasants. If the bourgeoisie emerged as the principal beneficiaries it was the revolutions that made the bourgeoisie and not the other way round. Moreover, in the English case this argument is only sustainable if the gentry and aristocracy who remained politically dominant in the eighteenth century are considered as bourgeois by virtue of the fact that they were no longer feudal but capitalist landowners who invested in other capitalist enterprises. This problem impinges on complex and sometimes pugnacious historical debates about the nature of English society in the eighteenth century.

The contributors to this volume, it will be seen, vary in their approach to these issues. What remains inescapable is that the early modern revolutions occurred in the context of increasingly commercialised economies – indeed in the most advanced European countries – leaving historians with a problem of working out what the relationship was between these two phenomena – if any.

Revolution and modernisation

A possible response to the problem, entertained more seriously by some revisionist historians than the contributors to this volume, is to minimise the significance of social and economic change by stressing the impact of 'external' forces and events. Thus 1688 may be treated as an episode in European dynastic politics brought about by William of Orange and the Revolution of 1917 as a consequence of the First World War without which it is sometimes suggested Russia might well have developed into a liberal capitalist democracy. Of course it would be foolish to deny the way in which 'external' pressures contributed to creating revolutionary situations. In the case of the Dutch and American rebellions which were precipitated by the fiscal demands of imperial rulers, they are self-evident. Both France and Russia were embroiled in what proved to be disastrous foreign policies which sapped the prestige and resources of their respective rulers. Yet there were strong inducements for the Dutch and American rebels to retain the advantages brought by imperial protection and leadership. The unexpected transformation of these rebellions into national revolutions is only explicable, as our contributors show, through a careful analysis of the distinctive social and political structures of both countries and the tensions in their midst.

In the French and Russian cases the crucial question which arises is why formerly powerful monarchies no longer had the resolve or the means to carry out the reforms required if they were to sustain their position as great powers. Gwynne Lewis and Maureen Perrie draw attention to the structural weaknesses of the French and Russian states which both made necessary and impeded political and/or economic 'modernisation'. This is a concept to which they return on several occasions. Its value is that it makes possible an analysis of 'external' pressures which does not merely simply counterpose them to social explanations. Modernisation in fact only makes full sense, as Skocpol has insisted, when employed to compare one regime with another.[3] The problem facing the French regime in the eighteenth century was the need to match the superior economic, administrative and naval capacities of Britain or lose the competition for colonial or commercial supremacy. In the event it proved unable to do this; and the government's somewhat belated attempt at major reform precipitated a series of political blockages which opened the way to revolution. The Russian state in the late nineteenth century was similarly confronted by the need to 'catch up' with Western Europe and likewise ran into a political impasse. For a time a planned economy appeared to have succeeded where the Tsars failed but, despite putting the first man in space, the over-centralised and technologically limited Soviet economy proved unable to sustain the arms race with the USA whilst continuing to raise living standards. It was this realisation which impelled Gorbachev in 1985 to embark on the process of reform which less than six years later ended in the dissolution of the entire regime. All these examples confirm the old adage that states are often most vulnerable when they begin to reform. They may also confirm Skocpol's view that the underlying process which, at certain critical junctures, makes reform unavoidable is the uneven spread of capitalism. For states which are lagging behind, a burst of modernisation becomes essential with a risk that this will expose and intensify existing structural weaknesses.

The revolutionary process

Of course not all moments of pressure and structural crisis lead to revolution. Indeed not all potentially revolutionary situations where an existing regime has lost its grip on the levers of power mature into full revolutions. During the minority of Louis XIV, with the Spanish pressing at the door, opposition to the fiscal policies of the Crown flared into open revolt, involving virtually every social group from great nobles to peasants. In January 1649 (just three weeks before Charles I of England was executed) the young King was forced to flee the capital city, leaving the sovereign law court the *parlement of Paris* in *de facto* control. Bouts of civil war followed. Yet there was never any likelihood, despite a temporary paralysis of the fiscal system, that this rebellion would become revolution. Indeed, given the benefits of hindsight we know that this was the prelude to the greatest assertion of kingly power and prestige in French history.

It is almost impossible to generalise about what does transform a rebel-lion into a revolution. Although we may recognise a revolution when we see one and even take the risk of defining a revolutionary moment when state power is irretrievably lost – the moment of political rupture – there has been no prescribed sequence of steps for getting to this point. On the contrary, what emerges from the revolutions studied here is the way in which the participants often lurched from one crisis to the next so that, even in retrospect, one cannot be dogmatic about the point of no return. Marjolein 't Hart's account of the Dutch rebellion begins in the year 1566, which she describes as a major 'turning point' when resistance to the religious and fiscal policies of the Spanish authorities was fanned by economic recession and political repression into open revolt. But the prospect of turning the rather fractured centres of resistance into a national uprising remained remote until the situation was transformed by the almost accidental capture of the strategic seaport of Brill by a band of water beggars in the spring of 1572. The catalytic effect was immense, broadening the basis of revolt and paving the way for the 'revolutionary meeting' of the Estates of the province of Holland in July at which they asserted their authority over their territory. Even then the fiction of the formal superiority of the Crown was maintained. Sovereign power was not assumed by the new federation of the United Provinces until 1579 and Philip II was not deposed until 1581. It was 1648 before Spain formally recognised the sovereign status of the Dutch republic.

Even the Russian Revolution, which was long anticipated by many and consciously prepared for by Lenin, was unpredictable in its evolution. One critical event followed another to produce an outcome which he certainly did not foresee: the abdication of the Tsar in February 1917, the over-throw of the provisional government by the Bolsheviks in October, their forcible dispersion of the Constituent Assembly the following January, foreign intervention and civil war and the rise of Stalin. As Maureen Perrie observes, the Russian Revolution was a process rather than an event, an observation which may readily be applied to nearly all the revolutions examined here. Even the transfer of the English throne to William of Orange in 1688 which is deceptively like an abrupt *coup d'état* in its final execution was, as Bill Speck makes clear, the ultimate outcome of a complex political process. This was driven by James II himself as he lurched from one stratagem to another in an unsuccessful endeavour either to secure a sufficiently broad basis in the country for his divisive religious policies or to impose them on his increasingly exasperated subjects.

An examination of the elements which push revolutions along from one stage to the next quickly makes apparent the difficulty of creating any general model of the revolutionary process which can incorporate them all. There are of course features which recur: ill-judged tax demands; the refusal of rulers to compromise; attempts, often bungled, at intimidation or repression; conversely, the defection of the armed forces; divisions among the upper classes; divisions inside the revolutionary movement; economic distress; the pressure exerted by the populace as normal constraints on them evaporate; outside intervention or the threat of it. Yet the mix of these elements is not sufficiently constant across all revolutions to make possible the elaboration of a model which is universally applicable. Perhaps the nearest we can get to one is with Charles Tilly's suggestion that revolutions are like traffic jams. These 'happen in different circumstances for a number of different reasons' which nevertheless display 'strong regularities . . . each of which is somewhat independent of the others' although 'relatively predictable on its own'.[4] This conception of revolution as a series of inevitable but unpredictable blockages is certainly suggestive, but the model remains an abstraction which may be thought inadequate.

The French Revolution: a model and a watershed

Historians have frequently taken the French Revolution as a starting point for more general reflections. The sense that the French Revolution offers the most 'complete' example of a real revolution is in part justified by the determination of the revolutionaries to sweep away every vestige of the *ancien régime* and to start again. The most symbolic if not the most significant consequence was the introduction of a new, more 'rational' calendar based on a ten-day week and dating Year 1 from the inauguration of the Republic on 22 September 1792. However, the completeness of the French Revolution has been largely discerned in the fact that by com-parison with preceding ones 'the people' played a decisive part. The revolt of the peasantry in the summer of 1789 destroyed feudal relations in the countryside while the people of Paris intervened first to save the newly created National Assembly and later to destroy the monarchy. With the revolutionary crowd came the turbulence of street politics, a violence screwed up to fever pitch by the threat of foreign intervention, fear of betrayal and a culture of denunciation. Finally, the French Revolution became a European affair plunging Europe into decades of war and setting a political framework encapsulated in the terms 'Left' and 'Right' still used today, despite the fact that in the post-1989 world it is far less clear what these terms signify.

The protracted nature of the revolutionary struggles in France has also encouraged historians to delineate distinct phases which might provide a model of the revolutionary process applicable to other times and places. As articulated by Crane Brinton, this model hinges on the idea that after a 'moderate' but unsuccessful experiment with constitutional government, the revolution moved to the Left and gave rise to the 'extreme' Jacobin dictatorship before the Thermidorean reaction (July 1794 to November 1795) led to the reintegration of many of those excluded by the previous regime. However, for the reasons discussed by Gwynne Lewis, Thermidor did not produce a stable form of government, thus paving the way for Napoleon's *coup d'état* in November 1799. Some historians have concluded that the revolutionary process will invariably end up with a Napoleon, a Cromwell or a Stalin. Robert Daniels on the other hand extends the revolutionary cycle down to the final moderate settlement embodied in the July monarchy of 1830. It is left to our readers to assess the extent to which the 'cyclical' patterns of the French Revolution were reproduced elsewhere and the value of general models of the revolutionary process.

Revolutionary ideology

The prime purpose of this book is not to engage in systematic model building but to consider in historical sequence the most revolutionary moments in the context of a developing revolutionary tradition. But in this context, too, the immense significance of the French Revolution is unavoidable simply by virtue of the fact that it bequeathed to succeeding generations a new concept of 'revolution' as such. Although the term 'revolution' had been applied to political upheavals from the fifteenth century, it now became attached to larger views of historical change which assumed that this was both natural and desirable, in other words to a concept of progress. Prior to the Enlightenment, change was generally thought to be a bad thing, an alteration of a God-given natural order. As the chapters on the earlier revolutions make clear, justifications for revolt had focused on the defence and restoration of ancient liberties or privileges, words which could be used almost interchangeably. At the outset of our period, these were understood to be corporate or collective liberties – enshrined in the charters of towns and provincial customs, in the rights which came with membership of the noble estate and sometimes in the rights of representative assemblies to assent to taxation. Monarchs who attacked such rights and failed to preserve the traditional order of things were considered by many to be abusing the power placed in their hands by God for this very purpose. The difficult question for contemporaries, passionately debated through the sixteenth and seventeenth centuries, was whether kings were responsible only to God for their misdeeds or whether they could be called to account by their subjects.

Nonetheless, despite an outpouring of monarchical propaganda defending the Divine Right of Kings and their absolute power to abrogate old laws and customs and despite the hesitations of those embarking on the unthinkable, enough ideological conviction was summoned up not simply to challenge the idea that monarchs had unfettered power but to wrest it from them or impose severe limitations on its use. Much of this ideological conviction, as the chapters on Holland and England suggest, was provided by Protestantism in a variety of forms. There is not the space here to embark on what would be a complex discussion of whether Protestantism was inherently subversive or whether it was a religion particularly well suited to increasingly commercialised societies. What is clear is that religion and politics were inseparable in the minds of both rulers and ruled. For monarchs, religious uniformity was fundamental to the preservation of their authority, a view which led both Philip II and Charles I into what would might appear to be foolish and irredeemable confrontation with their subjects. For the latter, the open or covert promotion of popery by their kings became synonymous with tyranny or absolute monarchy.

Both Philip II and Charles I were accused of failing to fulfil their 'contract' with the people by trampling on ancient rights. One of the more significant ironies of the events of 1688 is to find William of Orange justifying his invasion of England on the grounds that those on whom authority is bestowed were 'bound to endeavour to preserve and maintain the established laws, liberties and customs' (see p. 55). Even more ironic is the way in which nearly a century later American revolutionaries exploited the idea that prior to the Norman Conquest the rights of the freeborn Englishman had been protected by a system of representative government. The theory of the 'Norman Yoke' had after all been one of the stock arguments deployed by defenders of Parliament against the absolutist pretensions of Charles I; but now it was turned against the sovereign pretensions of the same Parliament which had become entrenched and conservative.

Although some historians have suggested that the choice between absolute monarchy and constitutional forms of government was not a significant one before the nineteenth century, this view is clearly not sustained in the contributions to this volume. Early modern rebels implicitly, often explicitly, challenged the idea that royal authority was unlimited, even if their arguments were frequently diluted by the device of attacking the King's 'evil counsellors'. Moreover, new ideas crystallised during the course of struggle and it became necessary to justify different systems of government. The concept of sovereignty, which rested on the idea much exploited by royalist writers that there could only be a single source of law, could be put to other uses. The Dutch defence of local autonomy flowered under the pressure of events into a defence of the sovereignty of the provincial estates. In England the royal assertion of prerogative rights proved very costly. Charles I was executed on the grounds that he had exceeded the limits of his powers, and James II, who seems not to have absorbed the lesson, precipitated a chain of events in which even the power to determine the succession passed to Parliament.

Another idea which emerged slowly over the two centuries spanning the Dutch and American revolutions was that individuals as well as corporate bodies had rights. Moreover, such rights were rooted not in a mythical ancient constitution but were natural; that is, they were possessed by men when they entered civil society from a state of nature and set up governments for their protection. Colin Bonwick notes how the defence of American liberty developed into a defence of natural rights once independence was claimed. When such ideas, which assumed the natural equality of all, became attached to the Rousseauist notion that sovereignty lay with the people and was inalienable, the ideological ingredients for the explosion of 1789 to 1794 were in place.

These years constituted an enormous watershed, ushering in an age in which the concept of revolution as such acquired a life of its own. It was now possible for intellectuals of every sort, from historians to revolutionaries themselves, to debate the nature, causes and objectives of revolution. Political movements, sects and parties came into being whose aim was the conscious overthrow of the existing order in the name of progress and human liberation; an almost inevitable consequence of such developments was the potential for division on the Left about revolutionary tactics and strategy which became a sort of theology, the cause of endless, sometimes bitter debate and of major splits on the Left, particularly in the opening decades of the twentieth century. The French Revolution also brought into being modern conservative ideology, an articulated defence of the established order which no longer depended on religious assumptions about its God-given nature (although such attitudes can be traced well into the twentieth century).

The 'social question' and 'the people'

Following Hannah Arendt, Dick Geary and Gwynne Lewis also emphasise the way in which the French Revolution brought to the fore the immense problem of poverty and social equality. For Arendt, the way in which the 'social question' displaced the pursuit of liberty which had inspired the American Revolution was little short of a disaster. Whether the pursuit of liberty and social equality are ultimately incompatible is a large and critical issue, beyond the remit of this introduction or the powers of historians to resolve.

What can be said is that, although the scale and impact of popular interventions reached an unprecedented level in the French Revolution, the presence of 'the people' was certainly felt in some of the earlier ones. As Marjolein 't Hart shows, popular pressure frequently driven by economic distress played a critical part in pushing some municipal authorities into the rebel camp. In England the intervention of the people of London on behalf of the parliamentary cause in the early 1640s offers some interesting parallels with the early stages of the French Revolution. Although Leveller agitation might be thought not to be comparable in scale and impact to that of the sansculottes, their social egalitarianism was certainly frightening to men of property. Ann Hughes shows that the gentry who led the revolution already faced the problem which was to confront the liberal middle classes in subsequent revolutions and which became unmanageable during the French Revolution: how to maintain an alliance with the populace without losing control. In fact the only revolution in which the relationship between the revolutionary leaders and 'the people' appears not to have been at all problematic was that of 1688, and this was partly because the former were determined not to repeat the experiences of the 1640s.

In more recent times, although the demand for the elimination of poverty and social equality may have become the central driving force, revolutionary movements and parties have not been composed, and certainly not led, by the poorest or most downtrodden sections of the population. Artisans and more latterly skilled workers have been more typical of both rank and file and leadership. In some cases the deskilling and impoverishment of craftsmen overtaken by the increasing speed of technological change was a motivating factor. But as Dick Geary points out, revolutionaries were more likely to be drawn from those with a sense of their own worth and the resources and time to invest in radical politics. Rising but unfulfilled expectations as much as absolute misery may explain the power of modern revolutions. Be that as it may, the 'social question' did become central to revolutionary ideology. 'Revolutions', notes Crane Brinton, are about 'increasing promises to the common man'.[5]

The power of ideas

The hugely significant part played by ideas in making revolutions emerges very clearly from the contributions to this volume. This is worth stressing, given the tendency of writers like Skocpol and Charles Tilly to concentrate on power relationships and state structures. States were legitimated and sustained by an entire range of social, political and cultural ideas. Chris Wrigley shows the important part played by popular assumptions, values and prejudices in limiting the prospects for revolution in Western

Europe between the wars. Conversely, nothing could be more destabilising than the development of new ideas which sapped the convictions of those in authority and emboldened their opponents. The ideological 'isms' already noted and discussed at greater length in the following pages bear repeating: Protestantism, republicanism, liberalism, nationalism, socialism, Marxism, fascism, together with the daunting concepts of liberty and equality. Of course the presence of these ideas in itself does not necessarily result in revolutions and, as a number of contributors suggest, their development might be an outcome rather than a cause of revolutions. But as long as the political and social elite retained their belief in the established order and in themselves, then significant change was unlikely. On the other hand, when nobles and royal office holders lost their faith in Divine Right, Communist governments in their conviction that they the represented the interests of the working class or the German middle classes became uncertain about the value of parliamentary government ideological spaces opened up for subversive ideas. That such ideas might themselves be contradictory and lead in many different directions is perhaps less important than the fact that it became possible to imagine a different and better way of ordering things.

If the Enlightenment bequeathed to modern Europe a concept of progress, this intellectual inheritance was accompanied in Gwynne Lewis' words by 'the belief that political regeneration could not be achieved without moral regeneration' (see p. 90). The Rousseauist desire to create virtuous citizens, the Marxist belief that the abolition of capitalism would overcome human alienation, the fascist vision of a rebirth of the nation and the creation of a new man all drew on the belief in moral regeneration. They also afforded their adherents an overriding conviction that they represented the interests of humanity as a whole, with devastating consequences for those who did not agree. Perhaps it is this ideological certainty and the political oppression which followed rather than a misguided attempt to end poverty by political means that has really bedevilled modern revolutionary regimes. It was certainly not the often impressive welfare policies of Communist regimes that forfeited public support, while events since 1989 lend support to those who argue that an unregulated capitalism will simply widen the gulf between rich and poor.

It would be easy to conclude on this somewhat negative note. Not only does Europe's revolutionary tradition appear to have run out of steam – at least for the foreseeable future – but it could be argued that little has been achieved by way of greater freedom, democracy and social equality that might not have been achieved by other means. We shall of course never know, as it is not possible to rerun the history of Europe through a computer minus the revolutions to see what might have been. But some words of caution are required. First, as John Dunn has pointed out, if revolutions do not fulfil their declared objectives, neither do non-revolutionary regimes.[6] Moreover, the inescapable fact remains that revolutions occurred precisely when old regimes either failed to respond to pressures for change or proved unable to carry through a belated programme of reform. Monarchs were particularly prone to hanging on to their power until disaster overtook them. Even after the lesson had been repeated, ruling houses could be very slow to absorb it. Parliamentary regimes have been more susceptible to public pressure and have shown a greater capacity for reform. This was recognised at various moments by Marx and his followers, some of whom concluded that the working class could exercise sufficient pressure to reduce social inequality without revolution or even achieve socialism in peaceful fashion. It is arguable, however, that the development of the welfare state in Western Europe would have been much slower had it not been for the fears and inspiration generated by the October Revolution. This was the event which shaped the social and political agenda of Europe (and beyond) for most of the twentieth century, just as the French Revolution shaped that of the nineteenth century.

Notes

1 Hannah Arendt, *On Revolution*, London, 1990, pp. 114, 180.
2 Francis Fukuyama, *The End of History and the Last Man*, London, 1992.
3 T. Skocpol, *States and Social Revolutions*, Cambridge, 1979, pp. 5, 19.
4 Charles Tilly, *European Revolutions, 1492–1992*, Oxford, and Cambridge, MA, 1995, p. 7.
5 Crane Brinton, *Anatomy of a Revolution*, New York, 1938, p. 262.
6 John Dunn, *Modern Revolutions, An Introduction to the Analysis of a Political Phenomenon*, Cambridge, 2nd edn, 1989, p. 246.

Further reading

Hannah Arendt, *On Revolution*, London, 1990 (first published New York, 1963).
Crane Brinton, *Anatomy of Revolution*, New York, 1938.
John Dunn, *Modern Revolutions, An Introduction to the Analysis of a Political Phenomenon*, Cambridge, 2nd edn, 1989.
E.J. Hobsbawm, *The Age of Revolution: Europe 1789–1848*, London, 1973.
R.R. Palmer, *The Age of the Democratic Revolution. A Political History of Europe and America, 1760–1800* (2 vols), Princeton, NJ, 1959, 1964.
T. Skocpol, *States and Revolutions*, Cambridge, 1979.
Charles Tilly, *European Revolutions 1492–1992*, Oxford, and Cambridge, MA, 1995.

2 The Dutch Revolt 1566–81

A national revolution?

Marjolein 't Hart

Introduction

> Truly, it almost drives me mad to see the difficulty with which your Majesty's supplies are furnished, and the liberality with which the people place their lives and fortunes at the disposal of this rebel. (Governor-General Alva to the King of Spain, 11 February 1573)[1]

On 19 July 1572, the Estates of the Province of Holland assembled in a truly revolutionary meeting in the old town of Dordrecht. For the first time ever they asserted sovereign powers over their territory, even though they continued to pretend loyalty to the King. Refusing a royal summons to appear at The Hague, the Dordrecht delegates also decided to proclaim William of Orange as their new *Stadhouder* (the representative of the lawful sovereign) instead of Count Bossu, appointed by the Governor-General, the Duke of Alva. The assembly also furnished William of Orange with the means to pursue his armed resistance by providing him with a more or less consolidated territory, with regular funds for warfare (taxation!), and with a sound political base. Without the Dordrecht meeting the Dutch Revolt would merely have constituted a curious mixture of local rebellions, piracies, religious strife and civil warfare with which the superior Spanish forces, aided by the typically factious nature of urban government, might well have coped. As it was, the revolt of the townspeople of Holland in the spring of 1572 and the subsequent convention of the independent Provincial Estates in the following summer created a focal point of resistance against Spain; this encouraged other towns and provinces to join the Revolt, and culminated in a veritable national revolution. Following Charles Tilly, I am here using the term 'revolution' to mean a forcible transfer of power over a state in the course of which two blocks of contenders make incompatible claims to control the state, while both blocs enjoy the support of a significant part of the population.[2]

It is however necessary to go back to 1566 in order to place the meeting at Dordrecht in the widest context and to give the revolution its full significance. At that time, the Netherlands belonged to the Spanish Habsburg

Empire, constituting a loose federation of seventeen provinces, ruled by the court and bureaucracy of the governor general in Brussels. Flanders, Brabant and Holland were among the most wealthy, commercialised and urbanised regions of Europe; over 50 per cent of the population of the Province of Holland lived in towns. In their dealings with the King, representatives of the provincial elites (nobles, the higher clergy and the urban magistrates) met at regular intervals in their various Provincial Estates. Every year the King sought their consent to levy taxes, and government policy touching upon provincial interests was also discussed. Under Philip II discussions centred on two highly contentious projects: first, the forceful promotion of the Catholic religion, and second, the remodelling of the tax regime.

Both were a necessary part of Philip II's political strategy. In his view, an uncompromising enforcement of the Catholic religion served to preserve the peace, the coherence and the prosperity of the region. Tax reform was equally indispensable, as the Spanish Empire was increasingly embroiled in a Mediterranean war with the Turks. Although both projects tended to alienate major groupings in the Provincial Estates, the proposals do not in themselves constitute a sufficient explanation for the Revolt. Belonging to a powerful empire also brought significant benefits: secure borders, sound coinage, and advantages of scale in trade as peace and order tended to prevail throughout the empire. For the influential merchant class, these benefits far outweighed the attractions of an uncertain future under a revolutionary regime. As will become clear, the Revolt was sparked off by the way in which the discord over government policies coincided with serious economic distress, the agitation of the religiously discontented and the frustrated ambitions of some nobles, whose armed bands roved around causing severe disruption. In the course of struggle new ideologies then emerged.

The following analysis concentrates on explaining how it was that the inhabitants of the towns of Holland – in many ways less radical than their co-revolutionaries of the southern Netherlands – were mobilised in revolt. Whereas the south was reconquered and reincorporated into the Spanish Empire, the revolutionary achievements of Holland endured. After 1572, several provinces in the northern Netherlands joined it in revolt. By 1579 a new federation of provinces under the leadership of the Estates General had been forged. But in this polity the provinces remained sovereign and there was no unitary head of state; the *Stadhouder* received his authority from each of the Provincial Estates separately. For several decades, the independent United Provinces continued the war with Spain, until a peace was finally signed in 1648.

1566: The irrevocable turning point

The way was prepared for widespread revolt by the crisis which gathered momentum from 1566. Religious issues were at the heart of it. In its various tendencies, the Reformation had already spread among a significant minority of both the lower and the upper classes. The growth of dissent was facilitated by the high literacy rates of the urban population and their access to sophisticated networks of publishers and bookshops. The local authorities were increasingly reluctant to impose severe restrictions upon the Protestants, the more so as increasing numbers of the ruling elite were themselves becoming involved in the reformed faiths.

Economic distress added to the tension. In the 1560s a Danish–Swedish war disrupted trade through the Sound, which was of prime importance for the supply of grain to the Dutch towns. Textile manufacture also languished because of English embargoes, the effects of which were felt above all in the Flemish industrial centres. Furthermore, 1565–66 was a period of extreme dearth and price inflation because of disappointing harvests. Nor did the situation improve much in the following years. In 1570 a terrible flood on All Saints' Day destroyed extensive tracts of land, killing 25,000 people in the northern coastal districts alone. In 1571 and 1572 plagues, piracy and an extremely severe winter disrupted the supply of foodstuffs, pushing up prices once again. In sum, the early 1570s were characterised by a sustained economic depression.

This certainly added to the general level of discontent among the lower classes while also contributing to a decline in the estate revenues of the ruling elite. At the same time the nobles sensed a general reduction of their political influence. Foremost among them was William of Orange, who had inherited the French princedom of Orange along with rich manors in the Netherlands. From 1559 to 1567 he held the post of *Stadhouder* for the King in the provinces of Holland, Zeeland and Utrecht. While William had been a favourite of Philip II's father Charles V, the Spanish-oriented court frustrated his ambitions, the more so as the *Stadhouders'* powers were reduced too. Appointments of bishops, abbots and government officials was increasingly restricted to a small circle at the Brussels court, thus reducing both the political influence and powers of patronage of the local nobility. Furthermore, the secrecy surrounding plans for a territorial reorganisation of the Church, involving the creation of fourteen new dioceses and the strengthening of the position of Louvain University, stimulated rumours that the Spanish Inquisition was about to be imposed. Although it never in fact operated in the Dutch territories, rumours that it was about to do so were rife, particularly as Protestantism was making thousands of new adherents, and new anti-heresy laws were also mooted. The Inquisition, it was feared by many of the deputies to the Provincial Estates, would push aside local jurisdictions, and subvert both the traditional autonomy of the towns and the judicial powers of the lesser nobility in the countryside.

Discontented nobles formed leagues in order to oppose the increasingly authoritarian policies emanating from the central government. Most famous was the Compromise of 1565, in which around 400 lesser nobles,

Catholics, Lutherans and Calvinists alike came together to demand a moderation of the anti-heresy decrees. In April 1566 they presented a petition to this effect to Philip's half-sister Margaret, the Duchess of Parma, governess-general of the Netherlands at that time. They warned her and the King – of whom they declared themselves to be his 'very humble vassals' – that, should the decrees not be moderated,

> the people are so exasperated that the final result, we fear, will be an open revolt and a universal rebellion bringing ruin to all the provinces and plunging them into utter misery . . . the evil is meanwhile daily augmenting, so that open revolt and universal rebellion are imminent.[3]

Apparently, in order to reassure the governess, one of her councillors dismissed the petitioners as *gueux*, the French word for beggars. Hence, the discontented and indeed often impoverished nobles acquired the term *Geuzen* which they wore as a badge of honour. Margaret for her part accepted the petition, albeit hesitantly, and succeeded, albeit temporarily, in diminishing the threat of religious repression.

But during the summer of 1566, the rapid spread of the hedge-preachings (open-air meetings) of the Calvinists alarmed the Brussels government. Viglius, the President of the Privy Council, wrote on 2 August:

> The town of Ieper, among others, is in turmoil on account of the daring of the populace inside and outside who go to the open-air services in their thousands, armed and defended as if they were off to perform some great exploit of war. It is to be feared that the first blow will fall on the monasteries and clergy and that the fire, once lit, will spread.[4]

The first blow came on 10 August. Rebellions flared up, first in Flanders, but soon spread to the other provinces, largely provoked by militant Calvinists. Churches and convents were plundered, images pulled down, paintings and tapestries destroyed. In the face of these anti-Catholic and anti-Spanish demonstrations, Philip II's wrath was predictable. A much more austere governor-general came to replace Margaret: the Duke of Alva.

In order to avenge the iconoclastic outburst, Alva created a special court, rapidly nicknamed 'the Bloodcouncil', which made irrevocable the rupture between the King and local elites. Although the council was not an instrument of the Spanish Inquisition, its activities, together with those of the many local 'inquisitions' which came into being, generated immense unrest. Within two years 12,000 Netherlanders had been tried before the council, and over 1,000 executed, including the influential grandees Egmond and Hornes and despite their protestations of loyalty to the King. Those who had reason to fear for their lives fled, among them a significant number of lesser nobles who had signed the Compromise. Estimations as to the number of fugitives range from 50,000 to 60,000. Some took up arms against Alva's rule under the name of *Geuzen,* or *Watergeuzen* when they roamed the seas.

William of Orange, who had been greatly involved with the opposition, decided to leave the country too. From his family lands in Germany he organised a mercenary force. He sought and obtained support for his cause among German and French Calvinists and engaged numbers of *Watergeuzen* to lead privateering activities in the Dutch coastal waters. Meanwhile, Alva moved on with his religious 'pacification' and with plans for fiscal reform, including the introduction of a sales tax deemed necessary to pay for the Spanish forces in the Low Countries. The superiority of these forces and their tactics compared with those at the disposition of Orange at first seemed to be confirmed in a sequence of ill-fated campaigns for the rebels. The indiscipline of most of the *Geuzen,* whose piratical ventures were frequently directed against friend and foe alike, made the prospects for the rebels seem very poor. Yet the whole situation was suddenly transformed with the unexpected capture of the small port of Brill (see Map 2.1) by the Sea Beggars in April 1572.

Sea beggars and the first urban revolts in Holland

In 1571 this town of around 3,500 inhabitants had been home to a Spanish garrison. However, during wintertime no attacks were feared and most Spanish troops were lodged further inland. For several months, a major grouping of Sea Beggars had been able to find refuge on the other side of the English Channel, until Elizabeth I decided to turn these pirates out. The winds brought twenty or so of their ships, operating under Count Lumey de la Marck, an exile from the southern Netherlands, with hundreds of armed men to the mouth of the Meuse. While the magistrates of Brill hesitated over whether or not to allow the pirates within their walls (choosing between possible plunder by the Sea Beggars or a likely bloody revenge by Spanish troops) the rebels, aided by a local ferry-man, forced an entry through one of the gates.

The majority of the inhabitants, aware of the notorious plundering raids of the Sea Beggars, did not wait for the attack, but sought refuge in neighbouring villages. However, on this occasion the Beggars, probably because one of the captains was an exile of Brill himself, did not follow their usual course of plunder followed by a quick withdrawal. The captains persuaded Lumey to remain, and the town was declared for Orange. Several Catholics were arrested and then executed, but looting was restricted to the churches and cloisters; grain found in the convents was confiscated and distributed among the poor.

Only a small minority of the Brill population may have welcomed the Sea Beggars. Most seemed to have feared them because of their rough and unpredictable behaviour. Certainly the execution of Catholics met with little popular support. William of Orange himself was reluctant to assume

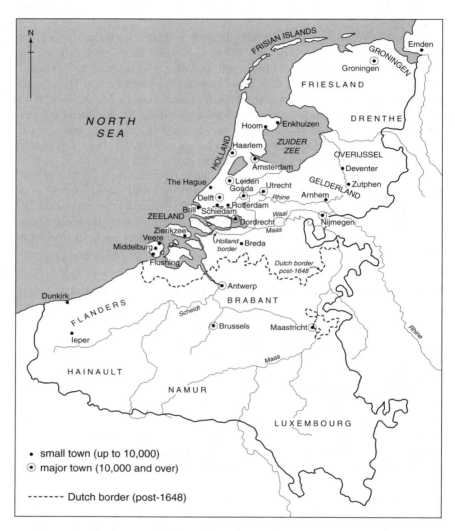

Map 2.1 The Habsburg Netherlands around 1570

responsibility for the capture of Brill which he thought was militarily premature. He was also anxious about Lumey's capacity to manage the
situation for he was prone to violent outbursts which, indeed, continued to
be a problem even after he became Orange's official deputy in July. Yet the
seizure of Brill was an enormous source of inspiration to the sympathisers
of Orange elsewhere. Its symbolic importance was reflected in some spirited
popular verse which played on fact that the Dutch word *bril* also means
spectacles: 'On April's Fool's Day, Alva's spectacles were stolen away.'

Following in Brill's wake, Flushing and Enkhuizen, two other small towns with populations of between 3,000 and 5,000, also rose in revolt. Between them these ports assured the *Watergeuzen* of a highly strategic position in relation to Holland's overseas trade routes. Brill itself brought control of the Meuse, and the shipping of Rotterdam, Delfshaven (Delft), Schiedam, Dordrecht and elsewhere. Flushing dominated the Scheldt estuary, the main gate to Antwerp, Middelburg and many other towns in the south; while Enkhuizen ensured rebel command of the major sea-route to Amsterdam and several other harbours in the far north.

While Brill's defection was undoubtedly imposed by the Sea Beggars, the uprising in Flushing and Enkhuizen acquired the character of a mass insurrection from below. After the loss of Brill, Alva rushed a couple of companies towards Flushing. But, forewarned and fearful of the burdens the troops would bring, crowds shut the gates and expelled the quarter-master together with the tax collector (6 April 1572). Two weeks later (22 April) they allowed the Sea Beggars from Brill to enter the town. Almost immediately some Spanish officers were hanged, along with a famous Italian engineer who happened to be in Flushing. In this way, Orange acquired a strong base in the province of Zeeland.

Enkhuizen was the next town to choose for Orange. In early May, apprehensive that troops from the warships in their harbour might be employed against the population, the urban militia refused entry to two Spanish soldiers. This was followed by the expulsion of all foreign troops already in town, the arrest of the admiral of the pro-Spanish fleet and the confiscation of ammunition and shot intended for the Spanish troops. However, it was not until the arrival of two exiles from Emden in East Frisia, which housed a significant section of Dutch Calvinist refugees, that the armed burghers decided to throw in their lot with the rebel forces. The restive inhabitants, among whom there were many unemployed sailors and fishermen, were then persuaded to declare their support for Orange. In so doing the fishermen may have believed that this was the best means of avoiding the perils caused by privateering for which the *Watergeuzen*, above all, were responsible. When *Stadhouder* Bossu demanded a new oath of allegiance to Spanish rule from the Enkhuizen burghers, the citizenry launched an open revolt. On 21 May the burgomasters were imprisoned and the Orange banner was unfurled from the town walls.

Bossu's attempt to recover the situation ended in failure. In an effort to retake Brill he sought the support of the neighbouring town of Dordrecht. But the gates remained shut; the authorities were both fearful of the reaction of the people and doubtful of the reliability of the citizen militia. All they would do was to provide three vessels to carry the soldiers to Brill. Then, on 8 April, Bossu demanded passage through Rotterdam. The magistrates gave permission but the crowds were so determined to keep the Spanish out that the gates were blocked. Not even the citizen militia, which here remained loyal to the authorities, could control them. After a day, through the mediation of a popular priest, the gates were finally opened, but the troops were so vexed that they savagely butchered some Rotterdammers on the spot. The casualties probably numbered forty, a figure that soon mushroomed to 400 in rebel propaganda. According to the lines of a sixteenth century song: 'The [Rotterdam] streets were red of blood, like herrings they were cured.'[5] Never before had Spanish soldiers struck so violently at the populace of one of the major towns in the north. News of the atrocities intensified anti-Spanish sentiment throughout the province of Holland.

Spread and consolidation of the 1572 Revolt

Most significantly, the massacre at Rotterdam consolidated the revolutionary disposition of many militia forces who were henceforth determined to keep the Spanish troops out of their towns. Many urban governments could no longer rely on their own armed forces. Militia captains were normally appointed by the town council, but some militias now began to choose new captains from their midst. In Hoorn, a town of about 5,000 inhabitants, the new captains of the urban militia formed a so-called Broad Council with the town councillors. From this board, a municipal *coup* was staged on 18 June in favour of Orange. By this time, local revolts were coming thick and fast. The exhausted and despairing Bossu wrote to Alva that 'even the stones rebel against me'.[6]

There were of course multiple and varied reasons for joining the Revolt, as can be shown by analysing the process of mobilisation in the larger towns; that is, of over 10,000 inhabitants. Gouda, the first of these to join the Revolt, was devoutly Catholic, with few adherents of the new religion. In 1566 it had not experienced any iconoclast revolts. Yet the insistence of the Brussels government on its uncompromising anti-heresy laws divided the community and exacerbated personal rivalries. The banishment and execution of so-called dissenters provoked profound anxiety among people and magistrates alike. Furthermore, the contraction of the economy reduced the amount of trade on the Gouda market, making large groups of the population extremely vulnerable to rebel propaganda.

News of the Rotterdam massacre led to attacks by a panicky crowd on the local castle, which was a Spanish stronghold, and on the Franciscan monastery whose friars were popularly associated with the Inquisition. These riots were suppressed with the assistance of the citizen militia. Yet at the annual militia parade in early June 1572 a number of the armed burghers, overly bold perhaps after the successes of the *Watergeuzen* in the smaller towns, openly declared their support for the Prince of Orange. As the town council had feared, the militia could not be trusted. Moreover, one of the four burgomasters became increasingly open about his sympathy for the Revolt. The capture of a small neighbouring town, together with the power of intimidation, did the rest: the people of Gouda were led to believe that a great lord from Sweden with an enormous army was coming to save the town from the tyranny of Alva. The watch on the gates was deliberately relaxed and before daybreak on 21 June a company of *Geuzen*, a mere sixty or seventy strong, simply entered Gouda.

The adhesion of this prestigious urban centre to the revolt gave an enormous fillip to the revolutionary movement. Other major towns followed suit. Among them was Dordrecht, a highly privileged city with an outspoken tradition of loyalty to the Crown. Like Gouda, it had avoided iconoclastic disturbances in 1566. While the militiamen were probably anti-Spanish they were not anti-Catholic. As in Gouda, a significant number of unemployed were found among the Dordrecht boatmen, 'rough and unreasonable men' with whom 'the heretics mix easily', according to one royalist agent.[7] As elsewhere the municipal government feared the crowds and was not sure about its militia. Several Protestants were members of the town council, some of whom enjoyed regular contacts with Orange. The actual defection on 25 June was a simple act by the revolutionary faction of the council together with the captains of the citizen militia.

The revolution at Leiden followed a different trajectory. Its flourishing textile industry languished in the 1560s, creating a massive number of unemployed textile workers. In contrast to the picture at Gouda and Dordrecht, fierce iconoclast disturbances broke out in 1566, sustained by a widespread reforming movement. During the ruthless repression that followed, large numbers fled the town. With most convinced Protestants in exile, renewed riots in early 1572 arose not out of religious or revolutionary fervour, but because Spanish soldiers were expected. Weary of this kind of 'forced hospitality', the populace erupted. Pressurised by the crowd, perhaps under influence of some returned exiles, the municipal authorities allowed rebel troops to enter the city on 26 June. Yet this was insufficient to assuage popular discontent. Now the anger of the crowd was vented in the plunder, not of the churches and convents, but of the houses of the wealthy.

After mid-June, urban revolts occurred in quick succession. In Haarlem the authorities were driven by popular support for the returned exiles to recognise Orange as their *Stadhouder*. On 3 July this town joined the Revolt. Other towns followed a variety of paths. Some were pushed by revolts from below, some were conquered by the Beggars, while others switched sides because of a *coup* or a simple political decision. From the middle of July the whole outlook improved for the revolutionaries of Holland, as Alva needed all his armed forces further south. Spanish troops were withdrawn from Rotterdam, Delft and Schiedam, which allowed these towns among others to side with the Revolt too. Geography also favoured the revolutionaries given the distance to Brussels and the difficulties faced by Spanish troops in operating in the low and marshy lands of Holland, under constant threat of inundation by the rebels. No doubt Alva calculated that he would be able to recapture the towns of the province at a later date.

Yet in these summer months a firm and decisive base for the Revolt was created. Formerly loyal authorities changed sides, clergymen decided to defect too, town councils or militias were purged in a revolutionary fashion, and the Dutch Reformed Church established its institutions everywhere. Above all, the Provincial Estates declared their independence from Alva at their revolutionary meeting in July 1572.

By the end of the summer Amsterdam remained the only major city of Holland in Spanish hands. This fact needs consideration as it also casts light on why so many other towns joined the Revolt. For many years Amsterdam had been home to a variety of reforming tendencies. In 1566, the iconoclast revolts had been unbridled and violent. In the course of the repression that followed, hired troops replaced the urban militia. A new unity was forged between the town council and the religious leaders, with the result that the whole city came to radiate a strong pro-Catholic attitude. All signs of anti-Spanish or anti-Catholic movements were checked at the outset. It is true that in 1572 the urban authorities decided not to receive Spanish soldiers in order to avoid unnecessary stress and expense for the inhabitants. Yet Amsterdam remained utterly loyal to the King until 1578, when it could no longer resist the pressure from the Sea Beggars who had cut off all connections with its former markets.

The example of Amsterdam showed the importance of upper-class unity. As long as the urban community, in particular its leaders (supported by the citizen militia, or as in Amsterdam by hired troops) were determined to withstand the rebels, the latter had little chance. The actual military threats of the Beggar forces were always negligible, because of their small numbers and poor discipline. While the *Watergeuzen* could disrupt trade and the fishing industry, this worked only in the very long run: in the case of Amsterdam the blockades had lasted five to six years.

The religious factor

As has already been suggested, the part played by religious belief in the process of mobilising the urban population varied from one town to the next. From the Catholic solidity of Amsterdam to the more equivocal stance of the Catholics of Gouda and Dordrecht, from the forceful convictions of the Calvinist exiles in Enkhuizen and Haarlem to the highly divided Protestant communities in Leiden and Brill, attitudes on both sides of the religious divide were far from homogeneous. Moreover, in general, political alignments rarely followed religious differences. Many Catholics supported William of Orange and most Catholics in the north were moderate in their views. A significant number of priests adopted a flexible attitude to Protestants as far as Church dogmas were concerned. A strong humanist tradition tended to minimise differences. On the other hand, the Protestants were divided, ranging from the highly accommodating Lutherans through the various Calvinists to the more radical Anabaptists. Even the latter had shed their earlier militancy in favour of a pronounced pacifism. Overall, the number of Protestants was small, probably nowhere exceeding 10 per cent of the population, even when all dissenting denominations are included. The large numbers appearing at the hedge-preachings during 1566 included many who were simply curious.

Although in a minority, Dissenters belonged to all classes and were to be found in virtually all towns and villages of the north. From the earliest moments of the Reformation, the Anabaptists had established a strong presence particularly among the urban lower classes. The nobility tended to favour Lutheranism, although quite a number of lesser nobles, including some notable Sea Beggars, became fierce supporters of the Calvinist religion. After the popular hedge-preachings in the summer of 1566, a number of Calvinist churches were established in the north, but this development remained limited before 1572. Yet numerical weakness was more than compensated for by the impressive organisational skills of the Calvinists, who gradually dislodged the more other-worldly Anabaptists from centre stage, particularly through the popularity of hedge-preaching and their leading role in the riots of 1566.

However, not all image-breakers were Protestants by conviction. Attacks on churches and convents, particularly in the south but to some extent also in the north, were sometimes the rather orderly work of small bands of unemployed workers who had been hired for a day. In those places where the Calvinists did not control the iconoclasm, religious disturbances could easily overflow into wider social unrest. Some local authorities even had the churches and convents stripped by their own officers, thus removing a potential cause of popular unrest. It remains noteworthy however that in several towns in the north, notably Gouda and Dordrecht, no iconoclasm occurred at all.

Because of Alva's repressive measures a large number of Protestants had gone into exile. As a result, during the urban revolts of 1572 no mass demonstrations or street actions were mounted by Dissenters. Yet some individuals did exert significant influence, in particular a number of exiles returning from Emden. Even though they comprised only a tiny minority, and by themselves could not stage a revolution, they were persistently reported to have found support among the ranks of the discontented. Perhaps their influence was so large precisely because of the clarity of their solutions, which came from their experience abroad.

The Dutch Reformed Church drew massive advantages from the international Calvinist network, which linked them to the powerful French Huguenots among others. Not only did exiled communities exchange experiences and provide models of church organisation,[8] but William of Orange was able to use the international network to mobilise foreign military support. Upon the news of the taking of Brill, exiled communities, particularly in London, Norwich and Emden, reacted swiftly, raising funds, ships and troops. With the establishment of independence, the Dutch Reformed

Church became the privileged church of the United Netherlands. This was not because of its majority position, for up to the seventeenth century its members were outnumbered by Catholics, but because of the success of its leaders and institutions in pressing their claims. They were however helped in this by the enormous influx of Calvinist refugees from the south after Flanders and Brabant had been reconquered by the Spanish.

The formation of exile communities, particularly in Emden, also contributed to the development of a distinct nationalist feeling. As the Calvinists came from quite different places in the Netherlands, their shared experiences tended to transcend their sense of local identity. This new nationalism lent itself to a more broad-ranging anti-Spanish consciousness than that felt by most of their fellow countrymen. Many Sea Beggars also openly proclaimed their Calvinist faith primarily because being a Calvinist was indicative of an extreme anti-Spanish attitude.

The religious issue had the clear effect of dividing the elites. In particular under Alva, the policy of religious repression isolated the government in Brussels from the majority of the urban authorities in Holland. The latter were generally rather reluctant to come down hard on heretics. As long as Dissenters behaved modestly and calmly, the local authorities preferred to leave them in peace. They were aware that several lawsuits against the Dissenters had resulted in serious popular unrest. In some cases religious prisoners were liberated from gaol, executions impeded, and condemned books saved from the fire. The authorities were also anxious to ensure that the economic activities of possibly unorthodox foreign merchants should not be disturbed.

Not surprisingly, the urban elites were much attracted by the idea that William of Orange offered a compromise between Calvinist radicals and 'Alva's tyranny'. The eldest son from a Lutheran family, William favoured a less militant Protestantism while accommodating the Catholic majority. He continually opposed the hedge-preachings of the Calvinists, and personally contributed to the repression of the Calvinists in Antwerp. He abhorred iconoclastic movements; and during the Revolt he continuously denounced the anti-Catholic actions of the *Geuzen*. When he turned to Calvinism in 1572 it was only for want of military support and not because he was a Calvinist by conviction. Contrary to many Calvinists who aimed at the imposition of the 'Only true religion', Orange's explicit aim was to establish a religious peace founded on a remarkable degree of religious toleration. This would have permitted considerable latitude to the external expressions of freedom of conscience, including freedom of worship.

Many local rulers therefore believed that support for Orange offered a reasonable expectation of peace and order in the near future; on the other hand, they were deeply disturbed by Alva's insistence on the strict implementation of the anti-heresy laws which entailed a continuing risk of riot. Furthermore, they were offended by the way in which the religious inquisition interfered with ordinary judicial procedures. At Haarlem in 1570 the bailiff arrested a religious exile who had temporarily returned to the town. Liberated by Haarlem burghers the man fled, whereupon the bailiff arrested his wife and demanded that she be put to torture. The municipal court refused his demand. Alva's response to the complaints of the bailiff was to enhance his power but the burgomasters, though not particularly anti-Spanish, refused to comply.[9] At a more general level, the Duke launched in 1567 a recodification of the law and a consolidation of the procedures for lawsuits which might also serve the religious inquisition.

The resistance against the Tenth: uniting the opposition

The directives of the central government in relation to religious policies both reflected and contributed to the general tensions between a centralising state and decentralising town governments. The potential reorganisation of the legal procedures for lawsuits was a major threat to the traditional authority of the burgomasters and town councils. So too was Alva's proposal for the introduction of the Tenth or general sales tax. Not only would this constitute a new burden on the commercial prosperity of the towns but it would subvert the Provincial Estates which had traditionally determined the distribution of the tax burden. Customarily, the King had always been obliged to request funds from the separate Provincial Estates showing why the central government was in need of them. If the Tenth, as a permanent tax with significant yields, was voted for once and for all, the whole procedure would be circumvented. The King, as Alva wrote to him, would finally become the 'señor assoluto'[10] and the political influence of towns and provinces would be savagely reduced.

If the Tenth was highly controversial in itself, so was the method by which Alva decided to implement it. In 1569, after long deliberations, the Provincial Estates of those regions which formed part of the Habsburgs' Burgundian inheritance, notably those of Holland, Brabant and Flanders, had all agreed to pay the Crown a lump sum in lieu of the proposed tax to cover the period to 1571.[11] But in 1571 Alva was not prepared to accept a further redemption, and insisted that the tax should be levied everywhere. His view was that in 1569 they had agreed to the Tenth in *principle*, the lump sum being only a temporary concession. The alleged consent to the Tenth was contested by the Estates, and Alva's high-handedness provoked widespread uproar. Some of the representatives to the Estates gambled on their long tradition of loyalty to the Spanish Crown, expecting to obtain exceptional concessions, particularly as Philip II had sworn at his coronation that he would uphold the tax privileges of the provinces and towns. Several magistrates held the opinion that the Spanish King would never agree to such a levy which was only Alva's doing.

This attitude allowed the provinces and towns to play for time, yet the expectations about the Spanish King proved false. By the end of 1571 no concession had been made. Alva did reduce the rates for primary goods and for some exports, but the Tenth remained. Town councils refused to publish the decree or to appoint the collectors, but by March 1572 the possibilities of protest had run out. Collectors were appointed by Alva's agents, bypassing the local authorities, which were threatened with punitive fines should they obstruct the levy. These ranged from the equivalent of a year's salary for a high civil servant to twenty-five times as much. Such intimidation added to the sense of bitterness and injustice, affecting the morale and prestige of the urban authorities.

The Tenth also caused serious unrest among the lower and middle classes. As opposition against the Brussels government mounted and soldiers threatened to mutiny, fears grew that troops might be employed to enforce the collection of the funds. As a result, Spanish soldiers were denied entrance to towns. In the case of Flushing, for example, the hatred of the tax and the fear that it might be imposed by government troops was an explicit justification for the revolt in April 1572. The urban authorities, fearful that popular disturbances would force them to appeal to the Spanish forces to restore order and further reduce their independence, proceeded with caution. So too did many of the tax collectors who found themselves unprotected by the burgomasters or the local militia. In the end, not a penny of the Tenth was collected. Alva decided to cancel the plans in June 1572.

Yet the political damage was done. The battle of the Tenth brought together opposition from different layers in society: the clergy, the elites of the towns, the middle and the lower classes. Prominent members of the clergy, among them several bishops in the southern Netherlands, raised their voice against the tax and declared it to be unlawful. Some priests excommunicated collectors of the Tenth together with those municipal leaders who had not done enough to oppose it. The urban authorities condemned the unconstitutional nature of the imposition, as well as the heavy fines which affronted their status. The middle classes resented the burden placed on their sales and exports. The lower classes, fearful of a rise in the cost of bread and beer, rioted. Finally, the Beggars used the Tenth in their propaganda against Alva in almost all of their declarations and in their songs and ballads.

The disagreements and debates over the Tenth furthered the development of a new ideology. Liberty was the term that became writ large, and freedom came to be regarded as the 'daughter of the Netherlands, the source of prosperity and justice'.[12] The Estates of Holland were increasingly seen as the true guardians of the country. In order to fulfil this indisputable function, in 1572 the towns and local nobility granted them sovereign powers, first temporarily and from 1581 without limit. Meanwhile, all 'foreign' rule was rejected, although formal allegiance to the King endured until then. Orange wrote in a pamphlet in June 1572:

That people be given back their houses, possessions, hereditary estates, their good name, their freedoms, privileges and laws, by which liberty is maintained. . . . That political matters will be dealt with by the King himself and by the [E]States which are chosen in every province and not dispatched secretly by hired foreigners through whose faithless-ness and greed present troubles have come about.[13]

The great weight attached to the Provincial Estates can also be seen in the address made by the Prince a few weeks later at their famous meeting at Dordrecht:

They [the Provincial Estates] shall further discuss and ordain the best and most suitable means of restoring and reestablishing in their old form and full vigour all the old privileges, rights and usages of the towns, which may have been suppressed and taken away by Alva's tyranny or otherwise, in accordance with the privileges and rights the King has sworn to maintain.[14]

The revolutionary nature of the Dordrecht meeting also reflected the char-acter of many of the delegates. Most of the urban deputies were attending a meeting of the Provincial Estates for the first time. After 1572, alongside the former six major towns and the nobility, twelve new towns were repre-sented.[15] Coming from this fresh political background, almost no one was hampered by a tradition of cooperation with Alva. The fact that the meet-ing was held in Dordrecht was by no means a coincidence either. Dordrecht possessed the oldest town charters and privileges of Holland, was widely known for its age-long attachment to peace and order and was regarded as the traditional 'capital' of this province. By the late sixteenth century, Amsterdam may have become the most important economic centre in Holland, but Dordrecht was held in greater political respect.

During the 1570s the delegates to the Provincial Estates continued to interpret their representative position and their sovereign rights in a most radical way; more radical even than Orange wished, for with the expansion of the authority of the Provincial Estates his own control diminished. In fact, the enormous power of the Estates proved to be a constant impediment to the monarchical ambitions of the later princes of the Orange-Nassau dynasty. Up until 1795, the power of the *Stadhouders* was severely restrained by the members of the Provincial Estates, thus bequeathing to the European states of the nineteenth century a suggestive model for 'limited monarchy'.

A religious, a bourgeois or a national revolution?

In each town of Holland, the actual outbreak of revolt in 1572 was the result of a specific mix of causes, each of varying weight. In the seafaring towns the hardships caused by the *Watergeuzen* in the fisheries and trade was significant; class divisions were particularly strong in industrial Leiden; individual exiles proved more convincing in one place than in another; here new ideology outweighed religious views, there the opposite was true. Decisions to join the Revolt were always taken during a period of confusion and stress. Small incidents such as a minor disagreement between Spanish soldiers and the local militia, false rumours about the imminent arrival of thousands of Beggar troops or of Spanish troops intent on imposing new taxes and suppressing resistance, were the typical triggers for a sequence of events which could lead to yet another declaration of support for Orange.

Economic distress should not be overlooked as an important element in the situation, fuelling the discontent with Spanish rule. Given the widespread hunger and dearth, coupled with fears of troops and wandering beggars, riots would have occurred regardless of the conflict. Yet economic conditions in themselves have little to tell us about the direction of the resistance. What gave the Dutch Revolt its character were the elements that determined its anti-Spanish perspective, above all the more or less concerted actions of the Beggars, the opposition to the Tenth from all social strata, and the fear of a Catholic inquisition.

Contrary to later myths, the Dutch Revolt was not a Calvinist revolution. Only in the course of the struggle did the Dutch Reformed Church come to play a central role. Most religious exiles were still abroad when the Dordrecht delegates met in July 1572. Moreover, the majority of the population was still Catholic, and among the Dissenters the pacifist Anabaptists outnumbered the militant Calvinists. Generally speaking, the Revolt did not have its roots in religious discontent, although the clash over royal policy towards Protestantism constituted the main rationale behind the crisis of 1566.

Nor was the Dutch Revolt a bourgeois revolution. Of course Holland was a rapidly developing capitalist society and the urban elites performed a crucial role in deciding to send delegates to the revolutionary Estates. Yet nothing about their grievances was specifically bourgeois and most of the social structures remained intact. No ideological stance was developed against the nobility as such. On the contrary, most leaders of urban communities shared their distress with the local noblemen. In the Provincial Estates, they joined together to attack Spanish rule. Almost all nobles in the north, most of them of lesser rank, rallied behind Orange; most of them signed the famous Compromise of 1565. Another thing which bound the bourgeoisie to the nobility was their shared fear of unrest and the uprisings of the lower classes. Contrary to what was later assumed, Dutch merchants and entrepreneurs drew significant advantages from belonging to the Spanish-Habsburg Empire and they favoured peace and order as long as possible. The most outstanding example of this is provided by the merchant community of Amsterdam which remained loyal to the King after the whole province had already joined the Revolt.

A national revolution is a much more appropriate term for the Dutch Revolt. Its anti-Spanish character counted for much more than Calvinism or 'bourgeois demands' in bringing together rebels from various social strata and many towns. In large measure the townspeople of Holland were reacting against the implementation of Alva's policies: they opposed Spanish troops, the payment of new taxes to a distant regime and the insistence on dogmatic and alien religious attitudes. Yet to think that independence from Spain was a considered option from the start is a mistake. The new ideology expressed in the demands for 'liberty' and 'sovereignty', of which the Provincial Estates came to be regarded as the true guardians, was only developed during the struggle itself, probably from as late as 1572. Within an increasingly autonomous political environment, William of Orange's views on religious toleration found fertile ground as did the nascent nationalism developed by Calvinist exiles. Thus, as several points of no return came and went, the idea of establishing an independent United Netherlands became increasingly attractive.

To conclude, the Dutch Revolt was the product of several strands of conflict none of which were exceptional in early modern Europe. Almost everywhere there was a tension between centralisation and a desire for greater local autonomy. Religious issues had also come violently to the fore in many countries since the start of the Reformation. Tax increases and the presence of troops caused widespread revolts in all early modern states. Still, the outcome of the Revolt was extraordinary and revolutionary in the early modern European context. This may be explained by the concerted action of the towns of Holland and its nobility in the Provincial Estates. Their example was to be followed by neighbouring northern provinces when they came together in 1579 in the Union of Utrecht. In the course of this national revolution, revolutionary notions of freedom of conscience and of limited monarchy were developed, notions that were to play a part in both the English and French revolutions before becoming much more fashionable in the nineteenth century.

Chronology

1425   Death of the last independent count of Holland.

1433   Holland and some other provinces of the Low Countries incorporated into the Burgundian Empire.

1477   The provinces of the Netherlands draw up the Grand Privilege, asserting their rights within the Burgundian Empire against the centralising power of the Duke of Burgundy.

1506   Charles V of Burgundy inherits the Netherlands.

1516–19 Charles V becomes King of Spain and Habsburg Emperor.

1531	Charles V establishes the government in Brussels.
1548	Treaty of Augsburg: Charles V unites the seventeen provinces of the Netherlands.
1555	Philip II, King of Spain, succeeds his father Charles V as overlord of the Netherlands.
1558	Start of church reform in the Netherlands; continuation of repression of Protestantism.
1563	Open resistance of Dutch nobles against Brussels government.
1566	Iconoclast revolts in the Netherlands.
1567	The Duke of Alva becomes Governor-General over the Netherlands; commences severe repression of rebels and Protestants.
1568	First armed invasion by William of Orange; first activities of the Beggars at sea.
1569	The Duke of Alva introduces a highly contested tax system.
1572	Revolt of the towns of the Province of Holland.
1573–75	Spanish troops forced to retreat from large parts of the northern Netherlands.
1579	Establishment of the Union of Utrecht, the fundament of the independent Republic of the northern Netherlands.
1581	King Philip II is abjured by the northern Netherlands.
1648	Peace of Westphalia, end of the Dutch War of Independence against Spain, general recognition of the United Provinces as an independent republic.

Notes

1 Cited in John Lotrop Motley, *The Rise of the Dutch Republic. A History*, London, 1873, p. 478.
2 Charles Tilly, *European Revolutions, 1492–1992*, Oxford, 1993, p. 8.
3 Original wording of the Petition of 5 April 1566, translated by E.H. Kossman and A.F. Mellink, *Texts Concerning the Revolt of the Netherlands*, Cambridge, 1974, p. 63.
4 Cited in Geoffrey Parker, *The Dutch Revolt*, London, 1977, p. 76.
5 T.S. Jansma, 'Dordrecht wordt Geus', in *Economisch-Historische opstellen geschreven voor Prof. Dr. Z.W. Sneller*, Amsterdam, 1947, p. 36.
6 17 June 1572, cited in J.J. Woltjer, *Tussen vrijheidsstrijd en burgeroorlog. Over de Nederlandse Opstand 1555–1580*, Amsterdam, 1994, p. 52.
7 Cited in J.C. Boogman, 'De overgang van Gouda, Dordrecht, Leiden en Delft in de zomer van het jaar 1572', *Tijdschrift voor Geschiedenis*, 1942, vol. 51, p. 95.
8 Andrew Pettegree, *Emden and the Dutch Revolt. Exile and Development of Reformed Protestantism*, Oxford, 1992, pp. 230, 241.
9 Joke Spaans, *Haarlem na de Reformatie: stedelijke cultuur en kerkelijk leven*, The Hague, 1989, pp. 38–9.

10 Ferdinand H.M. Grapperhaus, *Alva en de Tiende Penning*, Zutphen, 1984, p. 309.
11 These are sometimes described as the patrimonial estates inherited in 1477 as opposed to those acquired later.
12 Martin van Gelderen, *The Political Thought of the Dutch Revolt 1555–1590*, Cambridge, 1992, p. 263.
13 Translated by Kossman and Mellink, *Texts*, pp. 96–7.
14 'Instruction and advice (. . .)', translated by Kossman and Mellink, *Texts*, p. 99.
15 J.W. Koopmans, *De Staten van Holland en de Opstand. De ontwikkeling van hun functies en organisatie in de periode 1544–1588*, The Hague, 1990, pp. 36–9. Eventually, the Provincial Estates chose The Hague as their seat.

Further reading

A. Duke, *Reformation and Revolt in the Low Countries*, London, 1990.

Martin van Gelderen, *The Political Thought of the Dutch Revolt 1555–1590*, Cambridge, 1992.

Gordon Griffiths, 'The revolutionary character of the Revolt of the Netherlands', *Comparative Studies in Society and History*, vol. 2, 1959–60, pp. 452–72.

Marjolein 't Hart, *The Making of a Bourgeois State. War, Politics, and Finance during the Dutch Revolt*, Manchester, 1993.

C.C. Hibben, *Gouda in Revolt. Particularism and Pacifism in the Revolt of the Netherlands 1572–1588*, Utrecht, 1983.

Jonathan I. Israel, *The Dutch Republic. Its Rise, Greatness, and Fall, 1477–1806*, Oxford, 1995.

Henk van Nierop, 'Similar problems, different outcomes: the Revolt of the Netherlands and the Wars of Religion in France', in Karel Davids and Jan Lucassen (eds), *A Miracle Mirrored. The Dutch Republic in European Perspective*, Cambridge, 1995, pp. 26–56.

Geoffrey Parker, *The Dutch Revolt*, London, 1977.

J.W. Smit, 'The Netherlands Revolution', in Robert Forster and Jack P. Greene (eds), *Preconditions of Revolution in Early Modern History*, Baltimore and London, 1970, pp. 19–54.

3 The English Revolution of 1649

Ann Hughes

Introduction

On a bitter winter's day, Tuesday 30 January 1649, in an extraordinary and unprecedented drama, Charles I, the anointed King of England, Scotland and Ireland, was executed at Whitehall. The King's death was not some furtive, private murder. It was not 'done in a corner', but as, one radical later insisted, 'as he sinned openly, so he should be tried, sentenced and executed in the face of the world, and not secretly made away by poisonings and other private deaths'. Charles was tried for crimes against his people and the laws of England. 'Trusted with a limited power to govern by and according to the laws of the land, and . . . for the good and benefit of his people', he was accused of a 'wicked design' to establish 'an unlimited and tyrannical power to rule according to his will'. Charles had attacked the fundamental constitution of the kingdom, under which frequent parliaments were the remedy for misgovernment, and had embroiled his people in 'unnatural, cruel and bloody wars'. The Scots and Irish subjects of the King had not been consulted, and his son was soon proclaimed Charles II in Edinburgh, but in England the execution had been preceded by a military *coup*. Parliament's own politicised army, in alliance with London radicals, had invaded the city and purged the Parliament of those MPs (a majority) who, in December 1648, were prepared to make an unsatisfactory peace with Charles. In ringing tones the purged House of Commons had declared:

> That the people, are, under God, the original of all just power. . . . That the Commons of England, in Parliament assembled, being chosen by, and representing the people have the supreme power in this nation . . . whatever is enacted, or declared for law, by the Commons . . . hath the force of law; and all the people of this nation are concluded thereby, although the consent and concurrence of King, or House of Peers, be not had thereunto.[1]

This would seem to be a clear-cut, revolutionary act, but on closer examination qualifications are needed. The King was tried, and his death voted, before monarchy as an institution was abolished. Charles' execution was indeed delayed for some hours while a law was rushed through to prevent the proclamation of a new monarch. Sir Thomas Fairfax, the nominal commander of Parliament's army, was among those involved in desperate last-minute moves to save the King's life. The formal abolition of the monarchy and the House of Lords was not complete until Acts of 17 and 19 March. Regicide was not an act willed or anticipated by anyone in the summer of 1642 when Parliament had reluctantly organised for war against 'the king, seduced by wicked counsel, [who] intends to make war against the Parliament'.

The ambiguities surrounding even the climacteric scene of a reigning monarch on the scaffold highlight the problems in interpreting these events. There are profound disagreements over whether developments should be characterised as a revolution; whether they should be seen as an explicable outcome of earlier trends, or as a brief and bizarre episode in English history. Here it will be argued that what happened in 1649 was clearly revolutionary in that it produced, at least in the short and medium term, a distinct shift in the nature of English government. There was no simple replacement of one king by another but alterations in the structure of power, with the establishment of collective rule by a single chamber Parliament whose members elected an executive Council of State. Second, there was a massive shift in the social status of England's rulers who for the next decades came not from the ranks of the aristocracy, but mainly from relatively obscure members of the landed classes, men who before 1640 would have been important only in their immediate neighbourhoods. Third, and crucial in an early modern context, the Revolution of 1649 confirmed both the collapse of a compulsory and inclusive National Church and the existence of unprecedented religious liberty for Protestants. I will also argue in this chapter that the 1640s witnessed the emergence of new political practices, and new forms of political communication and mobilisation that amount to revolutionary processes. Political and religious ideas facilitated the conception of radically different futures. Whether these developments produced a revolutionary outcome, in the form of permanent or long-term shifts in the social and political development of England (or Britain) is more debatable, but this might apply to all revolutions.

The causes of revolution

Much historical controversy has developed around the causes of the 'English Revolution', where explanations are inextricably connected with definitions of the nature of the conflict. Are we explaining a civil war, a rebellion or a revolution? Did the 1640s witness one revolutionary process, or a series of distinct ruptures, some of them decidedly 'unrevolutionary'? Historians such as Conrad Russell have argued that we need to distinguish different stages in the political crisis, with different explanations as appropriate. In 1640 when the reforming Long Parliament met, its survival secured by the presence of an occupying Scottish army in the north of England, the main problem, he suggests, is to account for the breakdown of Charles' government in at least two of his kingdoms. But with the outbreak of civil war in 1642, the focus shifts to the King's ability to raise forces (representing a recovery since 1640) and Parliament's willingness to organise against him. Revolution came, argues Russell, only in 1649, initiated by a minority radicalised by the experiences of civil war. For some historians even the regicide when it came was not a revolution: it was a desperate attempt to escape from the insoluble dilemma of how to achieve a settlement with a transparently untrustworthy king and secure some result from the years of war, in a situation where war weariness had brought most to yearn for peace at any price.

Until twenty-five years ago, it was commonplace within influential historical traditions to emphasise the distinctiveness of England's upheaval compared with earlier revolts or contemporary struggles on the Continent. Within a Marxist tradition the English Revolution was in some sense a 'bourgeois revolution' connected with the replacement of a feudal social structure by a modern capitalist system. For 'liberals' or Whigs, its distinctiveness lay in its contribution to the birth of modern liberty – to constitutional monarchy, individual rights and religious freedom. Much recent historical scholarship has, on the contrary, stressed the old rather than the new, connecting the English civil war to the past, to traditional rebellions, rather than to the future. The central role played by religious commitment in determining allegiance in the civil war has prompted the famous judgement by John Morrill that the conflict was Europe's last great war of religion rather than its first great revolution; while the prominence of peers in petitioning for a Parliament in 1640, or in Parliament's military command until 1645 and its political councils until 1648, has led John Adamson to argue that the civil war should thus be seen as a baronial conflict of a traditional, medieval kind, a breakdown in trust between Charles and the great men who should have been his closest supporters.

The now common judgement that the opposition to Charles was not radical but rather a conservative defence of traditional liberties against an ambitious if not terribly effective absolute monarch has been underlined through comparisons with contemporary events in continental Europe. Charles' problems have been presented as one example of the difficulties which many European monarchs faced in dealing with the diverse territories of their multiple kingdoms. Rather than an English civil war or revolution, we should perhaps be exploring a 'British problem'. Charles ruled three (or four if we include Wales) very different kingdoms, and 'normal' problems of war, finance and taxation, along with the difficulties of incorporating remote elites into patronage networks, were made yet more intractable by complicated religious tensions involving Catholic Ireland, Calvinist Scotland and divided England. Charles' botched attempt to impose an unpalatable prayer-book ignited a widespread national revolt in Scotland, a revolt regarded with much sympathy by zealous Protestants in England who consequently did little to support the government's attempts to repel the Scots' invasion in 1640.

The stress on what Conrad Russell terms 'Unrevolutionary England' has been challenged in other recent work. It would, of course, be too simplistic to argue that England was heading inevitably for revolution in 1603 or 1640 or 1642. Russell may be right to emphasise the enormous impact that the civil war itself had on men and women as unprecedented events opened up new possibilities for both. Nonetheless, it may be argued that the Revolution developed potentialities which were already present within English political culture by 1640. Far from being an aberration from the normal quiescent and hierarchical pattern of English life, the events of the 1640s can be understood in terms of broader trends in England's social, religious and political development. The remainder of this section will elaborate on this argument.

If we examine, first of all, economic and social change, it is clear that much research has made it difficult to defend an older Marxist case that civil war and revolution were directly connected to a shift from feudalism to capitalism. Certainly, studies of the social characteristics of allegiance in the civil war have shown that the conflict was not between a royalist and feudal class and a parliamentarian capitalist bourgeoisie. It is nonetheless the case that a capricious personal monarchy whose main priority in social and economic regulation was to raise revenue, rather than promote trade, colonial or industrial enterprise was likely to offend important elements among the propertied. Zealously Protestant peers with colonial interests in America or the Caribbean, such as Lord Brooke or the Earl of Warwick, had economic as well as religious common ground with new mercantile elements in the City of London who did not benefit from the privileges granted by the Crown to the great companies. More generally, a century of change had prompted possible defiance of the King through a parliamentary cause that involved broad social groups. Rising population and economic expansion created anxiety among elites about social mobility and social distinctions, and about the 'threat' to hierarchy apparently posed by the increasing numbers of the poor. At the same time, many among the peerage and the landed gentry had prospered, becoming self-confident, powerful figures in their localities. Such men wielded power as unpaid servants of the Crown rather than as dependent pensioners; a monarch lost their support at his peril. Below them, for the 'middling sort' of smaller landholders, craftsmen and merchants who have been the object of much recent historical attention, the impact of social change was also ambiguous. Some had faltered through inflation and rising indebtedness, but in most parishes by 1640 there were several householders who had profited from a more commercialised society, the village notables, active on local juries, as churchwardens, constables or overseers of the poor. A broad range of propertied male householders had developed an understanding of legal processes and local politics through their participation in the structures of government. This did not make them a revolutionary class or inevitably parliamentarian, but it did mean that they were capable of responding to and acting upon the political messages aimed at them in the 1640s. It is also relevant that economic expansion ended in depression and stagnation from the 1620s; as in other revolutionary situations, economic hardship contributed to a worsening political situation. Finally, the years around 1649 were among the most desperate in English economic history, with poor harvests and trade dislocation made much worse by the depredations of a long and bitter war. Fear of social unrest and of the fertile royalist recruiting ground in a war-weary population hardened the radical resolve to achieve a ruthless political settlement.

Further discussion of radical potential within English political culture will be necessary, but it should be stressed at the outset that complex and contradictory assumptions about the nature of political power are present from the 1590s at least. A commitment to authority, order and hierarchy was countered by a belief in fairly broad political participation especially through regular, freely elected parliaments, as a safeguard against evil counsellors who might encourage royal arbitrariness. It was not so much that there were conflicting and distinct ideologies; a commitment to the rule of law and an approval of consensus, for example, were commonplace among the politically active. Contradictory tendencies are often to be found within the same individuals. But at times of heightened dissension, as during the conflicts over the administrative and financial demands of war in the 1620s, or when fears about the direction of religious change intensified, cleavages based on contrasting political ideologies became more clear-cut. At such times significant elements among elites presented themselves as public servants, defenders of the 'country's' interests and traditions against the private interests of the court. But the 'political nation' – those people whose opinions and actions mattered – was not confined to those who sat in Parliament, or as local magistrates. There was an insatiable hunger for news and gossip about political and religious events among most sections of the population, while necessarily fragmentary evidence of seditious talk and the spreading of slanderous stories and rhymes about the powerful suggests that it was not necessary to be literate or wealthy to have opinions, often disrespectful, about political figures. Much of the political news and talk was crude and unsophisticated, consisting of salacious attacks on courtiers and royal advisers such as Buckingham, Strafford and Laud; but of course notions of politics here were often more polarised than those expressed in the more measured views of elites. Again we can discern much potential for political mobilisation among broad groups, whose influence was already seen in parliamentary elections and resistance to royal exactions in the 1620s, and was to be fully demonstrated in a range of activism in the 1640s. A long-standing lack of respect for authority and a view of English political structures as essentially collective and partici-patory helped make the drama of 1649 possible.

Religious divisions, also of long standing, were crucial in creating opposing sides in the civil war. The King himself, and many of his followers, adhered to a hierarchical and sacramental vision of the English Church expressed in communal, parochial ritual. For them the Reformation had gone far enough, or even in the wrong direction, with too much stress on the naked preaching of the word and arid speculation about theology. On the other hand, the most zealous Protestants who by the 1640s had grown to welcome the label Puritan, initially given them by their opponents, believed that the Reformation was but half-finished, and was being reversed by Charles and his Archbishop William Laud. Puritans combined a strong individual sense of God's acting on their souls and in their lives with an equally strong sense of the need to build a community of the godly, working together in the world to fulfil God's purposes. A Calvinist, predestinarian creed, dividing humanity between God's elect saints, and the reprobate or damned, inspired many Puritan activists. Crucial also to zealous English Protestantism was fear of the 'other' – the dark forces of Antichrist rep-resented by Catholicism or 'popery'. Whereas James I had been a prime intended victim of Catholics in the Gunpowder plot, a terrible and disturbing suspicion developed that his son Charles was an enemy of true religion. The failures and hesitations of the King's foreign policy as Catholics advanced in Europe was important here as well as his support for popish 'innovations', such as the railing off of altars as sacred places in the east end of churches. For a significant section of the population, Charles was an idolater whose encouragement of 'sports' or (in his terms) 'lawful recreations' on the Sabbath was a horrific profanation of the Lord's Day. When the Irish rebels of 1641 claimed the King's commission for their rising against Protestant oppression, their claim seemed all too plausible to many in England. Again Charles' nemesis in 1649 does not, in this framework, appear so extraordinary. A 'man of blood', against whom God had so clearly testified in crushing defeats in two civil wars, was brought to the scaffold by men convinced they were God's saints fighting the Lord's battles.

To distinguish too sharply between religion and politics would be misleading. Parliamentarians, who frequently associated popery with absolute monarchy, believed that the former popery's triumph would only be possible through an attack on Parliament and on the English laws and liberties that defended true religion. As the Grand Remonstrance, the controversial declaration denouncing Charles' personal rule, passed by Parliament in the wake of the Irish rebellion of 1641, insisted: 'The root of all this mischief we find to be a malignant and pernicious design of subverting the fundamental laws and principles of government, upon which the religion and justice of this kingdom are firmly established.' For the King and his supporters there was a parallel fear that presumptuous

Calvinist Puritans would inevitably attack all authority; a fear that was fulfilled for him in the Scots' rebellion from 1638. For parliamentary Puritans, on the other hand, the Irish rising confirmed all their worst fears of popery.

Both King and Parliament sought to gain backing from broad sections of the population from the opening of the Long Parliament, and especially as they organised for war in 1642; propagandist appeals to religious and political opinion were as necessary as money or coercion by local notables in gathering forces. There were anxieties on both sides about the subversive implications of appeals to the people; a proposal to print the Grand Remonstrance was initially defeated in the House of Commons. But appeals for support occurred more naturally, or less reluctantly, on Parliament's side. A role as representative of the people was a central part of the self-image of the House of Commons and promulgated in Parliament's declarations, which were based on the belief, however qualified, in participation and consent. The King's assumption that the political process involved the transmission of orders from the top down made rallying support somewhat more complicated. It was on Parliament's side, in any case, that new forms of mobilisation were to have a revolutionary impact; methods, structures, ideas and people will be explored in turn.

Revolutionary methods

Parliament sought to bind people to its cause through oath-taking, building on precedents from Elizabethan England, and on the Scots' National Covenant of 1638. These were not oaths of individual loyalty to the King, but collective endorsements of specific ideological positions. The Protestation of May 1641, intended to be sworn by all adult males, bound its adherents to support the true reformed Protestant religion, the privileges of Parliament and the subjects' liberties, as well as the King's person and estate. The 'Solemn League and Covenant', imposed from the autumn of 1643 as a seal of the alliance with the Scots, included a commitment to religious reformation; in some London parishes at least, women as well as men subscribed to it. All oaths before 1649 included support for the monarchy, but they implied a vision of kingship very much at odds with Charles' authoritarian view, a vision where the collective aspirations of subjects had to be taken into account.

Petitioning was another crucial element in revolutionary mobilisation from the petitions for religious reform in the early months of the Long Parliament, to those calling for judgement on the King in the winter of 1648. Many people were involved in political and religious debate through being required to sign a petition (or put their mark to one if they could not write). In nineteen counties petitions were organised against episcopacy, while twenty-two counties sent in petitions in defence of bishops, with 6,000 names on the one from Cheshire. Almost all counties sent in some response to the Grand Remonstrance – in Derbyshire it was based on a month's soliciting of support parish by parish. Petitioning on Parliament's side became more partisan, divisive and radical during the war. In London large-scale petitions were organised for and against a reformed national church on Presbyterian lines. Members of radical, separatist congregations mobilised against religious authoritarianism, and a broader democratic political movement, the Levellers, emerged, defending the rights of modest householders against oppression by clergymen, lawyers, great merchants and even an ungrateful Parliament itself. Leveller, like Puritan, was a term of abuse, and the movement's self-definition was based on the centrality of the petition: Levellers described themselves as 'Presenters, Promoters and Approvers of the Large Petition of September 11 1648'. Parliament's New Model Army petitioned against precipitate attempts to disband them without addressing their grievances in the spring of 1647. The Commons' fatal judgement that this activity made the soldiers 'enemies to the state and disturbers of the public peace' poisoned relationships irrevocably.[2]

Revolutionary rituals surrounded oath-taking and petitioning. Mass takings of the covenant like that by the Earl of Denbigh's soldiers in Coventry in December 1643 were a vivid enactment of commitment to the cause. The influence of petitions derived from their status as ritual activity as well as texts. Provincial petitioners processed solemnly through the City of London to Westminster: a London artisan Nehemiah Wallington watched many hundreds of Kentish men coming across London Bridge in February 1642, 'with their protestations sticking in their hats and girdles'. Wallington also witnessed many demonstrations in the city; Dr John Bastwick, one of the martyrs of Charles' personal rule, was met at Blackheath on his return from prison in December 1640 by 'many coaches and horse and thousands on foot with their rosemary and bays in their hands', commemorating the suffering of the 1630s and celebrating their victory.[3]

In the first place a petition was a text, usually printed, and the effervescence of cheap, rapidly produced religious and political print in the 1640s is a defining characteristic of this revolutionary culture. Early modern England was a partially literate society, but print was ever-present and oral and written forms of communication were closely related. In most communities a significant minority could read even if they could not write, while a bare majority of London men and women were probably literate by the mid-seventeenth century. Print technology made for a responsive press reacting speedily to events and polemical attacks, so that news books or rebuttals of an opponents' position, as well as petitions, parliamentary orders, and letters from military commanders poured on to the streets to be read aloud, debated and, in some cases, systematically collected by men who realised that the times were exceptional. Print very quickly became a way of conducting divisive and radicalising debates within the parliamentarian cause, not simply a means of presenting Parliament's case against the King. Until the 1650s however, Parliament's attempts to crack down on illicit and subversive printing were only intermittently successful.

Revolutionary structures

Parliament was the more ready to fight a civil war because it had been gradually assuming executive powers since November 1640 when its committees played a major role in negotiations with the Scots and in raising the money needed to pay off their occupying army. This was in effect a revolutionary process by which an institution previously meeting erratically and for short periods at the monarch's command became a collective, permanent executive as well as legislative body, reluctantly but inexorably organising for war. After Parliament's formal alliance with the Scots, a Committee of Both Kingdoms was established in early 1644 to oversee the war effort. There were thus precedents for the Council of State established in 1649 as England's executive authority.

On Parliament's unofficial, radical wings, new structures also emerged. Some were based on existing parochial or ward bodies, especially in the City of London. The pioneers in mobilising opinion to put pressure on the city authorities and on Parliament itself were Presbyterians who petitioned and lobbied for repressive measures against the radical religious sects and for a speedy reformation of the Church on Presbyterian lines, akin to the Scottish model. This movement is often seen as 'conservative' because of its religious stance within the parliamentarian spectrum, but its methods were undoubtedly novel. Political agitation in London testified to the fragmentation of earlier networks which had campaigned in the early 1640s for more zealous prosecution of the war. In opposition to Presbyterian mobilisation there developed an undoubtedly radical movement in London based on the newly emerging separatist gathered churches of London. Some remained within a Calvinist tradition, but the most radical – the General Baptists – believed in overall redemption. It was from this milieu that the Levellers developed. The sects' habits of participation and self-government made a vital contribution to democratic political possibilities. All London factions made extensive use of print, the radicals relying often on illegal, underground presses.

Finally, Parliament's New Model Army produced new structures for advancing its political influence. From the spring of 1647, each regiment and later each foot company or horse troop elected two rank and file 'agitators' or representatives to draw up grievances and coordinate protest. Later that year, the agitators along with an equal number of officers formed the General Council of the Army, where in October 1647 soldiers, officers and Levellers engaged in the 'Putney Debates', eloquently discussing the future of the kingdom and the nature of political power. From December 1647 the Army Council comprised officers only, but it remained a remarkable arena for political debate and revolutionary organisation.

Revolutionary ideas

The ideological content of the 'parliamentary cause' was complex and flexible, and thus capable of radical development. After the Bible, the book most quoted by the Leveller leader John Lilburne was a collection of Parliament's own declarations. To some extent Parliament's justifications for fighting the King were traditional, even 'backward-looking'. They were defending the historic rights and liberties of the kingdom against the attacks of evil, popish counsellors, with liberties understood as being specific privileges in a corporate, medieval sense, rather than modern freedoms. The Grand Remonstrance denounced a 'malignant and pernicious design of subverting the fundamental laws and principles of government, upon which the religion and justice of this kingdom are firmly established'. Nonetheless, a stress on liberties and on a representative parliament could be developed into direct claims for political rights by men whose previous experiences had focused on local resources and power structures. Similarly, a mode of argument based on appeals to the past was by no means 'backward-looking' in its content; idealised pasts could be used to justify a variety of new departures.

One example of such a flexible historical doctrine was the 'Norman Yoke'. For mainstream parliamentarians, the Norman Conquest had eclipsed English rights and traditions, such as regular parliaments and orderly legal processes. These rights had been confirmed or restored through Magna Carta, and it was now Parliament's duty to preserve them. Political radicals like the Levellers, however, extended the concept of Saxon rights – the rights of freeborn Englishmen – and argued that many were still kept from ordinary men: Magna Carta, 'itself being but a beggarly thing, containing many marks of intolerable bondage'. For the 'True Leveller' or Digger leader Gerrard Winstanley, who argued for economic equality, the 'Norman Bondage' included private property. The complexities of the use of history can be demonstrated from the Act to abolish the kingly office in England. This presented the end of the monarchy as the nation returning 'to its just and ancient right, of being governed by its own representatives or national meetings in council'. This was in itself a historical myth of legitimation, but the act also used history differently, to provide education or evidence against the monarchy:

> it is and hath been found by experience, that the office of a king in this nation and Ireland, and to have the power thereof in any single person, is unnecessary, burdensome, and dangerous to the liberty, safety, and public interest of the people, and that for the most part, use hath been made of the regal power and prerogative to oppress and impoverish and enslave the people.

Finally, this Act was founded on an abstract concept of natural rights, on the assumption that 'the just freedom and liberty of the people' should not be infringed. Equally, Levellers could reject the past when it did not support their aspirations: 'Whatever our forefathers were, or whatever they did or suffered or were enforced to yield unto, we are men of the present age.'[4]

Religious commitment was crucial to the English Revolution. Even at its most prosaic, zealous Puritanism had enormous potential for encouraging individual determination and self-sacrifice in the Lord's cause. It also offered a collective vision (or rather competing collective visions) of a society reformed as God would approve. Again past and future were mingled. The search for a scripturally based church in succession to the Apostles was compatible with a belief, central to the Reformation, that part of God's purpose was the progressive illumination of his people. Throughout the 1640s, the sense grew among the godly that God had blessed their cause and witnessed against Charles. At an army prayer meeting in May 1648, the soldiers noted how the Lord had 'led and prospered us in all our undertakings this year'. It was their duty to 'call Charles Stuart, that man of blood, to an account, for that blood he had shed, and mischief he had done, to his utmost, against the Lord's cause and people in these poor nations'.[5] Suspicion of Charles' antipathy towards true religion, already noted above, had been dramatically exacerbated by war. Religion was also a source of bitter division among parliamentarians. Puritanism fragmented in the 1640s and 1650s between those who wanted a reformed national church and those, often themselves divided, who supported religious liberty and argued that the true church was a voluntary community of the godly. The majority of those who pushed forward to revolution in 1648–49 belonged to these latter groups. A strong sense of personal identification with and illumination by Christ was held by many, ranging from Lord Protector Oliver Cromwell to the Digger Winstanley. Also widely shared were millennial hopes that these extraordinary times were the last days, presaging Christ's second coming to rule this world with his saints for a thousand years, performing marvellous things for his people. For some, such as Cromwell, millennial hopes focused on inward, spiritual change, but some radicals in the 1650s – the 'Fifth Monarchy men' – expected a literal political transformation. Millenarian expectations certainly helped to make possible and explicable the execution of the King, and were connected to a variety of utopian proposals. Gerrard Winstanley's vision of an egalitarian commonwealth which eliminated all forms of 'kingly power' is one memorable example.

As discussed above, secular and religious ideas combined in certain pervasive themes such as anti-popery. Similarly, a quasi-republican current in English political culture drew on both a classical humanist and a zealous Protestant commitment to the values of public service, expressed in the wide participation of male householders in legal and political processes. The sense of the political community as a collective body, and of political authority as abstract and accountable, was already present in 1642. In refusing Charles' admission to Hull in May 1642, Parliament denied that the King had

> the same right and title to his towns . . . that every particular man hath to his house, lands and goods, for his Majesty's towns are no more his own than his kingdom is his own, and his kingdom is no more his own than his people are his own . . . [Kings] are only entrusted with their kingdoms.[6]

A vision of a commonwealth is implicit here, and was to be enacted in 1649.

Revolutionary people

The parliamentary cause was a social alliance, ranging from peers, gentry and merchants to many humbler men and women. Londoners' support for Parliament was vital in the early 1640s as we shall see and, although radicals were in a minority by the mid-1640s, there was always to be a militant constituency in the City and, to a lesser extent, in provincial England, willing to underwrite revolution. To some extent economic interests can be related to political and religious allegiance: for parliamentary peers with colonial interests, as with smaller, independent city merchants, economic and religious views came together against royal government and in support for a rousingly Protestant foreign policy. Parliamentary peers such as Brooke or Warwick did not depend on medieval social power for their role, but on their status as popular leaders of the godly cause. Some social alliances were perhaps opportunistic: in both Derbyshire and Gloucestershire, miners seem to have joined the civil war party opposed by their local oppressors. Nonetheless, Parliament's role as 'representative of the people' and its commitment to the laws and liberties of England appealed to many smaller property owners, artisans and merchants for whom customary rights and liberties were of pressing importance and who were used to independent participation in a range of economic, administrative and legal processes. The English Revolution was made possible by the actions of many who were not members of traditional elites. It had some crucial popular support, but we should not assume inevitable popular enthusiasm for revolution. The King's appeal to social stability and hierarchy, and to an English church distinguished from popery and from strange and subversive sectaries, won some success in 1642. As in France, the most numerically impressive mobilisations were for 'traditional' or 'conservative' ends: by 1645–46 war weariness had created support for idealised good old days, and anti-war 'club' movements arose in the West Country and on the Welsh borders, resisting military exactions, taxation and religious upheaval.

A narrative of revolution

From 1640, two rival authorities competed for political legitimacy and political support in England, prompting profound and troubling reflections on the origins and nature of authority. People were required to make decisions of escalating significance and personal danger, from whether to agree with a petition about episcopacy, or to demonstrate against Bishops sitting in the House of Lords, to the ultimate dilemma of whether to take up arms for one side or another. To be a royalist in London in 1642, or a parliamentarian in north Wales, was rarely an option, but in many parts of England – the Midlands, the north-west, and parts of the West Country – this was a real choice, as two sides competed for control of local militias, the main armed force available.

In this increasingly turbulent decade, there were certain decisive ruptures that made war and revolution increasingly likely. The mass mobilisations in London in 1641–42 drastically weakened the King's position. In May 1641, thousands of Londoners took to the streets to force the House of Lords to convict Charles' chief minister the Earl of Strafford and then pushed the King, fearful for the safety of his Catholic wife, to sign the warrant sending Strafford to his death. In the winter of 1641–42, London was clearly a revolutionary city: in December 1641, the Bishops were removed from the Lords by popular pressure, and then the King himself was driven from London in January 1642 after his failure to arrest five leading members of Parliament. Nehemiah Wallington vividly described how citizens 'shut up our windows and doors', and stood upon their guard to preserve Parliament from attack. This act of revolutionary pressure iron-ically allowed Parliament to underline its defensive case for civil war: the King had deserted the government, and it therefore fell to Parliament to carry it on for the time being. The King's departure from his capital gave stark physical reality to the competing authorities in England. He was to return to London only for his trial and beheading.

The second decisive rupture was within the parliamentary cause itself, with the radicalisation of the New Model Army in 1647. The attempt by factions in Parliament to disband the bulk of the Army, without satisfying the troops over their arrears of pay or their vulnerability to legal challenge for actions committed during the war, followed by the contemptuous rejection of the Army's petitioning, prompted the Army to take public responsibility for the settlement of the kingdom and the defence of the principles for which they believed the war had been fought. Army leaders, notably Oliver Cromwell and his son-in-law Henry Ireton, acquiesced in this army revolt, but the initial impetus came from below. As part of their campaign the Army seized control of Charles from his parliamentary captors. But there was a simultaneous contrary political mobilisation in the City of London against the Army; this culminated in July 1647 with the violent coercion of Parliament, forcing it to demand peace and the

King's return to London. Leading members of both houses who fled to the Army in alarm were then escorted back to London by the military. On 7 August the Army paraded through a cowed city in an all-day show of strength – in practical terms London's acquiescence had been secured days before.

August 1647 was a dress rehearsal for purge and revolution. Even after a second civil war provoked by Charles in alliance with the Scots and English provincial discontent, a majority in Parliament still worked for peace. An enraged Army presented a Remonstrance to Parliament on 20 November 1648 calling for a more equally elected parliament to be the supreme authority in the nation and for justice against the King. The Army moved ever nearer as Parliament ignored its Remonstrance – Windsor, Kensington, Hyde Park – to arrive in Westminster on 2 December. Nonetheless, on 5 December, the Commons voted by 129 to 83, after an all-night sitting, that the King's latest answer to the peace propositions was a basis 'for the settlement of the peace of the kingdom'. The following morning, Colonel Thomas Pride stood at the Commons door supported by two regiments and with a list of MPs in his hand. By the end of the day forty-one MPs had been arrested, and many others prevented from entering. The stage was set for the surviving MPs (perhaps 40 per cent of those sitting in December 1648) to establish a court to try the King and to push through the Revolution.

To conclude this section on revolutionary processes, it is important to stress their many links with 'normal' or 'everyday' experience. Established religious and political ideas, habits of participation in parish and village affairs, understandings of law and history, all fed into the revolutionary experience and were transformed by the unprecedented circumstances. Again, Gerrard Winstanley and the Digging experiment are an instructive example. For Winstanley himself, visionary and mystical religious traditions inspired a campaign for social transformation presented as a triumph of human reason. More broadly, the Diggers drew on and radicalised generations of struggle over access to common lands. The movement emerged in 1649 propelled by a fierce sense that the death of the King should mean the overthrow of all kingly power.

War and revolution

Winstanley's London business failed in the 1640s, perhaps as a result of heavy taxation and the dislocations of war. While the French Revolution led to war, in England as in Russia war led to revolution. Something of the ideological development prompted by war has already been suggested; it is now important to stress how its practical impact contributed to radicalisation. As many as one in four Englishmen took part in the fighting (if we include activity in local sieges); almost 200,000 English people died as a direct or indirect result of war, a proportionately higher total than in twentieth-century conflicts. The impact in Ireland or Scotland was even more devastating. Taxation in England was at ten times peacetime levels, while plunder and the billeting of troops through free-quarter cost more money and trouble. 'What a multitude of precious lives has been lost? What a mass of monies has been raised?' asked the Levellers. What radicals wanted was some recompense for the sacrifices that had been made – some reward for ordinary people.

This impulse can be seen most clearly, and was to have most impact, in the Army. War had facilitated the upward political and social mobility of many men, among them the impoverished country gentleman Oliver Cromwell, who discovered a genius for military command and thereby became the ruler of three nations. By 1647 at the latest, this was a politicised army. Of course, as contemporaries and later historians have stressed, it was not uniformly radical, including pressed men and some who had previously fought for the King. But for many, military service in Parliament's cause had been a creative and liberating experience: as the soldiers proclaimed in a famous declaration of June 1647: 'we were not a mere mercenary army, hired to serve any arbitrary power of a state, but called forth and conjured, by the several Declarations of Parliament, to the defence of our own and the people's just rights, and liberties.' Political and religious debate under 'praying and preaching Captains' had produced a citizens' army that was also God's army:

> We are not soldiers of fortune, we are not merely the servants of men: we have not only proclaimed Jesus Christ, the King of Saints, to be our King by profession, but desire to submit to him upon his terms, and . . . to follow him whithersoever he goeth.[7]

Radicalism was not necessarily the most characteristic response to the burdens of war: many, as I have already suggested, yearned for a return to old ways and hierarchies. But it was the radical response that made the Revolution. From 1640 on there were fissures in parliamentarian alliances, and moderates drew back at many stages, but there were always enough who were prepared to go on, to secure or advance the causes for which the war had been fought. In 1642 many who had supported reforms of royal government would not fight the King, but Parliament could still conduct a victorious war-effort. Other moderates retreated in 1647, and many of course could not stomach regicide, but the more radical leaders in Parliament and the Army (themselves often cautious and reluctant men) always had 'allies on the left', well-placed minorities who underwrote revolution. As the Army officers moved against the King in the desperate winter of 1648–49, their Remonstrance commended the Leveller 'large' petition of 11 September, and the Army Council conducted negotiations with the Levellers and with leaders of radical congregations as well as with sympathetic MPs.

Revolutionary outcomes

In the short and medium term there was a clear political revolution: the monarchy and the House of Lords were removed and England was 'governed as a commonwealth and free state by the supreme authority of this nation, the representatives of the people in parliament'. The hopes of the more secularly minded radicals were rapidly disillusioned with Leveller denunciation of the purged Parliament as a corrupt oligarchy imposing 'England's New Chains'. Leveller-inspired army mutiny failed while Winstanley's 'Digger' communities were dispersed by force. But no revolution has satisfied its most radical adherents as its leadership has inevitably sought consolidation and compromise.

The Army itself became dissatisfied with the Rump, but many radicals were aghast at Cromwell's assumption of personal power in late 1653, after some months of political experimentation. After Cromwell's death in 1658, the parliamentarian cause fragmented and the monarchy was restored unconditionally in 1660.

But political practice could never be quite the same again after 1649, even if the impact of civil wars and a decade of non-monarchical rule was often deliberately muted or negative. When struggles against arbitrary rule and the fear of popery drove another king from the throne in 1688, ruling elites acted as quickly as possible to avoid civil war and a radicalising popular upheaval. Parliamentary monarchy was, however, established in 1688–89. Equally, the events of the mid-seventeenth century provided a context and inspiration for massive changes in thinking about politics. In contrasting and not always accepted ways, both Hobbes and Locke insisted that political arrangements were not established by divine laws, but by human contrivance based on notions of contract or consent.

In the 1650s a broad, parish-based national church coexisted with liberty of conscience for a range of Protestant sects. At the same time a more self-conscious and aggressive 'Anglicanism' developed, spurred on by the rigours of 'orthodox' Puritan reformers as well as the insolence of lay or mechanic preachers and radical sectaries. When the Bishops were restored with the monarchy in 1660, elements in the Church of England worked for the suppression of Presbyterians and more radical dissenters. But the revolutionary impact of the decades of religious fragmentation could not be gainsaid. Significant Protestant minorities would no longer be accommodated within the national church, and religious toleration for many Protestants was granted in 1689. Civil and political disabilities were not removed and the second half of the seventeenth century inaugurated the split between church and chapel, Anglican and Dissenter, which was to have profound implications for English culture, education and politics over the ensuing 250 years.

Almost no one in the 1640s and 1650s wanted thoroughgoing social revolution. The Diggers were a tiny group of visionaries who made connections with particular local grievances. There was no wholesale confiscation of the property of defeated royalists, but much qualified and often avoided penalties. There was no fundamental critique of familial or sexual hierarchies: women played an important but clearly subordinate role in radical religious congregations and in the Levellers, a movement led decisively by 'honest' male householders. There was no bourgeois revolution in the sense of the victory of a self-conscious capitalist class over a feudal hierarchy. However, clear structural shifts in English economic and social development occurred in this period and were closely influenced by political upheaval. Population stability after a period of expansion was the result of an extensive civil war as well as of general economic cycles. The problems of small landowners were intensified by civil war losses, and these same losses encouraged the trends among the propertied classes towards more aggressive, commercial exploitation of their estates. As Robert Brenner has long argued, some of Parliament's most important and determined support came from newer London merchants with close ties to members of the aristocracy equally committed to colonial expansion backed by a dynamic foreign policy. One result of the upheavals of the 1640s and 1650s was to weaken the ability of the Crown to interfere with economic development in order to raise revenue for itself. At the same time, there was no successful radical egalitarian assault on private property. In the sense that the world became safer for economic expansion, backed by government, the term 'bourgeois revolution' has some validity.

Civil war and military transformation, along with novel and unpopular governments, inevitably necessitated a stronger state. The 1650s also saw governments that consciously promoted England's expanding trading and commercial activities. This stimulated, in turn, a new political rhetoric of 'interest', arguing that the state should foster wealth creation that harmonised individual interests with the general good. This rhetoric was characteristic of many republicans of 1649–53, and was continued by radical Whigs in the later seventeenth century. It can be argued that the economic legacy of the Revolution thus combined stronger state input, particularly in colonial and trade expansion, with a more individualised, commercialised society. The Revolution also confirmed the dominance of England, perhaps even lowland England, over the rest of the British Isles and Ireland, and the centrality of London in an emerging British Empire. English soldiers conquered both Ireland and Scotland in the 1650s, and Ireland certainly underwent a social and economic transformation with immense and tragic consequences.

Conclusion: revolutionary traditions

As one of the most enthusiastic regicides, Major-General Thomas Harrison approached the scaffold where he was to be hung, drawn and quartered, he claimed,

Next to the sufferings of Christ, I go to suffer in the most glorious cause that ever was in the world. And one, as he passed by, asking him in derision where the good old cause was, he with a cheerful smile clapped his hand on his breast and said, Here it is, and I go to seal it with my blood.[8]

One reason why the English civil war or Revolution has been so controversial is that it has become tangled up in rival political traditions, viewing the good old cause with pride or derision. For monarchists, the events of the 1640s and 1650s were best forgotten, but for radical Whigs or eighteenth-century radicals, the Commonwealth was a proud heritage. One later radical, the historian Catherine Macaulay, produced a *History of England from the Accession of James I to the Revolution* in ten volumes from the 1760s. Her work was much admired by leaders of the American and French Revolutions and was suggested as a school prize in France in 1798. All revolutions were contested in their own time, all were more contradictory and qualified than models of revolution would imply. There seems to be no reason why we should not join eighteenth-century revolutionaries in assigning the events in mid-seventeenth-century England to the modern revolutionary tradition.

Notes

1 Quotations are from Edmund Ludlow, *The Voyce from the Watch Tower* (Camden Society, Fourth Series, 21, 1978); John Keynon, *The Stuart Constitution* (Cambridge, 1966); S.R. Gardiner (ed., *Constitutional Documents of the Puritan Revolution* (Oxford, 3rd edn, 1951).
2 Ian Gentles, *The New Model Army in England, Ireland, and Scotland, 1645–1653* (Oxford, 1992), p. 151.
3 Paul Seaver, *Wallington's World. A Puritan Artisan in Seventeenth-century London* (London, 1985), pp. 150–1.
4 Leveller ideas here and below are taken from *The Remonstrance of Many Thousand Citizens* (1646), often reprinted: see Andrew Sharpe (ed.) *The English Levellers* (Cambridge Texts in the History of Political Thought, 1998); the Act for abolition of the monarchy is in Keith Lindley, *The English Civil War and Revolution. A Sourcebook* (London, 1998).
5 Lindley, *The English Civil War*, p. 167.
6 Kenyon, *Stuart Constitution*, pp. 242–3.
7 A Declaration or Representation, in William Haller and Godfrey Davies (eds), *The Leveller Tracts* (reprinted Gloucester, MA, 1964), p. 55; Declaration of the English Army in Scotland, August 1650 in Kenyon, *Stuart Constitution*, p. 327.
8 Ludlow, *Voyce from the Watch Tower*.

Further reading

The literature available on the English civil war is enormous. The following works give guides to further reading and represent a range of views.

Richard Cust and Ann Hughes, eds, *The English Civil War*, London, 1997.

Christopher Hill, *The World Turned Upside Down. Radical Ideas During the English Revolution*, first published 1972, Penguin edn, London, 1975.

Ann Hughes, *The Causes of the English Civil War*, 2nd edn, Basingstoke, 1998.

Mark Kishlansky, *A Monarchy Transformed Britain 1603–1714*, London, 1996.

Keith Lindley, *The English Civil War and Revolution. A Sourcebook*, London, 1998.

Brian Manning, *The English People and the English Revolution*, first published 1976, Penguin edn, London, 1978.

John Morrill, *The Nature of the English Revolution*, Harlow, 1993.

Conrad Russell, *The Causes of the English Civil War*, Oxford, 1990.

Conrad Russell, *Unrevolutionary England 1603–1642*, London, 1990.

4   1688: A political revolution

W. A. Speck

Introduction

On 11 December 1688 James II fled from his capital city and made his way down the Thames hoping to escape to France. His departure produced the first breakdown of government in the Glorious Revolution. For a time a group of peers agreed to 'take upon them the Government for the preservation of the Kingdom and this great City'. As one of them noted, 'we had otherwise been a state of banditi, and London had certainly been the spoil of the rabble'. This alternative administration did not last long, for the King returned to the capital on 16 December. He had been intercepted by fishermen at Faversham, from whom he had been rescued by a party of guards sent to bring him back to London. James tried to resume the reins of power and even held a meeting of the privy council. But when William of Orange entered the capital on 18 December he asked the King to remove himself from the seat of government and James agreed, retiring to Rochester. Once more there was a vacuum of power, which the peers, meeting in the House of Lords, again attempted to fill. When James fled to France on 23 December, however, this time successfully, they met on Christmas Eve and asked William to call a free Parliament to meet on 22 January, and meanwhile to take upon himself 'the administration of public affairs, both civil and military, and the disposal of the public revenue'. He delayed acceptance until former Members of Parliament of King Charles II's time also asked him to govern the country on 26 December. William then carried out the task not just until the Convention assembled, for it too asked him to be chief executive until the constitutional position had been resolved. He therefore governed the country by virtue of these informal *ad hoc* arrangements until 13 February, when he and his wife Mary, James' daughter, accepted the Convention's offer of the Crown.

For seven weeks, therefore, England was without a king or queen. This was a unique era in constitutional history, for the rule was 'the king is dead, long live the king'. No interregnum was recognised legally even between the execution of Charles I in 1649 and the Restoration of 1660. Charles II dated his reign from the day of his father's death. The Convention elected in 1689, however, accepted that the throne was vacant between the flight of James II and the acceptance by William and Mary of the Bill of Rights. This was arguably the most telling sign that 1688 was a truly revolutionary year.[1]

The collapse of James II's government in December 1688 was due immediately to William of Orange's invasion of the country on 5 November and the King's total failure to cope with this challenge to his authority. That the Prince had been able to invade at the head of a Dutch army was largely attributable to the European situation. That James failed to withstand the threat posed by the invading forces was very much his own responsibility and the outcome of his domestic policies.

The Dutch invasion

The Revolution of 1688 can only be properly understood against the background of events in Europe. Its international context was clear to contemporaries like the Marquis of Halifax who claimed that William took London on his way to Paris. Louis XIV, King of France, was perceived by his neighbours as a menace. In order to contain French aggression they had formed the League of Augsburg in 1686. Although the Dutch did not join this alliance it was welcomed by the Prince of Orange. The French Army and Navy could have prevented his invasion, and until September the proximity to the Dutch Republic of troops under the duc d'Humieres made the States General of the United Provinces reluctant to support William's project. Fortunately for him, Louis XIV ordered Humieres to attack Philippsburg on the Rhine nearly two hundred miles from the Dutch border. This attack was a pre-emptive strike against the League of Augsburg, and precipitated a war with it which lasted until 1697. It tied up Louis XIV's army in such a way as to remove obstacles to William of Orange taking Dutch troops with him to England. At the same time the French Navy, which might have been used to intercept the invasion, was stationed not in the English Channel but in the Mediterranean. It was there to put pressure on the papal states at a time when relations between the French King and the papacy were fraught. The immediate cause of friction between Louis XIV and Pope Innocent XI was the outcome of the election of the Archbishop of Cologne. Two candidates had emerged, one backed by France, the other by the Holy Roman Emperor. To Louis' chagrin the imperial candidate had been successful, thanks to the Pope's support. Ironically, James II's backing of Louis XIV in this dispute alienated Innocent XI from him, and William's invasion did not get papal disapproval despite its taking on the character of a crusade against Popery. William's Declaration, issued from The Hague on 20 September, gave religion as the main motive for his actions:

> It is both certain and evident to all men that the publick peace and happiness of any state or kingdom cannot be preserved where the law,

liberties and customs, established by the lawful authority in it, are openly transgressed and annulled; more especially where the alteration of religion is endeavoured, and that a religion, which is contrary to law, is endeavoured to be introduced; upon which those who are most immediately concerned in it are indispensibly bound to endeavour to preserve and maintain the established laws, liberties and customs, and above all the religion and worship of God that is established among them, and to take such an effectual care, that the inhabitants of the said state or kingdom may neither be deprived of their religion, nor of their civil rights.[2]

The Declaration blamed the King's advisers rather than James himself for policies which had overturned the religion, laws and liberties of his subjects. They had advised him to exercise his dispensing and suspending powers to get round the penal laws and Test Act in order to place Catholics on an equal footing with Anglicans. Dispensations had been given to individuals to make them immune from prosecution for holding office, despite the Test Act confining office-holding to communicating Anglicans. The penal laws had been generally suspended by Declarations of Indulgence issued in 1687 and 1688 which were virtual Edicts of Toleration. The fiction that it was evil ministers, and not the King himself, who had devised the arbitrary policies was upheld with the Declaration's claim that they had revived a commission for ecclesiastical causes, which had suspended the Bishop of London from the exercise of his episcopal duties, and had deprived the Fellows of Magdalen College Oxford of their Fellowships for not electing a Catholic as their president.

A regular plan had been carried on for the establishment of popery in England; for monasteries and convents had been erected, colleges of Jesuits founded, popish churches and chapels openly built, public stations crowded with papists, and a person who was a papist, a priest and a Jesuit (Father Petre) avowed to be one of the King's ministers of state.

The judiciary had been purged, and finally an attempt had been made to pack Parliament 'the last and great remedy for all those evils'. 'Therefore,' the Declaration concluded, 'we have thought fit to go over to England and to carry over with us a force sufficient by the blessing of God, to defend us from the violence of those evil Counsellors.'

How great a force William carried over, and whether or not it was sufficient to achieve his purposes, are now disputed questions. It was once believed that he had between 14,000 and 15,000 troops under his command when he landed at Brixham.[3] Recently, however, the estimate has been revised upwards to 21,000.[4] Such an army would have been 'sufficient' to take on James' forces, for though the King had some 40,000 men in arms these were scattered about the country, and only about 25,000 were at his immediate disposal in the south of England. The claim that there were 21,000 men in the invading army, however, has not been generally accepted. Further investigation of its basis has rather reaffirmed the traditional view that the Prince of Orange had enough troops to defend himself but not sufficient to attack James.[5]

Certainly William seems to have been very cautious about challenging the King to battle. He rested for over two weeks after reaching Exeter. The sojourn was partly to refresh his troops, who had been confined on board ship not just for the immediate invasion, but ever since the abortive expedition in mid-October, which had been forced by contrary winds to return to the Netherlands. At the same time William was hoping for reinforcements, not just from the local gentry but also, and more particularly, by desertions from James' army. He had been assured in the Invitation from the Immortal Seven that 'the most part' of the King's troops would desert to him. In the event very few came over, though these included the crucial figure of Lord Churchill, the future Duke of Marlborough. William's clear disappointment at the meagre increase in his ranks and his slow progress across southern England indicate his reluctance to engage his adversary. Of course, the goodwill which his expedition had fostered from its avowed intention to call a free Parliament could be dissipated overnight if the rival armies actually fought. William could lose the battle for the hearts and minds of Englishmen even if he won the battle against their king. Yet his whole strategy seems to have been defensive rather than offensive in his march across England. His cavalry units had been badly affected by the storm which wrecked the first invasion attempt, when many horses had suffocated under the ships' hatches. This alone made a frontal attack on the King's army hazardous. William acted like a commander who felt he had sufficient men to defend himself from attack but was unprepared in every sense to confront the enemy directly.

Had James taken the offensive, therefore, the military outcome of the Revolution might have been very different. Instead, after advancing to Salisbury with a view to engaging William, he withdrew to London. This lost him the initiative and ultimately his throne. Why he chose to retreat is one of the crucial questions of the Revolution. It does not appear that he felt himself to be outnumbered by the Prince's forces. Insofar as his decision was determined by the military situation, and not by the nervous breakdown which he apparently suffered at the time, it appears to have been his suspicion of treachery in his own high command rather than the threat posed by William. Given the behaviour of men like Cornbury and Churchill who went over to William, he was right not to trust his own officers. Militarily, the notion of the Revolution as 'Lord Churchill's *coup*' is at least as convincing as the view of it as a Dutch conquest.

Indeed, the idea that England was subjected to a Dutch 'occupation' after William entered London is as far-fetched as anything the Jacobites cooked up at the time. It is true that William stationed Dutch troops in the capital and that this caused resentment. But civilians resented military men in their midst anywhere. James' troops had caused friction between themselves and citizens in Bristol, Hull and York. The fact that William's were Dutch simply added xenophobia to the usual resentment. The reaction of most of James' subjects to his flight and William's arrival was relief. As Sir George Treby, the Recorder of London, put it to the Prince on 20 December, 'Reviewing our late danger, we remember our Church and State overrun by Popery and Arbitrary Power and brought to the point of destruction by men (that were our true invaders).'[6] William's army was not an army of occupation but of liberation.

Vital though the invasion was to the outcome of the Revolution, it cannot be said to have decided the result, despite claims that the crucial decisions had all been taken before the Convention was even elected, and that when it met it simply put its seal of approval to a *fait accompli*.[7] It is true that the replacement of James by William had effectively taken place in December. Although the Convention deliberated how to fill the vacuum of power left by the King's flight, and scouted alternatives to offering William the Crown, the Prince's determination not to settle for less, and to leave the country if he were not made king, made the final outcome inevitable. Few, even of James' most ardent supporters, were prepared to accept his unconditional restoration, and there was no way that he would have accepted any conditions. Most, however reluctantly, agreed that there was no alternative but to replace him with William.

However, merely to exchange King James for King William would have been a dynastic *coup* rather than a revolution. The settlement of 1689 was no mere replacement of King Stork with King Log but a fundamental alteration in the constitution. Not only was the monarch changed but so was the monarchy. A tendency towards absolute kingship was arrested, and limited or mixed monarchy was established.

Royal policies in the 1680s

During the 1680s there had been a drift towards absolute kingship in England under Charles II as well as under James II. Absolutism is not, of course, a technical term (nor for that matter is revolution) and different definitions of it are given by various historians. To some, Louis XIV was the embodiment of the idea. Theoretically there was no check on his authority other than his duty to God. The Sun King combined executive, legislative and judicial power in his own person. His ministers executed his policies. There was no legislature as such. The Estates General had last met in 1615, and were not to meet again until 1789. Of the seven major Provincial Estates which existed in the early seventeenth century, three were no longer summoned, and two had been replaced by truncated bodies. Louis governed by decree. It is true that his edicts had to be registered in the *parlements*, or supreme courts; but they too had been reduced to rubber stamps by only being allowed to object after rather than before registering them. Louis XIV therefore never had to resort to the process known as a *lit de justice* whereby his predecessors had obliged the *parlements* to register their edicts.

In practice, admittedly, even Louis had to compromise. Thus his duty to God was no mere abstract concept, but required the maintenance of the Catholic Church in France and the principle of the hereditary descent of the Crown. Many officials whom he relied upon to execute his policies had secure tenure of their offices and could not be removed. Hence his resort wherever possible to *intendants* who were directly responsible to himself and whom he could remove at pleasure. There was a limit to how far he could push the nobility around. Such restrictions on the French King's power in practice have led some historians to deny that Louis was an absolute ruler. But this is to reduce the concept to absurdity. It is absurd to measure him up to some ideal of absolutism and to find him wanting. Historically, Louis XIV was *the* model of an absolute monarch.

How far the later Stuarts emulated him is also debatable.[8] They clearly lacked his enormous fiscal resources which enabled him to maintain a large standing army, perhaps the acid test of an absolute ruler. Nevertheless there are signs of emulation in the 1680s. Charles II was able to dispense with Parliament after the dissolution of 1681, never meeting another before his death in 1685. This was in defiance of the Triennial Act of 1664 which required Parliament to meet at least once every three years. He was able to get away with this because the commercial boom of the decade increased customs revenues to the point where he at last realised the £1,200,000 income from taxation voted him by Parliament in 1660. James II's Parliament voted him the same revenue in 1685, and increased it to nearly £2,000,000 with the addition of short-term supplies to pay for the suppression of Monmouth's rebellion. Thus when he dispensed with Parliament's services that November he could afford to do so. Perhaps the most striking parallel with the French King was not the evasion of Parliament between 1681 and 1685, but James' attempt to pack it between 1687 and 1688. Had he succeeded he would have reduced the Lords and Commons to the level of the Provincial Estates of, say, Languedoc. The regulators of corporations whom he used for the purpose of packing Parliament were paid officials directly responsible to him, and were compared with *intendants* by contemporaries.[9]

Both Charles and James used the revenues voted to them for the purpose of raising a standing army. This was a modest force under Charles, amounting to no more than 8,500 men. James, however, thanks to the generosity of the Commons' response to Monmouth's rebellion, was able to increase it to nearly 20,000 by the end of 1685. This was a sufficient force to intimidate any of his subjects who might be tempted to follow Monmouth's example. The Army was used as a police force in garrison towns like Bristol, Hull and York. These centres were effectively under martial law during James' reign. In March 1688 a standing court martial was set up, which indemnified the Army from common and statute law, making it an instrument of the royal will.

The judiciary was also brought under royal control. The judges of the common law courts – common pleas, exchequer and king's bench – could be appointed either on good behaviour or at the pleasure of the Crown. In the first years of Charles II's reign both forms were used; but increasingly in the later years and exclusively in James' reign they were appointed at pleasure. Thus they could be dismissed at will, and during the 1680s both kings used their right of dismissal to purge the bench in an effort to procure compliant judges. James even established a prerogative court, the commission for ecclesiastical causes. This was regarded by many as a revival of the Court of High Commission, which had been abolished by Act of Parliament in 1641. It even used a seal similar to that employed by the earlier court.[10] James delegated to the commission his authority as Supreme Governor of the Church of England, which it used to deprive the Bishop of London of his spiritual powers, and to discipline the Fellows of Magdalen College, Oxford when they refused to elect the King's nominee as their president. These deprivations were cited by William of Orange in his Declaration as notorious instances of James' arbitrary rule.

Where Charles II got away with his measures to strengthen the royal authority, James was brought to book in the Declaration of Rights. Thus it did not condemn the appointment of judges at pleasure but denounced the commission for ecclesiastical causes as 'illegal and pernicious'. One reason for this difference was that the framers of the Declaration were anxious not to make new law but to declare what the existing law was. It was not illegal to appoint judges at pleasure, so a clause to make their appointments on good behaviour was dropped in the committee which drew up the Declaration. But another reason why members of the Convention were reluctant to criticise Charles II, when they showed no such reluctance to condemn his brother, was that many of them approved of the former's King's actions.

Charles II's strengthening of the royal prerogative in the early 1680s was in reaction to attempts made in Parliament to exclude his brother from the succession. Not only did he dissolve parliament and refuse to call a new one after three years had elapsed, but he also took steps to try to ensure that if he did have to summon it there would be a majority in the House of Commons loyal to himself. Thus he issued writs of *quo warranto* particularly aimed at parliamentary boroughs which had returned Exclusionists, or Whigs as they had come to be called, to the last three parliaments elected between 1679 and 1681. By recalling their charters and issuing new ones in which he nominated the mayors, who were the returning officers in parliamentary elections, he attempted to rig the return of Tories who would defend the principle of indefeasible hereditary right.

He also purged Whigs from the county militias and commissions of the peace, replacing them with Tories. In the Tory reaction of the early 1680s these measures provoked little protest. On the contrary, they were popular with men who had feared that the Exclusion crisis presaged another civil war, and that the Whigs had a hidden republican agenda. These steps went far to bring about an overwhelming Tory majority in the House of Commons elected after James' accession in 1685.

James II's policies

As long as the assertion of royal authority was done in the interests of the Tories and the Church of England it proceeded virtually unchallenged. The Whigs were completely marginalised by the executive and judicial attacks upon them, while the Dissenters experienced the most severe persecution of the reign. Where Charles had tried to protect them previously, with Declarations of Indulgence issued in 1662 and 1672, now they were left to the mercies of Tory magistrates who vied with each other in their zeal to implement the penal laws.

It was when James employed the powers of the Crown to advance the interests not of the established Church but of Roman Catholics that he encountered resistance. As he told the Papal nuncio Adda, he would have been the most powerful ruler England ever had but for his religion. It was the mixture of absolutism with Catholicism, or as contemporaries put it 'popery and arbitrary power', which proved unacceptable to the majority of his subjects. The Revolution is often seen as a Whig revolution, but in fact the main victims of James' Catholic policies were Anglicans, most of them Tories. Almost all the measures denounced by the Declaration of Rights, from the suspension of Bishop Compton and the Fellows of Magdalen to the trial of the Seven Bishops, had affected men who in Charles II's reign had been among the most stalwart supporters of the King and of the hereditary principle. James strained and then snapped the link between the Crown and its natural allies.

When this became obvious even to him by 1687 he tried to forge an alliance with Whigs and Dissenters who had tried to prevent him from succeeding his brother in the Exclusion crisis. The extent to which he succeeded in obtaining the support of 'Whig collaborators', as they are rather pejoratively known, has been a matter of debate. Those historians who see the Whigs taking the initiative in 1688 and hijacking the Convention tend to play down their number. But there can be no doubt that, while some Whigs and Dissenters were dubious about the King's sincerity, many were prepared to cooperate with him. They were added along with Catholics to the commissions of the peace when James purged them of Tories, and similarly to the corporations of parliamentary boroughs in plans to pack Parliament with members sympathetic to repeal of the Test Acts and penal laws. They also served on a commission of enquiry into the conduct of those who had been engaged in the prosecution of Dissenters for breaches of those laws during the Tory reaction under Charles II.[11]

Many of these men were of obscure social origin who had never previously held public office. They came from below the level of the political elite, and in many cases replaced gentry and others who belonged to the ruling class. In this respect James embarked on a social revolution, and ironically the Revolution can be seen as a reaction which restored the traditional rulers of provincial England. The reign of James II thus repeated the pattern of the Interregnum and Restoration, demonstrating the truth of the saying that history repeats itself, the first time as tragedy, the second time as farce.

Not that all the so-called 'collaborators' were of humble origins. There were some forty-eight MPs among the commissioners investigating the persecution of Dissenters. One of the more prominent among the commissioners was the Quaker leader William Penn. He became a close confidante of the King, helping to draft the Declaration of Indulgence, intervening in the Magdalen College affair and even getting involved in the campaign to pack Parliament. His 'collaboration' throws much light on the motives of many Dissenters who played a role in these revolutionary years. What they sought was toleration. The question was: Where were they to find it? If they looked to the Cavalier Parliament elected in 1661, which lasted until 1679, they were doomed to disappointment. So far from offering relief from the penal laws against dissent, the bigoted Anglicans on the back-benches, determined to get their own back on those who had persecuted them in the civil wars and Interregnum, added to the statutes penalising non-attendance at the established Church.

The only hope of relief in those years came from the King, who twice offered Declarations of Indulgence, only to be obliged to withdraw them after protests from Parliament. The Exclusion parliaments by contrast had seen sympathy for the plight of Dissenters, and there were even bills to relieve them brought forward in 1680, only to be aborted by the prorogation of the session. Since then, however, the Whig Party which had dominated the Commons during the Exclusion crisis had been virtually annihilated, its leadership cut off by treason trials and its support eliminated by the purge of the parliamentary boroughs. Once more a parliament with an intransigent Anglican majority had been returned which again refused to cooperate with a king anxious to introduce toleration. As on previous occasions under Charles II, it made more sense for Dissenters to hope for help from the Crown than from Parliament. This is what makes the term 'collaborators', with its echoes of Europe under the Nazi occupation, so pejorative. Penn was not a quisling. James II's Declaration of Indulgence brought immediate relief to fellow Quakers who were suffering the severest persecution they had ever experienced during the 'Tory reaction' of Charles II's closing years. Penn even justified the packing of parliament on the grounds that it was the only way to bring about a Toleration Act as comprehensive as the King's Edict in the circumstances of the time. He also recognised the force of the Marquis of Halifax's argument in *The Character of a Trimmer* that toleration based on the mere word of the King was very precarious, since the royal word had twice been recalled under Charles II. Only an Act of Parliament could give a permanent guarantee of freedom from persecution. At the same time only a parliament of members who shared the King's views would enact his Declaration of Indulgence.

Penn's analysis of the situation might seem to have been invalidated by the Toleration Act of 1689. Yet on examination that measure was very restricted in comparison with the Declaration of Indulgence. Where the Crown offered virtually unrestricted toleration to all, including Roman Catholics, the Act did not extend to them or even to Protestants who did not accept the doctrine of the Trinity, thus excluding a growing number of deists and unitarians. Furthermore, where James II dropped the requirement of the Corporation and Test Acts which obliged office-holders in boroughs or under the Crown to take communion in the Anglican Church, the Toleration Act specifically upheld it. It even endorsed the obligation of non-Anglicans to pay tithes to maintain the ministers of the Church of England. Cooperation with the King even to the extent of assisting his efforts to produce a compliant parliament, therefore, was not a treacherous betrayal of Protestant principles but made perfect sense.

When James panicked on learning of the imminent embarkation of William's task force, and threw his policies into reverse, those Whigs who had cooperated with him were left high and dry. He abandoned the attempt to pack parliament, and restored charters to many parliamentary boroughs, including London. He wound up the commission for ecclesiastical causes and reinstated the Bishop of London and the Fellows of Magdalen college. This 'U-turn', as it would be called today, was intended to placate his 'old friends' the Anglican Tories. It mainly succeeded in revealing his total unreliability. Thus he won over very few of the clergy whom he had alienated with his Declarations of Indulgence, although these included the important figure of Archbishop Sancroft of Canterbury. At the same time he completely lost all credibility with the Whigs and Dissenters.

Reluctant revolutionaries

This produced a consensus against the regime which ensured that virtually the only bloodshed in the Revolution was James II's nosebleed at Salisbury. As one contemporary put it:

> I question if in all the histories of empire there is one instance of so
> blodless a Revolution as that in England in 1688, wherein Whigs,

Tories, princes, prelates, nobles, clergy, common people and standing army were unanimous. To have seen all England of one mind is to have lived at a very particular juncture.[12]

It was not that the nation rose in unity to rally to William III's cause. Very few people actively participated in the revolutionary events. The majority in any Revolution play a passive role. What is crucial is whether or not they support the regime or its opponents. In 1685 at the time of Monmouth's rebellion, before James had time to alienate his subjects, most of them favoured his crushing of the rebels and his rival stood no chance. In 1688 they were so alienated that they withdrew their allegiance, creating a vacuum which gave William and those who assisted him the opportunity to overthrow him.

Among the small minority who took an active part in helping William were nobles in the Midlands and the North of England.[13] The Earl of Devonshire mustered his tenantry and seized Derby, then marched to Nottingham which he took with the aid of Lord Delamere. The Earl of Danby overthrew the Governor of York and proceeded to Hull, where a *coup* in the garrison gained control of the town from its Catholic governor. Those who took part in the Revolution in the Midlands were mainly Whigs, whereas Danby, himself a Tory, had support from both parties. Again, this revealed a consensus among the subjects of James II in support of William III's Declaration for a free Parliament. This lasted through the elections to the Convention, though debates on how to repair the damage left by James' flight to France were to reveal fissures between those who simply wanted the Dutch invasion to bring him to his senses and those who were determined to replace him on the throne.

Though more Whigs than Tories were returned to the Convention, the results of the elections to it reflected the consensus among those of both parties who had opposed James ever since his prorogation of Parliament in 1685. Many two-member constituencies returned one Whig and one Tory, apparently without contests. Both could stand on a platform of condemning the King's arbitrary actions and of ensuring that in future monarchs would not be able to act in a similar way. Those who had fallen in with his measures found themselves in double jeopardy, for many who stood as candidates for the Convention were unsuccessful. Their cooperation with the King was held against them. Thus in Suffolk they were defeated at the polls, 'the former regulation having made all people sick of the folly and madness of the phanatique administration when they were in the saddle'.[14]

When the Convention met, however, there was a clear division among the members as to how to fill the gap left by the King's departure. There were a handful on the one hand who claimed that James still commanded the allegiance of his subjects by divine right and should be called back to resume his hereditary throne. Against these there was another handful of republicans. But the majority accepted that, while there was a constitutional impasse, neither of these solutions was acceptable. That is to say they accepted the concept of limited monarchy over absolute kingship and republicanism. This acceptance was reflected in the resolutions that in future no Catholic or spouse of a Catholic could be king or queen. Experience had confirmed that Catholics were inclined to rule arbitrarily. This acceptance of limited monarchy also found expression in the Declaration of Rights, which listed thirteen measures undertaken by James and declared them to be illegal. By condemning James II's use of the Crown's remaining prerogative powers, and asserting parliamentary limitations on the King's freedom of action, the Declaration of Rights stated a preference for limited over absolute monarchy. This crucial change in the conception of kingship was confirmed in the changes made to the Coronation Oath in 1689. James had sworn to 'grant and keep' the laws 'granted by the kings of England'. William and Mary swore 'to govern the people of this kingdom of England ... according to the statutes in parliament agreed on, and the laws and customs of the same'.

Where the agreement over the nature of the monarchy brought Tories and Whigs together, however, the question of who was to exercise the powers of the Crown provoked serious disagreement in the Convention. Many Tories argued that the only constitutional way to proceed was by way of a regency. Others accepted that James should be laid aside, but argued that the smallest breach with the hereditary principle would be made by offering the Crown to Mary. The Whigs would have none of this, and insisted that William should be king. In the end his threat to leave the country to its own devices if he were not given the Crown concentrated minds wonderfully, and he and his wife became joint rulers. How far they accepted the limitations of the Declaration of Rights as a contract between themselves and the people represented in Parliament has provoked debate.[15] However, the framers of the Declaration claimed that its limitations of the Crown were statements of fact and that they were in that sense not conditions at all. Moreover, William and Mary accepted the Crown before they gave their consent to the Declaration. Later, when the first regular Parliament was assembled after the elections of 1690, the Declaration was put on the statute book as the Bill of Rights. At that stage William could technically have refused his assent to it, as he still had the right to veto bills and was quite prepared to use it. That he was happy to accept the Bill of Rights suggests that he was not irked by its provisions in any constitutional sense. Limited monarchy, not contractual kingship, was established by the Revolution of 1688–89. The framers of the Revolution settlement sought to limit the monarchy by keeping monarchs dependent upon Parliament. This was established in the financial arrangement which they agreed. Where Charles II and James II had both been voted £1,200,000 for life at the outset of their reigns, William and Mary were only voted money for the short term. Thus the customs were not granted until 1690, and then for only four years, extended in 1694 to another five. By 1699 the traditional distinction between the 'ordinary' and 'extraordinary' expenditure of the Crown had been converted into the civil list and public finance. In 1698 a civil list of £700,000 per annum was voted to cover the domestic bills of the royal family. The huge sums, amounting to some £5,000,000, needed to finance the war against France were no longer the personal responsibility of the monarch but were assumed by Parliament.

These developments raise the question of when the Revolution of 1688 can be said to have ended. Some historians take its constitutional effects down to the Act of Settlement of 1701, which provided for the succession of the House of Hanover when Queen Anne died. It also further limited the royal prerogative, for instance, by not allowing the monarch to appoint judges at pleasure but only on good behaviour, which was a major step in establishing the independence of the judiciary. Others argue that such measures as the Triennial Act of 1694, which restricted the royal prerogative by requiring a dissolution of Parliament at least every three years, were the consequence not of the Revolution but of the war with France. They point out that William vetoed a triennial bill in 1693, and only gave his assent to one the following year as the price he had to pay for the passing of the Act establishing the Bank of England. The Bank was an essential linchpin of a system of public credit necessitated by the financial demands of the war against Louis XIV.

However, the Financial Revolution, as it has been called, was as much the result of the events of 1688 as it was of the fiscal necessities of warfare. Indeed, to separate them is very artificial. One of William III's main motives in invading England was to gain its help in his struggle with the French. The members of the Convention were only too aware that their decisions locked the country into a major war. They debated against a background of James II's landing in Ireland with the backing of France. To separate the Battle of the Boyne from the Battle of La Hogue, placing one in the dynastic context of British politics and the other in a European context of the War of the League of Augsburg, is absurd. In many ways that war could be more appropriately called the War of the British Succession.

Warfare was to transform the nation (England before the Union with Scotland in 1707, Britain thereafter) into a major European power. It did this by diverting economic resources from peacetime pursuits of estate development and commercial expansion into the revenues of what has been called 'the fiscal-military state'.[16] This process brought into being a new interest, that of the state's creditors, which initially seemed to threaten the hegemony of the landed elite and was only slowly absorbed into an element in the ruling class. Whigs welcomed this transformation while Tories resisted it. There was a germ of truth in Swift's claim that by 1710 'all disputes which used originally to divide whig and tory were wholly dropped; and those fantastical words ought in justice to have been so too, provided we could have found out more convenient terms whereby to distinguish lovers of peace from lovers of war'.[17]

Swift was of course exaggerating. There were still religious and constitutional issues which divided Tory from Whig. Tories championed the Church of England against other sects, Protestant as well as Catholic, and hankered after divine right kingship. Whigs sympathised with dissent and were quite prepared to set aside the hereditary descent in favour of parliamentary monarchy. Whig ideology in the long run became the dominant political creed because Whigs were much more ready to accept the Revolution of 1688, and its consequences, than were their rivals.

Whatever their differences, however, Tories and Whigs accepted that there had been a revolution in 1688. Indeed, looking back they saw it as being *the* English Revolution, dismissing the events of 1640 to 1660 as a rebellion. Where the institutions of monarchy, the established Church and the House of Lords had then been swept away by violence from below, in 1688 they had been preserved against threats to them from above. Lesser gentry, merchants and even Levellers had been responsible for the complete overthrow of the ancient constitution and its replacement with a republic during the Interregnum. The Crown was seen as threatening to undermine it in the reign of James II. The King himself planned to replace the limited monarchy implicitly restored in 1660 with absolute kingship. His drive to put his fellow Catholics on an equal status with Anglicans was seen as a deliberate design to return the established Church to Rome. In order to achieve these ends he had initially tried to work with the traditional ruling classes, but when they became uncooperative he had set them aside and allied with lesser gentry, merchants and even men of humble origin to force his policies on the country. Determined to stop the process, and at the same time to avoid a repetition of the events of the 1640s and 1650s, the political elite temporarily put aside their partisan differences to unite in the preservation of what they perceived to be the constitution, and in the Revoluton settlement did their best to preserve it against future threats to it whether from above or below.

Notes

1 Robert Beddard (ed.), *The Revolutions of 1688*, Oxford, 1988.
2 Ibid., p. 125.
3 J. Childs, *The Army, James II and the Glorious Revolution*, Manchester, 1980, p. 175.
4 Jonathan Israel, 'The Dutch role in the Glorious Revolution', in *The Anglo-Dutch Moment: Essays on the Glorious Revolution and Its World*, ed. J. Israel, Cambridge, 1991, p. 106.
5 Stephen Webb, after considering Israel's reckoning, himself reckons William's task force at 14,000. Stephen Saunders Webb, *Lord Churchill's Coup: The Anglo-American Empire and the Glorious Revolution Reconsidered*, New York, 1995, p. 141.
6 W.A. Speck, *Reluctant Revolutionaries: Englishmen and the Revolution of 1688*, Oxford, 1988, p. 236.

7 Robert Beddard (ed.), *Kingdom Without a King*, Oxford, 1988, p. 65.
8 John Miller, *An English Absolutism? The Later Stuart Monarchy 1660–88*, Historical Association, New Appreciations in History, 1993.
9 Thomas Bruce, Earl of Aylesbury, *Memoirs*, ed. W.E. Buckley, 1890, vol. 1, p. 174. The prospects for James' attempt to pack parliament have provoked disagreement among historians. For a summary of views up to 1988 see Speck, *Reluctant Revolutionaries*, pp. 131–2. Two recent investigations continue the debate. M.J. Short concludes that they were good in 'The Corporation of Hull and the Government of James II', *Historical Research*, 1988 vol. lxxi, pp. 172–95. By contrast, Paul D. Halliday concludes that 'James's effort in 1687–88 to reshape the electorate in order to gain a Parliament ready to grant religious toleration . . . would not have worked. We know this because it did not work!' See *Dismembering the Body Politic: Partisan Politics in England's Towns, 1650–1730*, Cambridge, 1998, p. 239. Whether or not it would have worked is a question which can never be answered satisfactorily, since James abandoned it before it could be tested at the polls. That contemporaries feared it might have succeeded, however, is far more important when gauging its contribution to the Revolution.
10 J.P. Kenyon, 'The Commission for Ecclesiastical Causes 1686–1688', *Historical Journal*, 1991, vol. xxiv, pp. 727–36. Kenyon establishes that the commission was a court, where this had been denied previously, and that it met regularly to deal with matrimonial causes.
11 J.R. Jones, 'James II's whig collaborators', *Historical Journal*, vol. iii, pp. 65–73; Mark Goldie, 'James II and the Dissenter's revenge: the commission of enquiry of 1688', *Historical Research*, vol. cxvi, 1993, pp. 53–88.
12 Colley Cibber, *An Apology for the Life of Colley Cibber*, London, 1925, vol. i, p. 35.
13 D. Hosford, *Nottingham, Nobles and the North*, Hamden, CT, 1976; W.A. Speck, 'The Revolution of 1688 in the North of England', *Northern History*, vol. xxv, 1989, pp. 188–204.
14 Cambridge University Library, Add MSS. 4403: M.W. Bohun, 15 January 1689.
15 See Lois Schwoerer, *The Declaration of Rights*, Baltimore, MD, 1981.
16 John Brewer, *The Sinews of Power: War, Money and the English State*, London, 1989; see also D.W. Jones, *War and Economy in the Age of William and Marlborough*, Oxford, 1988.
17 Jonathan Swift, *The History of the Four Last Years of the Queen*, 1758, p. 7.

Further reading

Robert Beddard (ed.), *The Revolutions of 1688*, Oxford, 1991.
Lionel Glassey (ed.), *The Reigns of Charles II and James VII and II*, Basingstoke, 1997.
Jonathan Israel, *The Anglo-Dutch Moment: Essays on the Revolution of 1688 and its World Impact*, Cambridge, 1991.
John Miller, *The Glorious Revolution*, London, 1983.
Michael Mullett, *James II and English Politics 1678–1688*, Lancaster, 1993.
W.A. Speck, *Reluctant Revolutionaries: Englishmen and the Revolution of 1688*, Oxford, 1988.

5 The American Revolution 1763–91

Colin Bonwick

The question 'What was the American Revolution?' has been asked many times and been given many answers. At its simplest, it was a crisis within the British Empire: the loss of thirteen colonies when viewed from a British perspective, and the achievement of independence from the American stance. The second and more important component was the creation of an American republic. This in turn had three elements: the establishment of governments in each American state during the war, the creation of a national union, and substantial social change. Each raised important ideological questions concerning the source of legitimate authority, the protection of liberty, the necessity for government power and the nature of equality.

Victory over France in the Seven Years War created problems for Britain's North American policy from 1763 onwards. Thirteen mainland colonies were already mature and virtually self-governing, but acquisition of French territory persuaded successive governments to reorganise and consolidate the empire of which they formed the major part. Legislation attempting to raise revenue in the colonies, particularly the notorious Stamp Act of 1765, provoked the colonies to vehement resistance. In 1773 the Boston Tea Party encouraged both sides to turn up the heat rather than soothe angered feelings. Early the following year the British Parliament passed four Coercive Acts, which Americans significantly referred to as the Intolerable Acts. In response the colonies summoned the First Continental Congress which met in September 1774 to protest against the legislation and plan their responses. Their intention was to find a political solution to the dispute within the empire, but in April 1775, British troops and American militia clashed at Lexington, just outside Boston, Massachusetts. Fourteen months later, in July 1776, the Americans declared independence. The war dragged on for five more years. For a time it seemed that Britain would be successful in suppressing the colonial rebellion, but in 1777 General John Burgoyne was forced to surrender at Saratoga, New York. France entered the conflict in alliance with the United States early the following year, and what had been only a colonial rebellion became a world war in which Britain and France fought each other as

Map 5.1 The United States in 1783

far afield as India and the West Indies as well as in North America. In spite of considerable successes in the south after 1779 a second army, under General Earl Cornwallis, was surrounded and defeated at Yorktown, Virginia in 1781, thus effectively ending the war. Two years later, Britain formally recognised American independence. While the war continued, the states erected their own governments and began constructing a national union. They ratified the Articles of Confederation in 1781 which permitted Congress only limited delegated powers, but six years later the Philadelphia Convention drafted a new Constitution which came into operation in 1789. Much remained to be done, but its implementation during the 1790s marked completion of the Revolution.

Colonies within the British Empire

If the seeds of American independence were sown when the first English settlements were founded early in the seventeenth century, their flowering less than two hundred years later was unexpected. With hindsight their budding is easily visible during the 1760s, and the benefits of independence obvious, but there were many advantages to remaining within the empire. Economic, cultural and political circumstances provided a context for rebellion but did not compel it. True, the colonists looked increasingly towards the interior and constantly complained of their indebtedness to rapacious British merchants, and of navigation acts requiring them to trade through Britain. But they also enjoyed protected access to rapidly developing British markets, capital and entrepreneurial skills, and their ships could participate in the carrying trade under naval protection. When all things are considered their net trade deficit was easily sustainable. British taxes, even when successfully raised, were insignificant.

The colonies were also part of a highly successful transatlantic community. Thus Quakers and Protestant Dissenters had close associations with their overseas counterparts, Americans such as Benjamin Rush and John Dickinson were educated in Britain, and Benjamin Franklin represented several colonies in London and was prominent in the British intellectual world. But one particular feature of these Anglo-American connections illustrated the sharp social divide between all colonists and the imperial elite: they were all with the middling ranks and gentry, not the aristocracy which directed British society and controlled government policy. Two other characteristics bound the colonies to Britain. People on both sides of the Atlantic prided themselves on being free by comparison with the repressed peoples of continental empires, and being Protestant rather than Roman Catholic, a religion they associated with tyranny. Even the ideology which underpinned American resistance and the new republican regime was drawn from sources common to Britain and not inherently inconsistent with membership of the Empire – a point on which English radicals who defended the colonies insisted. Among its several elements were seventeenth-century Puritanism, the rational universe of the eighteenth-century Enlightenment and English legalism. In particular, the sources included the traditional English doctrine of a putative Anglo-Saxon ancient constitution which had allegedly provided a model system of representative government before being overthrown by the Norman Conquest in 1066. It had been given a fresh lease of life during the English civil wars and became the core of what became known as the 'commonwealth' or 'Real Whig' radical tradition; during the Revolution it inspired critics of government on both sides of the Atlantic. Republicanism, which stressed the importance of virtuous conduct and civic duty over private interest, was initially a component of this tradition rather than an attack on the monarchy. With such an intellectual inheritance, the liberty to which Americans were greatly attached before the war was the liberty of Englishmen and was only repositioned exclusively on to natural rights grounds when independence was claimed.

Similarly, the political framework of pre-revolutionary America was broadly consonant with that of Britain. Customary practice over generations had allowed virtually complete self-government in domestic matters, including in particular control over internal taxation. Local government in the counties and townships was largely autonomous, and at colony level each had a balanced system of government divided between executive, legislature and judiciary; all operated according to the rule of law rather than by royal fiat. But beneath the surface the possibility of dangerous conflict emerged during the dispute with Britain. Royal governors possessing extensive powers were appointed by the Crown and responsible to London for their actions, whereas legislatures were elected annually in each colony and their members were accordingly responsible to their respective communities. Colonial politicians developed sophisticated political machines which successfully curbed the extensive powers nominally possessed by the royal governors, but continual clashes were inevitable. The system generally worked well, but only where governors were tactful and respected local realities even if they conflicted with imperial instructions.

Colonial affairs were often stressful during the 1760s but not inherently revolutionary. Long-term processes such as rapid population growth, strong economic development and continuous territorial expansion were potentially unsettling. More immediately, trade recessions were only moderated by short recoveries, and difficulties were compounded by increases in the ratio of population to land and the rising price of both land and slaves in long-established areas. Urban America was undergoing stressful change at the same time. Wage rates for the less affluent often failed to keep pace with rising prices, and poverty increased significantly in New York, Boston and Philadelphia. Other disharmonies were more obviously political in character, and manifestations of factional divisions appeared in many colonies. The Paxton Boys, a group of Pennsylvania frontiersmen, marched on Philadelphia in 1764 to protest the legislature's failure to provide adequate defence against Indian attacks, and in New York two years later an anti-rent movement known as the Tenants Revolt had to be suppressed by force. Further south the Regulator movement in North Carolina in 1768–71, formed from small to middling planters who inhabited the interior, rebelled against attempts by the longer established gentry of the eastern seaboard to assert supremacy over them, and in South Carolina aspiring property-owners in the recently settled back country demanded the extension of civil government institutions to their region. None of these movements seriously threatened the local elite's authority, but all were warnings for the future. The hegemony of the elite was also being insidiously challenged in several colonies. Natural allies and supporters such as the established churches (the Church of England in New York and the south, and the Congregational Church in most of New England) were inherently weak and their authority increasingly challenged by other sects. Tensions such as these, not greatly serious in themselves, created an unstable context within which the imperial dispute took place. Conversely, the deterioration of relations with Britain heightened American sensitivities over the range of political, ideological, cultural and economic issues, and aggravated those tensions, especially between elites and their social inferiors, already present in colonial society.

Yet a sense of exclusive American nationalism was more a product than a cause of the Revolution. A feeling of continentalism and being distinctively American was undoubtedly growing, but nascent nationalism had not reached maturity before 1775. With few exceptions colonists were unashamed of being British as well as American; they sent men to fight in British wars on their own continent and were proud of their contribution to victory over France at Louisburg in 1745 and Québec in 1759. After Patriot efforts at the First Continental Congress failed to find a middle way which would allow a continued royal presence but ensure adequate protection of colonial liberty and interests, between 20 and 30 per cent of the population valued the British connection sufficiently to support the Crown in its attempt to suppress the rebellion. At the end of the war between 60,000 and 100,000 people had departed the United States rather than come to terms with the new independent republican regime.

Crisis of empire

The American Revolution was firstly a problem in British politics. Acquisition of vast new territory from France in 1763 and growing suspicions that the colonies were driving towards independence coupled to fears that this would end in national destruction led to a reformulation of official policy. Its controlling logic was that local interests should be subordinated to the broader interests of the empire as a whole and that direction of imperial defence should lie at the centre in Whitehall; all its members would benefit in the long run. Such views were reinforced by the conviction that the imperial relationship was one between a British parent possessed of superior wisdom, experience and knowledge, and colonial children whose interests should naturally be subject to her direction. The new policy necessarily raised questions concerning the constitutional structure of the British Empire. Heretofore, its fabric rested not on clearly defined and agreed principles but on customs and assumptions which were challenged as the crisis worsened.

The Declaratory Act of 1766 which accompanied repeal of the Stamp Act was particularly revealing, especially since it was legislation enacted by the Rockingham government whose supporters were known, then and later, for their sympathy with America. It rested on two axioms: that sovereignty was indivisible and by definition rested in a single place, and that Parliament represented the extended empire as well as Britain, so that even the colonists, who directly elected no members, were virtually represented in it and bound by its laws. Bluntly stating that Parliament possessed the right to legislate for the colonies in all cases whatsoever, the Act applied to colonial affairs the principle of parliamentary sovereignty – that is, the doctrine that parliamentary power extended to everything not naturally impossible.

This principle had grown from the need to justify parliamentary authority after the Glorious Revolution of 1688–89 and had become an article of faith accepted by lawyers and politicians alike by the mid-eighteenth century. In a British society that had become deeply conservative it legitimised the dominance of the landed aristocracy who owned the country's principal source of wealth, exercised social hegemony through the prestige of their property and titles, and maintained political control through their presence in both houses of parliament and dominance of the great offices of state. Yet the doctrines of parliamentary sovereignty and virtual representation, really legal fictions, were quite new and not so self-evidently inherent in British constitutional principles as their advocates insisted. Rather, parliamentary sovereignty was a convention whose utility was to defend Parliament against the Crown and challenges from surviving Jacobites, and to assert the authority of the controlling aristocracy against the generality of the population. In addition, it had significant if implicit limits. Custom and conventions were still important, common law was a practical rival, and Scotland possessed in its Church, its legal system and property law institutions which in the eighteenth century were practically immune from the principle of parliamentary supremacy. Nevertheless, successive British governments continued to assert the principle as essential to the integrity of both the British regime itself and the imperial connection, even to the point at which it could be sustained only by military force.

As the colonial dispute rumbled on, it appeared that concessions merely encouraged more demands and that the colonies could never be satisfied. It seemed essential to reassert British power after the Boston Tea Party of 1773 had flagrantly challenged royal authority in Massachusetts. Lord

North, the Prime Minister, could have relied on the royal prerogative by using orders-in-council, but preferred the legal process of parliamentary enactment. By the following summer the four Coercive or Intolerable Acts had been passed to general approval in Britain. The crucial legislation was the Massachusetts Government Act which reconstructed the colony's charter in order to strengthen the royal governor's control and influence in local politics. It seemed quite reasonable to British eyes since a charter was regarded as no more than a grant of privileges and concessions and thus susceptible to amendment if felt desirable. However, far from resolving the dispute, the Intolerable Acts aggravated Britain's difficulties, for other colonies feared that what had been done in Massachusetts could be extended to them. When the Americans began challenging royal authority, first by political protest, then by assembling arms for military resistance, North decided it was preferable to use coercion to enforce obedience rather than continue with negotiation. Given British assumptions and the presumed inconceivability of defeat, it was not an unreasonable decision – but undoubtedly it was unwise. Only in 1778, when it was too late, did he offer concessions which might have been acceptable three years earlier – and which implicitly abandoned the principle of parliamentary sovereignty.

American independence

The coming of American independence was not inevitable. Colonists accepted the 'true' principles of the British Constitution but understood them differently. Custom and practice over generations, which had culminated in the principle of parliamentary sovereignty in Britain, led to the very different principle of local autonomy in the colonies, and particularly to the conviction that Parliament could not lawfully raise internal taxation, for that would violate the principle which demanded the consent of those who were to pay. Americans also rejected the doctrine of virtual representation. Successive British efforts to reorganise the empire to the mutual benefit of all its members were consequently interpreted with alarm by the colonies.

Americans were pushed towards resistance by their developing interpretation of British policy. Beginning with the Stamp Act and coming to a climax with the Intolerable Acts, the colonists came to believe that there was system and purpose behind the policies of successive administrations which continually skirted their protests against successive legislation. They concluded that Britain intended to suppress American liberties and to establish an authoritarian regime which would subordinate America to her interests. In recent years it has been conclusively demonstrated that there was no such conspiracy on the part of British politicians – though it can be argued that the lack of intent did not render the consequence impossible. Rather, as I.R. Christie has argued, to a significant degree it was the inadequacy and misjudgements of British politicians that caused the loss of the colonies.[1] The Massachusetts Government Act is a good example of clashing principles. The British government believed colonial charters granted privileges that could be amended or withdrawn, but to Americans they had become virtual constitutions containing inviolable rights which could be changed only with their consent. Up to that point the initiative had been with Britain; thereafter it lay with America.

Claims to sovereign authority inherently include military power and the right and capacity to use it coercively. In this instance the government discovered, too late, that force was insufficient. The Americans eventually took up arms, declared their independence and successfully defended it. Authority which could resist parliamentary reform at home and be applied to the small West Indian islands, so dependent on Britain for defence against France and their slaves alike, failed in relation to the mainland colonies. The empire of which they were a major component had become a voluntary association dedicated to the advancement of mutual interests and affection, as English radical propagandists argued. The imperial connection rested on the willing consent of mature societies to accept central control in matters of general concern but not internal affairs, and should have been administered on that basis. In grand conceptual terms the loss of the American colonies represented the systemic failure of a profoundly conservative (but also successful and by contemporary standards liberal) regime to adjust to the changing realities of colonial maturity. Given the commitment to parliamentary supremacy which seemed to its supporters to be so central to its success, the American rejection of unlimited British authority within the colonies appeared to threaten the entire fabric of the regime. No government between 1763 and 1775 was willing to adjust to the altered requirements of the changing Anglo-American relationship. In that respect the loss of America was less a product of individual failings and more a consequence of the very success of the Glorious Revolution whose inheritance had ossified into comfortable self-satisfaction rather than continuing to adjust to changing circumstances.

In one respect there was a sharp contrast between events in 1688 and 1775. The Glorious Revolution in Britain was a revolution in which certain members of the aristocracy legitimately acted on behalf of the nation as a whole and ensured that they retained their authority against the Crown as well as over the mass of the population. Agitation for extended representation in Parliament at home could be confidently resisted, for Britain remained a deferential society. This was not the case in the thirteen colonies. American gentlemen – and, as will be seen below, most of the people – were no longer willing to accept aristocratic leadership and command from across the Atlantic. Instead, the British government provoked into rebellion well-intentioned colonists who had much to gain from continued membership of the empire. Thus the Revolution was in part a revolt of the gentry and the majority of Americans against the dominant imperial aristocracy.

As such it encompassed a violent and sometimes brutal civil war. The 20 and 30 per cent of the population who actively supported the Crown's attempts to suppress the rebellion posed continual difficulties for the new government, and the conflict between Patriots and Loyalists in the back-country of the Carolinas degenerated into savagery. Many Loyalists had their property confiscated, were banished or were victims of mob violence; a few were hanged. Since the United States had no professional army it depended on the willingness of ordinary Americans to volunteer for service; significantly for the future of civilian authority, their action was autonomous rather than the behaviour of social inferiors following the example of their betters. In all, armed service involved a very high proportion of the available adult males on the Patriot side, of whom 24,000 suffered service-related deaths and 24,000 were very seriously wounded. Desertion and changing sides were not unknown in the continental army, but discipline depended to an unusually high degree on persuasion and consent, rather than on the brutal punishment characteristic of the British army. Moreover, there was a shortage of 'gentlemen' to serve as officers, and many were drawn from lowlier sections in society than would have been possible in England. The experience provided many lessons for the future.

Revolutionary governments

What originated as an armed protest in defence of American liberty and interests within the empire became an outright bid for independence. The Loyalist solution to the colonial dispute, which would permit a continued British presence in American government, could be imposed only if the Crown was successful in suppressing the rebellion. During 1775 and 1776, royal jurisdiction disintegrated to the point at which it extended scarcely beyond the range of British guns; except in New York city it was only occasionally restored. But though independence was literally essential, it was primarily an enabling act which permitted the fundamental civil process of founding a new regime to take place. The opportunity presenting itself in 1776 was rare, if not unique. As John Adams, one of the leading radicals, said, 'When, before the present epocha [*sic*], had three millions of people full power and a fair opportunity to form and establish the wisest and happiest government that human wisdom can contrive?'[2] The previous elite and their government had lost control; rebellion against British authority became revolution within the United States. New sources of legitimacy had to be discovered, new relationships defined and new structures established; the new republic could not be merely the former regime adjusted for the metaphorical execution of the King.

The problem of lawful government was acute. Such authority as existed was increasingly exercised by local Committees of Safety, County Congresses and Provincial Congresses which were rapidly taking on some responsibilities of legislatures. Their *de facto* power was necessarily temporary and confirmed a central feature of the Revolution: no American elite could persuasively claim to represent the entire people as the British aristocracy had done in 1688. As the imperial dispute reached crisis point in 1775 men of all social ranks had been politicised, and in Philadelphia the independence movement was led by an artisan group, the Committee of Privates, rather than by a dominant elite group. Rising aspirations to political influence, coupled with a growing sense that elites often had different interests from their own, increased during the political conflict with Britain and were strengthened by the experience of war. Its nature also encouraged participants to claim a share in political administration and thus required important concessions by members of the Patriot elite.

In addition, any long-term system would have to conform to ideological principles articulated with especial clarity in the Declaration of Independence. These included the propositions that all men are created equal and are endowed with certain unalienable rights, including life, liberty and the pursuit of happiness, and that governments are instituted to protect those rights and derive their just powers from the consent of the governed. There was little argument about this philosophy since, as Thomas Jefferson, its primary author, correctly insisted, he was expressing commonly held principles, but there was another side to the problem of constructing a republican regime. If the United States was to survive and flourish, its government needed to be sufficiently powerful to execute its proper functions effectively in a way that the royal regime had failed to do. Thus, when the colonies transformed themselves into states they were obliged to construct governments capable of administering the daily affairs of civil society, introduce necessary republican reforms and cope with the difficult tasks of organising and directing armies, raising funds and conducting diplomacy. Yet the new governments could not impose their will on their communities since their army lacked the necessary capability. Coercion could be effective against Loyalists; it would be ineffectual against the majority. Successful government depended on consent. A balance had to be achieved between the ideological commitment to liberty, which required limited government dependent on popular will, and the need for strong government capable of implementing its policy.

The task was challenging, for the United States and its member states were literally creating themselves. The problem was complicated by the need to weigh the interests and functions of local state governments against some form of general government in a system in which power was dispersed rather than concentrated. The solution in this respect was to divide government, and thus power, between local and central administrations. Yet another dimension to the problem was the need to balance the corrosively equalitarian principle of the Declaration of Independence against the actuality of social hierarchy in American society within which were sharp conflicts of interest and aspiration between self-confident elites and their social inferiors whose contribution was literally vital to military victory.

The work was completed at two levels: first, within the individual states, since they remained the primary units of social and political organisation, and second, at the level of common interests which required construction of a national government.

The first stage was to create a fresh balance between the liberty of citizens and the need for effective power by framing republican governments within each state. A proposal that the Continental Congress should draft a standard constitution was rejected on the grounds that the states differed from one another. Instead, each constructed its own government in its own time. Superficially, the new systems were similar to those of the imperial regime and thus similar to the British structure of balanced components, in that each had a separated executive, legislature and judiciary. Yet their philosophy and thus their *modus operandi* were profoundly different.[3] Almost the only thing on which Americans agreed was that republicanism was more than government without a king. Separation from Britain was also a repudiation of prescription, whether of Crown or Parliament, as the source of legitimate authority, and thus it was necessary to seek an alternative source for the exercise of legitimate political power. The solution was to locate authority in the community itself. As the Massachusetts Declaration of Rights put it:

> The people of this Commonwealth have the sole and exclusive right of governing themselves as a free, sovereign, and independent state. . . . All power residing originally in the people, and being derived from them, the several magistrates and officers of Government, vested with authority, whether legislative, executive, or judicial, are their substitutes and agents, and are at all times accountable to them.

This replacement of parliamentary sovereignty by popular sovereignty represented a paradigmatic shift in the source of authority. The change eventually developed into a powerfully democratic and equalitarian ideology, but it did not immediately imply unequivocal majoritarianism: the people were still understood to be more a social collectivity than the numerical sum of politically equal individuals. The difficulty was how to articulate the principle in practice.

The outcome in every state was a written constitution. Such a process was a major innovation. It was different in kind from the uncodified and unwritten British Constitution formed by the accretions of centuries, whose character was so expansive in content that its most authoritative contemporary commentator, Sir William Blackstone, insisted that there was no distinction between the constitution and the current system of laws. The American system was more rapidly and deliberately constructed, albeit after some experimentation in the various states. All its distinctive features were displayed for the first time in the Massachusetts Constitution of 1780. For a start, it was drafted by a special convention elected on a universal male franchise on the grounds that constructing a new government was so fundamental that all men were entitled to participate. The Convention drafted a constitution which was sent to the townships for ratification and then put into effect. The document set out the principles of government and its structures, but also defined both the extent of power and the limits to power of administrations which would operate under them. Its essential principle was that a constitution was a delegation of the people's sovereignty; governments were subordinate to it, not co-equal with it. Responsibility to the people was recognised by annual elections, and their interests protected by a Declaration of Rights which set out philosophical principles and provided procedural protection. There was a further change compared with the British Constitution. In Britain power was theoretically regulated by a balance of estates (or social categories) between the monarchy (the Crown), aristocracy (House of Lords) and democracy or people (House of Commons). This traditional distribution did not match the structure of American society since it contained no crown, and elites were socially closer to the mass of white men than were their counterparts in Britain. In its place was erected a balance of functions divided principally between legislature and executive.

The experience of the states during the first decade of independence demonstrated the possibilities as well as limits of government authority. Their success in suppressing loyalism demonstrated their capacity to coerce dissidents, but the same policy could not be applied to the majority of citizens. Instead, the states, working individually, removed restrictions inherited from the colonial regime and encouraged autonomous activity by independent republican citizens. Thus northern states began the long process of emancipating their slaves, Virginia introduced extensive legal reforms, and several states encouraged economic development by chartering banks, and the franchise was extended. Several states improved their education systems on the grounds that republican government and popular sovereignty required an educated citizenry capable of performing their public responsibilities. The apotheosis of this liberalising process was the extension of religious liberty. At a time when men's relationship to society and the state was defined partly by membership of a particular church, the states went a long way towards dismantling confessional discrimination. Only Virginia went so far as to assert total religious freedom, but the Anglican Church was disestablished where it existed, the Congregational churches of New England had their privileges curtailed, and political discrimination against virtually all Christians and most Jews on grounds of belief was ended.

A national government

Thus far, the revolutionary changes took place separately in the individual states, yet there was clearly a need for a directing national authority to conduct affairs of common concern. It would have to balance the interests of the states against those of the central government and the need for strong authority against protection for the civil liberties of citizens. Like the states, it was constructed on fresh principles since the authority of the people flowed through their states rather than outwards from the centre or downwards from the Crown or Parliament. During the revolutionary war the United States lacked any coercive power comparable to that exercised by Paris governments during the French Revolution. In its absence Congress was obliged to conduct the war in conjunction with the states rather than solely on its own authority. Although it developed significant powers the wartime arrangement formed an inadequate base for long-term national development.

The first attempt at establishing a permanent system of central government, the Articles of Confederation of 1781, erected only a fragile central government. It was weak enough not to threaten the liberties of the citizens and the interests of the states, but inadequately effective at a time when the danger of disintegration was greater than that of concentrated centralism. Congress was granted only powers explicitly delegated by the states; it even lacked authority to tax and had to seek subventions from the states which were frequently not forthcoming. Thus although responsible for foreign relations it could not in practice bind the individual states, and it was unable to service the debts it had incurred during the revolutionary war. Crucially, the Articles explicitly acknowledged the sovereignty of the states, and required their unanimous consent for amendment.

In their place a stronger general government was needed that could meet certain criteria. It would require its own authority and responsibilities and coercive power without destroying the legitimate local interests of the states, have respect for the liberties of citizens, balance the sometimes conflicting interests of elites and the majority of citizens, and be adaptable to changing circumstances. Nationalist advocates of a stronger central government persuaded Congress to summon a Convention which drafted a fresh Constitution at Philadelphia in 1787; after ratification by the states it came into effect in 1789. It was radically different from its predecessor.

The new Constitution undoubtedly created a stronger general government, but not such a strongly centralist one as parliamentary sovereignty in Britain. It assigned the federal government authority in three crucial areas: revenue, interstate and international commerce, and the right to establish its own court system, but not absolute authority. Instead it introduced the new concept of divided sovereignty. For the first time the national government would act directly on the people, but so would the states; and the federal government and individual state governments would each be supreme within its own sphere of authority. The United States Constitution itself was defined as the supreme law, and the states' constitutions and their governments' and courts' actions were required to be compatible with it. But the states remained directly responsible to their own peoples as did the federal government to the American people at large. In practice thereafter, the states remained the primary units of social organisation and thus political and legal power, and exercised most of the powers of government throughout the nineteenth century. The Constitution also recognised the division between elites and the majority by allowing a broad electorate for the lower house of Congress, state appointments to the Senate and a filtering system for election of the President. Two further elements were added. The system of divided authority within the federal government required that the executive and legislature would have to cooperate if government was to function, but it also erected checks and balances among the three elements designed to prevent any branch going out of control. In addition, to provide explicit protection for the rights of citizens and states, a bill of rights was added in 1791, although initially it applied only to federal government.

Social change

The Revolution also included significant social change, though its extent varied from one group and state to another. Success in war itself prompted major social change since it brought repudiation of the imperial aristocracy, but that was only part of the process. The idea of equality contained in the Declaration of Independence, initially more nominal than substantive, began to take hold among white men as an ambition, and rhetoric sometimes became stridently egalitarian. Yet eighteenth-century American society was economically divided, and there were social hierarchies in urban and rural communities alike. Thus philosophical principles would have to be reconciled to social actuality – a task more difficult than establishing libertarian governments.

The range between the great wealth, privilege and power of the few and the poverty of the many was far narrower in colonial America than in Europe, but nonetheless clearly visible. One-tenth of the population owned more than half the total physical wealth of the community, while at the bottom one-fifth of the population were themselves a species of property, and the next 30 per cent above owned no more than 3 per cent of the total wealth. There were hierarchies among day labourers, artisans and rich merchants in the towns, and between great planters, affluent freehold farmers and tenant farmers in rural areas; in the south the principal labour force was enslaved. Yet hunger was rare, even among slaves, and desolating poverty unknown among free people. Gentlemen everywhere expected to govern their social inferiors, but many ordinary white men possessed the vote – which had to be solicited if wealthy men such as George Washington were to be elected to colonial assemblies. The Revolution triggered demands from people in the middling and lower ranks of society for greater recognition of their interests and greater participation in the political direction of their states.

Significant and permanent progress was made by the largest subordinate group: white men of modest to middling social status. They reinterpreted the term 'people', whose sovereignty underpinned the new state governments, to mean not only the community but also themselves as equal individuals. The traditional deference of inferiors towards their social superiors, never as strong in America as in Britain, melted away. Equality still did not mean complete equality of political influence or power, let alone property, but it did mean that in theory every white man became entitled to equality of respect, equality of freedom from domination by others, and equality of consideration for his interests, though practice often fell short of principle. Elites were challenged almost everywhere, and most deemed it prudent to take their social inferiors' interests and aspirations into account. In many states the exigencies of revolution coupled to normal population increases and the continuing dispersal of population attracted increased numbers of men into politics, and the size of legislatures increased accordingly. New counties, new offices, the need to replace Loyalist exiles, especially in New England, and limits on tenure of office in some states all created fresh opportunities. More men became entitled to vote. In part, rising prosperity and inflation made it easier to meet the suffrage requirements, but six states deliberately lowered the property qualifications. In consequence the electorate increased to between 60 and 90 per cent of free white men (a few were still unfree, indentured servants, though this system died out in the 1790s), depending on state and local area; in several states free blacks were permitted to vote. Turnout at elections also increased in most states, a tendency encouraged by wider use of the secret ballot and growing competition among candidates which rose through the 1780s to a climax during elections to the constitutional ratifying conventions of 1787–88. These democratising effects were also clearly visible at other levels of state politics. Before the Revolution, elites had controlled colonial legislatures; afterwards more than two-fifths of the legislatures were drawn from the ranks of men of modest means such as farmers and artisans.

Attempts by social elites to retain their control met with mixed success. Most states introduced property qualifications (sometimes very high) for holding office, a device which had some success, but another device for sustaining elite control proved very disappointing. Eleven states incorporated an upper house in their legislature in the belief that it would be a bastion for the rich, well educated and cosmopolitan, and thus mitigate what they feared would be the excesses of the more democratic lower house. However, the conflict between the rich and the many was only one division in American society; others derived from economic, cultural and locational differences, and these contributed substantially towards shaping the character of American politics. Complex political parties representing many interests quickly emerged. Each had representatives in both houses, thus destroying the exclusively social divide between an elite upper house and a popularly elected lower house of legislature. Their development accelerated the decline of social deference and diminished elite supremacy. The increasing commercialisation of American society further diluted the authority of traditional elites by substituting market relationships and individualism for traditional social deference. Elites were more successful in controlling national politics after 1789, but even here their command steadily crumbled.

If the general principles of republican government were fairly uniform, the manner in which they were implemented varied from state to state. The distinctive social structure of each state was a fundamental determinant, but there were others. Much depended on the relationship between elites and their social inferiors during the struggle for independence, and the degree to which elites were united.

Two adjacent states took drastically different paths, even though both were ethnically, religiously and economically diverse. By American standards, the Revolution in Maryland was strikingly conservative. The Whig elite led the battle for independence and thus were in a position to control the constitution-making process. They conceded that lawful authority derived from the people and permitted a broad franchise, but ensured their own continuing supremacy largely by incorporating ever higher property qualifications for office-holding; their assumption that wisdom was associated with wealth ensured that only rich men could become governors. This structure, coupled to shrewd concessions to the sentiments of lesser men, ensured their supremacy throughout the 1780s. In contrast, Pennsylvania, immediately to the north, underwent a radically democratic revolution. Its transformation flowed from certain distinctive features of its political structure on the eve of the Revolution. The province's social diversity was compounded by divisions among the elite between Quaker and anti-Quaker factions and between Loyalists and Patriots. Since the independence movement was led by artisans and men of modest means, the process of writing a constitution was captured by radicals based in Philadelphia. They drafted a document in which the executive was totally dependent on the legislature and the legislature was subject to popular will through the mediums of annual elections and a taxpayer franchise. However much the new system appealed to artisans, farmers and intellectuals, such a virtually democratic system was not fully congruent with the actual structure of a society which included men of considerable wealth. The outcome was a long political battle. By 1790 conservatives had succeeded in reconstructing the government in their favour – but democratic forces remained important. Changes in the other eleven states can be placed along the spectrum between these two extremes.

Other subordinate groups were less fortunate. White women contributed materially to the attainment of independence but shared very little in the political benefits of the Revolution. Many, especially poor women, performed vital support services such as nursing the sick for the army; the service of others was less direct. Their political views were assumed to coincide with those of their husbands, and they were expected to confine themselves to the traditional domestic sphere and be generally supportive of their menfolk. In spite of protests by women such as Abigail Adams (John Adams' wife), nowhere was there any significant improvement in their legal status, and if anything the ability of married women to control their property diminished as equity courts (which provided some protection) were merged with common law courts which were bound by customary male-oriented precedents. The effect of the Revolution on American women was felt in their private lives – familial organisation, responsibility for raising children according to republican values, their personal aspirations and their self-evaluation. Women were allowed to share the civil benefits of citizenship but not its political rights.

At the bottom of the hierarchy were about 500,000 African American slaves. Their position was rich in tragic irony since the prosperity of the richest and most influential southerners depended on their coerced labour, and their presence made it possible for poor whites to consider themselves in some sense the equals of their social superiors, thus maintaining a common front of racial solidarity. There was no slave rebellion, though more African Americans sided with Britain in the hope of freedom than with the United States. However, only South Carolina and Georgia did not recruit black soldiers in wartime, so pressed were the states for men. Slavery had been legal in all the colonies, but by the mid-eighteenth century white American opinion was beginning to turn against the institution in keeping with enlightened opinion in Europe. Anti-slavery agitation began before the Revolution, especially in the Quaker influenced province of Pennsylvania; building on these footings, substantial though incomplete progress towards emancipation was made. By 1787 every state except Georgia had prohibited the commercial importation of slaves or imposed prohibitive duties. Vermont banned slavery in its Constitution when it organised itself as a separate state, Pennsylvania abolished it by statute, and in a crucial legal decision Massachusetts declared it was incompatible with the new Constitution. Other northern states followed suit, though New York and New Jersey, which had possessed most slaves before the Revolution, did so very slowly. Emancipation in New England and the middle states did not necessarily imply equality of voting rights and social integration; nevertheless, the process had begun, and these early steps had profound significance for the long-term future. In the south, where the overwhelming majority of blacks lived, very little progress was made. Although most sophisticated southerners detested slavery, they were economically shackled to it, and many poorer but ambitious whites saw the ownership of slave labourers as their path to economic and social advancement. At the Philadelphia Convention, delegates from South Carolina and Georgia threatened to secede from the union if any attempts were made to interfere with the institution, and no one dared call their bluff. The slave-trade was abolished in 1808, but otherwise the institution spread deeper into the south as its territory expanded.

The revolutionary tradition

The record of the American Revolution is patchy – like that of other revolutions. Its record on political liberty and social equality was substantial but mixed. Most African Americans continued to be denied citizenship and remained the property of others (including a few free blacks). Yet significant progress was made towards abolishing slavery, and though discrimination and segregation remained common in the free states, some blacks even enjoyed full political as well as citizenship rights. The logic of liberty and equality expressed in the Declaration of Independence would also seem to extend to women, but it took more than a century for it to do so. White women enjoyed the civil rights of citizenship but (except very briefly in New Jersey) no political rights. New men entered politics in many states, and though the rich remained powerful (especially in national politics) the tradition of deference to social superiors had decayed in parallel with the extension of the franchise and expansion of a commercial economy. Elites were no longer able to demand obedience from their inferiors, but at most could offer their services as stewards promoting the national interest according to their own judgement, but were increasingly and rapidly subject to the electoral opinions of their social inferiors.

The independent United States was indeed a very different place from colonial America. Separation from Britain was in itself revolutionary but only a beginning. The accompanying internal revolution was what shaped the United States and moulded its future development. It created a republican system of government based on the supremacy of the people in place of traditional monarchic society, drastically altered the relationship between elites and their social inferiors, and introduced many major reforms. It constructed a federal union out of thirteen distinct and separate communities and created new authority, but ensured that it could not get out of control. Founding a republican regime created a nation very different from contemporary European societies, set an ideological agenda for the future, constructed a political framework strong enough to meet the different needs of later generations, and propelled the United States in a democratic direction.

Full democracy in the twentieth-century sense was neither expected nor achieved, but a profoundly democratising process had made great strides. Significant social and political development took place in the states within a decade. Social relationships and community values changed dramatically. Above all, the Revolution encouraged the white middling and lower orders (and some African Americans and women) to demand substantial advances in their status and influence in society. The mass of white men become active participants in politics, and the elites were obliged to share their power. The hegemony of government was separated from the hegemony of elites, and the people became the only source of legitimacy. Democracy in the United States was rapidly acquiring prescriptive status.

A final dimension also needs to be considered. Twentieth-century historians have disagreed sharply as to the international significance of the Revolution. Among them, Daniel Boorstin, a conservative American historian, declares that 'in the modern European sense of the word, it was hardly a revolution at all', while Hannah Arendt, a German refugee to the United States, sadly remarks that in comparison with the French Revolution, the American Revolution, 'so triumphantly successful, has remained an event of little more than local importance'. By contrast, R.R. Palmer, another American historian, insists the two revolutions had much in common and that both were leading actors in an eighteenth-century age of democratic revolution.[4] Americans were naturally concerned primarily for their own welfare, but were also convinced that their actions and achievements would be relevant to the broader world. Their judgement was soundly based. After as well as before the Revolution, they were members of a single cultural system that extended beyond Britain to continental Europe; thus Benjamin Franklin was renowned for his scientific work throughout Europe before the American Revolution and Jefferson was consulted by reformers during the early stages of the French Revolution. Their new republic, so different from any European society except possibly Holland, was seen by contemporaries as a general model for emulation elsewhere. It was not expected that every country would follow the American example exactly, since circumstances varied considerably: the nature of the *ancien régime* made the task of reform far greater in France, for example, and the outcome was more radical. But in one respect the United States was more successful: it overturned an empire yet succeeded in taming the necessary coercive power. The advantages of this became more apparent in Britain during the 1790s, when English radicals arguing for parliamentary reform used the American model as an example of the safety of change and as a middle way between the turgid conservatism of contemporary England and the violent radicalism of France whose ultimate outcome was the emergence of the Emperor Napoleon.

Notes

1   I.R. Christie, *Crisis of Empire: Great Britain and American Colonies, 1754–1783*, London, 1966, pp. 108–14.
2   John Adams, 'Thoughts on Government', in *The American Enlightenment*, ed. Adrienne Koch, New York, 1965, p. 260.
3   Bernard Bailyn, *The Origins of American Politics*, New York, 1968, pp. 61–105.
4   Daniel Boorstin, *The Genius of American Politics*, Chicago, 1953, p. 68; Hannah Arendt, *On Revolution*, London, 1990 (first published New York, 1963), p. 61; R.R. Palmer, *The Age of the Democratic Revolution: A Political History of Europe and America, 1760–1800*, Vol. I (Princeton, NJ, 1959), pp. 4–5.

Further reading

C.C. Bonwick, *The American Revolution*, London and Charlottesville, 1991.

I.R. Christie and B.W. Labaree, *Empire or Independence, 1760–1776*, Oxford, 1976.

H.T. Dickinson, ed., *Britain and the American Revolution*, London and New York, 1998.

J.P. Greene, *Peripheries and Center: Constitutional Development in the Extended Polities of the British Empire and the United States, 1607–1788*, Athens, GA, and London, 1986.

J.P. Greene and J.R. Pole, eds, *The Blackwell Encyclopedia of the American Revolution*, Cambridge, MA, and Oxford, 1991.

M. Jensen, *The Making of the American Constitution*, Princeton, NJ, 1964.

R.R. Palmer, *The Age of the Democratic Revolution. A Political History of Europe and America, 1760–1800*, Vol. I, Princeton, NJ, 1959.

G.S. Wood, *The Creation of the American Republic: 1776–1787*, Chapel Hill, NC, 1969.

6 The French Revolution 1789–99

Gwynne Lewis

Has the French Revolution a 'beginning' and an 'end'? For some historians, concerned with its place in the wider scheme of modern history, the Revolution has been traced back to the eighteenth-century Enlightenment, and forward to the Russian and Chinese Revolutions. The renowned *Annaliste* historian, Emmanuel Le Roy Ladurie, has suggested that the duc d'Orléans – Regent of France in 1715 – was an early enlightened despot who set the agenda for the French Revolution, while the equally celebrated, Marxist historian, Eric Hobsbawm, has argued that the entire period from the 1780s to the 1830s represents 'a *process* [my italics] of transformation that had already convulsed the continent and would go on convulsing it'.[1] Conservative or communist, there has been widespread agreement that the French Revolution is the 'mother of all modern revolutions'. But if there is agreement about the universal influence of the French Revolution, opinion remains very divided over its more immediate historical legacy. Did it lay down the foundations for twentieth-century 'totalitarian democracies'? Was it a political upheaval with social consequences, one that laid the foundations for a liberal world of representative government, parliamentary democracy and individual choice? Or was it the first of a series of 'social revolutions' with political consequences, whose ultimate objective was the extinction of mass poverty, the emancipation of men and women from the shackles of a developing, capitalist, world system?

The structure of this chapter, with its three chronological and thematic divisions, will enable us to engage with these interpretations of the Revolution. The conclusion will examine its legacy, which time, careless of historical compartmentalisations and controversies, has hardened into a single block.

The Revolution of the radical-liberal bourgeoisie

The Enlightenment and the Revolution

Nineteenth-century liberalism would revolve around four major 'freedoms': those associated with political and religious rights, property rights, and the right to free trade; *ancien régime* governments would be condemned for trying to control the political, religious, social and economic lives of their subjects. The work of the Constituent Assembly (September 1789 to August 1791) and the Legislative Assembly (August 1791 to September 1792) forms a historic bridge between the 'interventionist' policies of the monarchy and the increasingly *laissez-faire* policies of nineteenth-century liberalism. To what extent did the Enlightenment provide a blueprint for this revolution in the relationship between the state and its subjects?

It has been argued, of course, that Europe experienced several 'Enlightenments', beginning with the European Renaissance, followed by the late seventeenth-century English Enlightenment, and culminating in the mid-eighteenth-century European movement, spearheaded by the French *philosophes*. We should also note that the recent work of cultural historians, including Michel Foucault and many associated with women's studies, has thrown considerable doubt on the supposedly progressive nature of the eighteenth-century Enlightenment. Dorinda Outram has criticised Peter Gay for associating it almost exclusively with great, male thinkers, those *philosophes* who provided intellectual legitimation for the subsequent social domestication and political exclusion of women.[2] In other words, 'Enlightenment' could enslave as well as liberate. Finally, there were profound divisions between the *philosophes* and the economic theorists or physiocrats whose influence on the Revolution has frequently been understated. There was also no common agreement on the central proposition that rationalism was the essential key to an understanding of social behaviour. If the main body of the eighteenth-century Enlightenment was rationalist with Voltaire, its heart was often irrational and romantic with Rousseau. It is salutary to recall that Maximilien Robespierre, often invoked as a disciple of Rousseau, was of the opinion that 'philosophical enlightenment had made common cause with despotism and could in no way be considered the forerunner of the Revolution'.[3]

However, it would be silly to argue that 'the Enlightenment' exerted no influence on the Revolution. The difficulty lies in unpicking the threads of Enlightenment thought from the fabric of Revolutionary legislation. We shall argue that while the final pattern of the French Revolution was woven by the leaders of the Revolution, not for them, it is possible to isolate four important threads – religious, political, economic and social – that tie the Enlightenment to the successes and failures of the Revolution.

During the eighteenth century, the leadership of the Catholic Church lost the battle for the hearts and minds of the majority of the French population. With the advent of a more scientific and secular age after 1750, the Counter-Reformation policy of placing Jews in ghettos and Protestants in the galleys appeared increasingly gothic, to unbelievers as well as to believers like the Jansenists. A minority movement within the Catholic Church, Jansenism became extremely important in the battles between the Paris *parlement* and the Court during the reign of Louis XV

(1715–74). It contained in its doctrine and practice three elements that alienated it from the Court and the Papacy: it sought to attract the support of ordinary people; it leaned towards the nationalist 'Gallican' tradition of the French Church; and it was a profoundly moral movement. Peter Campbell has insisted upon the enduring influence of Jansenism, while Dale Van Kley has argued for a direct link between Jansenist thought and the constitutional democracy of the early Revolution.[4]

On the political front, many recent historians have concentrated on the 'political culture' of the *ancien régime* and the Revolution, arguing the Cobbanite, anti-Marxist case that revolutions retard rather than accelerate the march of democracy. It is now clear that a very diversified political culture did indeed develop in the *salons*, provincial academies, coffee-houses and reading-rooms of the *ancien régime* after the 1750s. It is equally clear, however, that it was geared more to the modernisation of an absolute monarchy than to the promotion of revolutionary change. Even Alfred Cobban believed that the early leaders of the Revolution derived very little in the way of specific political theory from the *philosophes*. What many leading revolutionary politicians did inherit was the belief that political regeneration could not be achieved without moral regeneration, a characteristic of most modern revolutions.

In many ways, the physiocrats exerted a more direct influence on the monarchy and on the Revolution than the *philosophes*. It was, after all, the *ancien régime* monarchy that first introduced – albeit spasmodically – the physiocratic/liberal policies of free trade, reform of the tax system and the abolition of the guilds. What the monarchy, after Louis XIV, lacked was the political will, as well as the appropriate government machinery, to convert theory into practice. The economic and fiscal reforms introduced in the mid-1770s by the impressive physiocrat first minister, Jacques Turgot, only received lukewarm support from the Court, while the reformulation of Turgot's plans by his successor Calonne in 1786 provoked the revolutionary crisis of the following year. As for the link with the Revolution, one of the main driving forces behind many of the new economic policies pursued in France throughout the reign of Louis XVI (1774–93) was Du Pont de Nemours, the 'spokesman of liberalism'. Du Pont, a junior minister, had supported Turgot throughout the trials and tribulations of the latter's ministry from 1774 to 1776, and he would continue to advocate liberal economic policies throughout the early years of the Revolution. In 1789, as a deputy to the Third Estate, Du Pont wrote that 'legislation in matters concerning manufacturing and commerce should be reduced to two phrases: "laissez-faire" and "laissez-passer"'.[5] From 1789 to 1792, and again from 1795 to 1799, revolutionary leaders would endeavour, in extremely difficult circumstances, to follow this advice, invariably with adverse consequences for the poor, thus providing us with one important clue to the failure of the liberal, bourgeois revolution of the 1790s.

Finally, on social policy, we should remind ourselves that the *philosophes* and the physiocrats were drawn, in the main, from the bourgeoisie and the nobility. Voltaire had no time whatsoever for the rabble, while Rousseau's political theories contained several radical, democratic ideas that were designed more to constrain and to educate the untutored masses than to emancipate them. In 1801, reflecting on the failure of the liberal revolution between 1789 and 1793, J-J. Mounier, one of its leading architects, reminded a critic that 'the *philosophes* had never called for rebellion; that their objective had never been to overthrow the social order; and that, on the whole, they had laboured to protect the State from disaster through modernisation and reform'.[6] One of the greatest mistakes the Constituent Assembly would make would be to 'modernise and reform' the Catholic Church without securing the support of either the Papacy or the people, thus providing us with another clue to the failure of the Revolution. Under the *ancien régime*, the Catholic Church, and its religious orders, provided for the social as much as the spiritual needs of its people, controlling schools and hospitals, providing charity for the poor, recording their births, marriages and deaths. It is true that the majority of peasants had good reason to hate the Church because it levied the burdensome tax, the tithe, and because many archbishops, bishops and abbots were numbered among the key manipulators of what David Parker has termed 'the mechanisms of economic domination and exploitation on which the rich and the powerful depended'.[7] Nonetheless, it ran the 'Welfare State' of the *ancien régime*, and the Revolution never really developed a satisfactory substitute.

The importance of economic and fiscal reform in an increasingly capitalist age is reflected in the project of reform that the *contrôleur général*, Charles Alexandre de Calonne, placed on Louis XVI's desk in November 1786, a project described by William Doyle as 'the most radical and comprehensive plan of reform in the monarchy's history'.[8] Its main provisions for a modernised, more equitable taxation system, a reform of provincial government and the introduction of free trade principles represented the last hope for a monarchy that was rapidly losing control, over its own supporters as well as its enemies. It would provide the blueprint for the radical-liberal revolution of 1789 to 1792. However, the King's failure to give Calonne and his successor, Archbishop Brienne, the wholehearted support they desperately needed placed his irresolute feet on the road that was to lead to the guillotine in January 1793. Admittedly, his position was not an enviable one, surrounded by a Court that was riddled with competing factions, lacking the power in the country to defeat the resistance of privileged institutions like the Church and the *parlements*. In addition, the entire local machinery of government had been mortgaged by the Crown for centuries through the sale of its offices, a ruinous policy that served only to keep the ship of state afloat rather than to propel it forward. Primarily as a result of the sale of offices, as well as the monarchy's socially inequitable and administratively inefficient taxation system, France in the late 1780s was on the verge of bankruptcy. The antiquated internal machinery of the Bourbon State, better at exploiting the residues of the poor than the ample reserves of the rich, was ill equipped to finance a foreign policy designed, after the humiliation of the Seven Years' War (1756–63), to defeat the British on the imperial seas. French participation in the American War of Independence proved to be the financial straw that broke the monarchy's back. When the Prussians moved into Holland in the critical year of 1787, the Court had neither the money nor the political will to react. The decision to call a meeting of an Estates General of the realm for May 1789 represented a fateful admission by the Court that its failure to defeat privilege at home had precipitated the collapse of its ambitious but misguided military policy abroad. The decision by the Paris *parlement* in September 1788 that the Estates should meet in more or less the same form as they had done in 1614 – with the first two Estates, clerical and noble, in a position to outvote the Third Estate – convinced Third Estate politicians and pamphleteers that the time for *serious* 'modernisation and reform' had arrived. The role of the press in shaping 'public opinion' – a creation of the Enlightenment for many historians – should not be underestimated when discussing the 'modernity' of the Revolution.

Reform and the constitutional monarchy

From a political standpoint, France was effectively 'nationalised' on 17 June 1789 when the Third Estate decided to call itself the 'National Assembly'. It was intended that representative democracy would now replace enlightened despotism. For the next two years, the Constituent Assembly (as the National Assembly soon called itself) was to undertake something bordering on the miraculous – the root-and-branch modernisation of France. It began on 4 August with the famous 'abolition of feudalism', an act that struck a death blow to *ancien régime* privilege, undermining the entire edifice of provincial and local government. The abolition of feudalism was followed on 24 August by one of the most famous documents in modern history: the 'Declaration of the Rights of Man and the Citizen', article one of which declared that men were born free and equal in rights. The document also recognised the need for freedom of political and religious thought, equality of taxation and equality before the law. However, article seventeen defended the rights of individual property-owners, while other articles stressed that liberty entailed duties as well as rights. Keith Baker refers to 'its ambiguities [that] served to inaugurate a radical dynamic that subverted representation in the name of the general will, constitutionalism in the name of political transparence, the rights of individuals in the name of the rights of the nation'.[9] There is no necessary link here with the Terror, but Baker is certainly right to stress the potential for conflict that existed between bourgeois 'representative' and popular 'direct' forms of democracy. Article seven of the Declaration defined the law as an expression of 'the general will', representing, for some historians, the missing link between Rousseau's 'totalitarian' political theories and the policies of the Jacobin Terror.

The economic and fiscal reforms of the early Revolution – a land tax to be levied on all classes, internal freedom of the grain trade, the abolition of the guilds and internal customs barriers, along with the anti-coalition Le Chapelier law of 1791 – would obviously facilitate the development of a modern capitalist society in the long run: the immediate problem, however, was that France was bankrupt. Partly to solve this major dilemma, the Assembly decided to 'nationalise' the Catholic Church. On 2 November 1789 it announced the seizure of two billion *livres*-worth of Church land. In order to facilitate the sale of these 'National Lands' the government ordered the printing of paper money called *assignats*, government bonds used to pay off the State's creditors who would then exchange them for Church property. All might have gone well had it not been that successive administrations, particularly after the outbreak of war, printed more money than there was land, provoking massive inflation. It has even been suggested that inflation, not Rousseau, produced the Jacobin Terror. Whatever the degree of truth in this assertion, the disastrous experiment of the *assignats*, along with the related religious settlement, the Civil Constitution of the Clergy, certainly 'produced a seismic fault in the political geology of the French Revolution, provoking repeated tremors throughout every section of French society, down to Napoleon's Concordat with the Papacy in 1801'.[10]

If the *assignats* brought inflation in their wake, the Civil Constitution of the Church (12 July 1790), which abolished the old archbishoprics, as well as fifty bishoprics, divided the nation from top to bottom, providing a major boost to a growing Catholic royalist counter-revolution. Although *curés* were given a half-decent wage, the stipulation that bishops should be elected, and by atheists as well as good Catholics, proved anathema to many. What was worse was the fact that the Papacy eventually rejected the settlement. The consequent legislation forcing priests to swear an oath of loyalty to the Constitution created one of the Revolution's enduring enemies: the non-juror priest. This divisive, not to say disastrous, religious policy of the Revolution explains, in large measure, the failure to create a national consensus for any lasting political settlement during the 1790s.

The Constitution of 1791 was intended to complete the work of the Constituent Assembly. The Revolution, it was fondly hoped, was over: the Legislative Assembly would now implement the necessary laws. France had undergone a juridical and administrative revolution: the *parlements* had been abolished; a modern judicial system, complete with juries, introduced; the old provinces had been replaced by departments and municipalities, effectively decentralising power, although this would provide political space for the counter-revolution. France had also been transformed into a constitutional monarchy, with a unicameral political system. The King retained considerable powers, including a suspensive veto over all legislation. However, as with the Declaration of Rights, the new Constitution contained ambiguities and contradictions that would prove fatal, the greatest being the fact that the Court never really accepted it. On 21 June 1791 the King attempted to flee abroad, only to be brought back a prisoner of the Revolution. The compromise between bourgeois liberalism and absolute monarchy was effectively over. On 16 July, the shooting of republican demonstrators in the Champ de Mars drove the point home. For the leaders of the more radical popular clubs, particularly for the Cordeliers who had organised the Champs de Mars demonstration, the article in the Constitution dividing the adult male population into 'active' and 'passive' citizens (in effect, those who could vote and those who could not) according to the amount of taxation they paid revealed the hypocrisy at the heart of the bourgeois, liberal revolution. Theoretical democracy masked the construction of a wealthy, male, property-owners' republic. Women, of course, were to be completely excluded from participation in the political process, for the first time in French history. Instead of creating a united nation, the Constituent Assembly, through its divisive religious, economic and political policies, was dividing France into warring camps – *patriotes* and *émigrés*, juror and non-juror priests, 'active' and 'passive' citizens. The constructive work of the early Revolution was being undermined by mounting popular unrest inside the country and a growing counter-revolution on its borders as nobles, priests and many bourgeois joined France's traditional enemies abroad to defend God, the monarchy and property, though not necessarily in that order. For both the Court, anxious to overthrow the Revolution with foreign assistance, and for the moderate republican faction, the Girondins, anxious to unite the country behind the Revolution, foreign war increasingly seemed to be the only answer to civil war.

War, the Jacobin state and the popular revolution, 1792–95

The Revolution, before and after the outbreak of war with Austria and Prussia on 20 April 1792 and the national insurrection that overthrew the constitutional monarchy on 10 August, was as different as day from night, as the English observer, Arthur Young put it. In just three years, the French people had been transformed from being the subjects of an absolute monarchy to citizens of a Republic, the First French Republic being declared on 22 September 1792. Three weeks earlier, over 1,100 prisoners, the majority ordinary criminals, had been massacred on the order of a popular tribunal created by the Paris Commune. Originally designed to administer and police the capital, the Commune by this time had been transformed into an 'insurrectional' body, one that would provide if not an alternative government to the National Convention (which had met for the first time on 20 September 1792), then certainly a focal point for mounting popular unrest. Parallels have been drawn with the situation that would exist in Russia in 1917, with the 'Soviets' representing the forces of insurrection and the Provisional Government of Kerensky attempting to hold the line between a return to the *ancien régime* and the threat of popular revolution. In both cases, war would help to resolve the impasse. The first nine months of the French National Convention's life would be dominated by the expansion of the foreign war – on 1 February 1793, war would be declared on England and Holland – as well as by the spread of counter-revolution in the west and south-east of France. The massive insurrection of the Vendée would begin in earnest in March 1793. From the autumn of 1792 to the early summer of 1793, the Girondin faction would control the Convention, conflict with their Jacobin rivals increasing as reversals abroad and at home threw doubt on the very survival of the Revolution and the state. As pressure increased, the Jacobins, guided by Maximilien Robespierre and Georges Danton, would move closer to the Popular Movement; the Girondins would fall back on their provincial bases. From 31 May to 2 June 1793, the latter would be swept from power by a popular invasion of the Convention.

The fundamental reason for the failure of the Girondins was their rejection of a closer alliance with the Popular Movement. For the majority of their supporters, the defence of property was a higher priority than the introduction of popular sovereignty. The Jacobins, on the other hand, realised that only the total support of the *patriote* section of the nation could save the Revolution, and the state. In terms of bourgeois class interests, there was no essential difference between the two factions. What the Jacobins envisaged was a temporary, wartime alliance with the Popular Movement. We should not, however, underestimate what might be called today a 'shift to the Left'. Hannah Arendt was not far off the mark when she wrote that the 'transformation of the Rights of Man into the rights of the *sans-culottes* was the turning point not only of the French Revolution but of all the revolutions that were to follow'.[11] In other words, the 'social question' lies at the heart of all modern revolutions, and it first became central to the process of a revolution in France between 1791 and 1792, and not in America a decade or so earlier.

A final, general point defines the period from 1792 to 1795. Ordinary people, peasants in the countryside and artisans in the towns, and not politicians, initially shaped the policies of the Terror, just as they had done in the summer of 1789. The historic role of the Jacobins was to harness the energies of the rural and urban movements in the defence of France, and by so doing save the Revolution for the propertied bourgeoisie. Unlike the Girondins, the Jacobins could count on the support of hundreds of clubs both abroad and in France, all professing allegiance to the 'mother-club' in Paris. The Jacobins saw their reflection in an international mirror.

In terms of political theory they had certainly inherited something from the Enlightenment, but far more from the experience of participating in a revolution. In 1917, the Bolsheviks would be armed with a revolutionary theory, not just with revolutionary experience. For example, the institutions of the so-called 'Jacobin Terror' – the two great committees of the National Convention, the Committee of Public Safety and the Committee of General Security, and the Revolutionary Tribunal – had been created before the Jacobins won a majority on the Committee of Public Safety. Like the Bolsheviks, however, the Jacobins would ultimately use the revolutionary state to emasculate the power of the *classes populaires*, once the survival of the Revolution seemed to be assured. In the modern conflict between 'state and Revolution', the former has invariably triumphed.

The Popular Revolution – (1) The peasantry

During the 1950s and 1960s, inspired by Marxist–Leninist theories of rev-olution, historical research was directed towards the urban crowd; in the 1970s, attention would shift towards the peasantry. It was in this decade that Albert Soboul concluded that the French Revolution was not a 'classic bourgeois revolution', but 'une révolution paysanne-bourgeoise'. Part of the reason for this shift in emphasis was the need to accommodate twentieth-century peasant revolutions in Russia, China, Cuba, Latin America and Africa.

To what extent can the French peasantry in the early 1790s be regarded as a truly revolutionary force? Historians as ideologically distinct as Alfred Cobban and Georges Lefebvre believed it was, both arguing that the theor-etical abolition of feudalism in 1789 would never have occurred without the greatest peasant *jacquerie* of the eighteenth century, the Great Fear. The Russian historian, Anatoli Ado, agreed, arguing that it was the succes-sive waves of peasant rebellion from 1789 to 1793 that forced politicians in Paris to transform this theoretical abolition into hard reality. More recently, John Markoff has insisted upon the dialectic that developed between peasant rebellion in the provinces and the legislators in Paris. It was this relationship, it is argued, that placed anti-seigneurialism at the heart of the Revolution, producing 'a mutual radicalisation'. Both Ado and Markoff suggest that continual pressure from ordinary peasants and artisans helps to explain the creation of the institutions of the Terror.[12]

There is some evidence, then, of an alliance between peasant radicalism and certain bourgeois, political groups in the revolutionary assemblies. At town and village level, however, we need to adopt a more cautious approach to the problem. On the one hand, the *cahiers* reveal that there was some common interest in abolishing the seigneurial system between many groups of urban, radical, professional bourgeois and the less wealthy, peasant proprietors. We can also discover links between rich tenant farmers or *fermiers* and urban bourgeois, either on the basis of commerce or because the *fermier* was acting as a steward for bourgeois-owned seigneuries. The situation obviously varied from rich, commercial farming areas like the Ile-de-France or Upper Normandy to the poorer regions of Brittany and the south-west. On the other hand, as the Revolution progressed, competition between urban landowners and many sections of peasant society over the purchase of national lands intensified, contributing in the west and the south-east to counter-revolutionary movements. Many of the bourgeois–peasant alliances of the early revolution did not survive the later competition for land and office. We must also take note of growing antagonisms within peasant society, over the purchase of Church land as well as the division of common lands. Two major conclusions can be drawn: (1) the significant increase in the number of peasant smallholders, through purchases of national lands, together with the massive investment of the bourgeoisie in the countryside, explains, in large measure, the peculiar evolution of French capitalism in the nineteenth and twentieth centuries; and (2) the emancipation of the French peasant from the burdens of 'feudalism', in just four years, when compared with the emancipation of his Russian counterpart in the 1860s, who was forced to go on making redemption payments for over forty years, must rank as one of the most significant social revolutions in modern history.

The Popular Revolution – (2) The sansculottes

Until the summer of 1792, the urban Popular Movement lacked a unified, coherent base. In May 1790, the sixty districts of Paris had been abolished and replaced by forty-eight *sections*, electoral and administrative organisations linked to the municipality of Paris, the Commune. The *sections* would provide the Popular Movement with its political base until its demise in 1795. Alongside the *sections* were the popular clubs and societies, linked in Paris and the provinces to the Jacobin Club. But there was also a very important, 'unofficial' popular movement, the Parisian crowd, traditionally suspicious of the police and prone to bouts of periodic violence if pushed too far. The Popular Movement did not invent violence, it was endemic in the history of the Parisian *classes populaires*. It was the bloody assault on the Tuileries Palace on 10 August that changed the face of popular politics. In the first place, the Paris Commune was transformed into a *Commune Insurrectionelle*; second, the membership of the forty-eight *sections* and of the National Guard, hitherto open only to 'active citizens', was now granted to 'passive' citizens; and finally, the armed crowd that stormed the Tuileries was strengthened by the arrival of the *fédérés* (volunteer batallions) from Marseilles and Rennes. The Popular Movement – and with it the Revolution itself – had been democratised and 'nationalised' in two weeks.

From the summer of 1792 to the peak of its power in the winter of 1793, the Popular Movement, in Paris and the provinces, developed something approaching a coherent political and social ideology. Adopting the Rousseauesque slogans of 'the General Will', 'the Sovereignty of the People' and 'the Sacred Right of Insurrection' (a right that pre-dated Rousseau for the Parisian crowd!), a very democratic, direct form of democracy developed in opposition to the liberal, representative democracy of the early Revolution. For the sansculottes – mainly artisans and shopkeepers representing the political elite of the 'unofficial' crowd – deputies were 'mandated' by the people, their mandate being immediately revocable if they strayed too far from the agreed line. In terms of social policy, the Popular Movement also espoused ideas that clashed with liberal, bourgeois ideology. Although there was widespread support for *small-scale* private property, the demand for a national system of education, the right to a fair wage, the attack on the principles of finance capitalism and a free-market economy all reflected a consumerist socio-economy in the early stages of capitalist development. Despite the 'male-chauvinist' attitude of most sansculottes, women contributed in no small measure both to the actions and the ideology of the Popular Movement. They were prominent in bread and wage riots, and although the great majority did not press for full voting rights they regarded citizenship as a right for all, not just for men. Several provincial women's clubs were formed (the club in Dijon had 400 members), while the Parisian *Société des Républicaines-Révolutionnaires* played a very active and important role in the development of the Popular Movement in 1793.[13]

War and the urban Popular Movement

However, we need to recall that the immediate objective of the Popular Movement was the defence of France and its Revolution, not the popularisation of Rousseau. It is not coincidental that the alliance with the Jacobin revolutionary government was forged during the summer and early autumn of 1793 when anti-revolutionary forces threatened the very existence of the French state. Externally, the armies of England, Austria and Prussia were invading France from the north and north-east, while those of Piedmont and Spain were threatening from the south. Internally, a federalist revolt, centred on the south and west and linked to the defeated Girondin faction, appeared to be making common cause with the Catholic royalist insurrection in the Vendée. By the end of July 1793 the Vendéean armies had crossed the Loire. The Revolution was, indeed, *en danger*.

It was during this critical period that the Parisian *sections* pressed the government to organise a conscript army. The Jacobins, however, were not keen on the idea of creating an eighteenth-century version of the Red Army; it decided instead, on 23 August, to organise a *levée en masse*, to be strictly under the control of the government. To attract wider support, the Committee of Public Safety – still not confident of its authority – had agreed on 24 June to introduce the most radical and 'sansculotte' constitution of the Revolution, the Constitution of 1793. Given the war crisis, and the eventual victory of the state over the Popular Revolution, it would never be implemented. In the months of June and July, laws were passed completely abolishing feudal dues and introducing the death penalty for hoarding. The temporary alliance of Jacobins and sansculottes was in the process of transforming a revolutionary war into a 'people's war'.

From August to December 1793, popular forces in Paris and the provinces continued to be the driving force behind the further radicalisation of the Revolution. Increasingly, however, radical measures to defend the Revolution were being adopted only with the grudging acceptance of the Jacobin-dominated Committee of Public Safety; indeed, two of these measures, the creation of popular and paramilitary *armées révolution-naires* to assist in the task of securing food supplies and 'evangelising' the countryside, and the introduction of a law fixing the price of basic neces-sities, the General Maximum of Prices, only reached the statute books after the sansculottes had invaded the Convention on 5 September 1793. The Parisian and departmental *armées révolutionnaires* were to be involved in some of the worst atrocities of the Revolution, the mass execution of thousands of 'counter-revolutionaries' in Lyon and Nantes, including hundreds of priests. Assisted by extremist 'representatives-on-mission' like Fouché, many *armées* promoted a policy of a wave of dechristianisation in town and countryside during the autumn and winter of 1793, the high peak of the Popular Terror. On 5 October 1793, the Convention agreed to the introduction of a new calendar, dating day one of the Year 1 of Liberty from 22 September 1792. Revolutionary time had replaced *ancien régime* time!

The anarchy of the autumn of 1793, however, had worried the govern-ment and divided the Convention into warring factions. Was the Revolution to be a 'popular revolution' or a 'property-owners' revolution'? Once again it was the fortunes of war that helped to provide the answer. By the end of 1793, the immediate – and the greatest – crisis of the Revolution was over. Abroad, the advance of the allied armies was checked and then reversed. In the north, the Dutch were defeated at the battle of Hondschoote (8 September), the Austrians at Wattignies (16 October); by the end of the year, the French armies had recaptured Alsace in the east; while, in the south, the Spanish army was forced back across the frontier. At home, the defeat of the Catholic royalists at Le Mans on 14 December provided confirmation that the Vendéan insurrection had virtually ended.

The successful offensive of the republican armies, internally and exter-nally, was matched by the equally successful victory of the Jacobin state over the Popular Movement; the origins of that victory may be dated from the Law of 14 Frimaire (4 December 1793) which centralised the Revolution in the hands of the now dominant Committee of Public Safety. The provincial *armées révolutionnaires* were dissolved, the undisciplined repre-sentatives-on-mission and, in their place, the *agent national*, the precursor of Napoleon's prefect, was installed in every town in France. Together with the police and surveillance activities of the Committee of General Security, the policies of the Committee of Public Safety were creating one of the most powerful and centralised states in the history of France, as Alexis de Tocqueville was to realise fifty years later. The period between the proclamation of the 'Jacobin Constitution' of December 1793 and the execution of Robespierre and seventy of his supporters in July 1794 witnessed the completion of the process. Everything was now sacrificed to the task of saving, and centralising, France and the Revolution.

The prize of total victory and the creation of the 'virtuous' Jacobin state was achieved at a high cost in human life. The revolt in the Vendée was mercilessly crushed: a few historians have even described the repressive policies of the republican troops in the west as 'genocide'. The struggle between the warring factions in the Convention was ended with the arrest and execution, on 4 Germinal Year 2 (24 March 1794), of the pro-Terror Hébertists, quickly followed, on 16 Germinal (5 April 1794), by the guillotining of their enemies in the Convention, the anti-Terror Dantonists: a strike against the 'Left Opposition', then against 'the Right Opposition', a tactic to be repeated in the 1920s in Russia as Stalin strengthened the Bolshevik state. Finally, the 'alternative government' of the Parisian Popular Movement was neutered by the 'voluntary' closure of the popular clubs, linked to the forty-eight *sections*, and the reversal of the popular economic policies of the summer and autumn of 1793.

By the late spring of 1794, the 'purified' Jacobin state was in a position to launch 'The Great Terror'. Between May and July 1794, more people would be executed than in the previous nine months. To facilitate this wave of repression, the Law of 22 Prairial Year 2 (10 June 1794) was introduced, denying prisoners any real defence. Two days earlier, Robespierre had led a procession in Paris to inaugurate the 'Feast of the Supreme Being', hoping that this capacious, spiritual umbrella would shelter many of those who had been alienated by the dechristianising policies of the Popular Movement. Ironically, as the armies of the Republic combined to achieve victory against their internal and external enemies (the turning point abroad was the victorious battle of Fleurus in Belgium on 26 June), the members of the two great Committees began to fall out. Robespierre closeted himself in his apartment in the rue Saint-Honoré as his enemies plotted his downfall. Denied the support of the Popular Movement they had abandoned to reclaim the bourgeois centre ground, denounced by former colleagues now fearful for their own lives, the Robespierrists went to the guillotine on 9 Thermidor (27 July 1794). The Jacobin Terror had saved France and the Revolution by manipulating the Popular Movement. Bourgeois 'Enlightenment' progress, involving the security of property-owners, could only be achieved through a strong state, as the *philosophes* had argued half a century earlier.

The Revolution of the conservative-liberal bourgeoisie

The Thermidorean transition

The word 'Thermidor' has come to represent a period of reaction, when the élan and popular enthusiasm of the radical revolution gives way to a conservative reaction, to the centralisation and bureaucratisation of the Revolution. Trotsky argued – not altogether convincingly – that the seizure of power by Stalin in the mid-1920s began the process of 'Thermidorianisation', of centralisation and bureaucratisation, that marked the death of the international, radical revolution of 1917. The Thermidorean period in France, which lasted for fifteen months from 9 Thermidor Year II (27 July 1794) to 12 Brumaire Year IV (3 November 1795) when the period of the Directory began, did not mark a new beginning, but the beginning of the end of the Jacobin system of terror; not a return to the principles of the radical-liberal revolution of 1789, but to those of the Republican 'nation-in-arms', before the temporary alliance of Jacobins and sansculottes shifted social policy too far from the interests of the propertied bourgeoisie. As the power of the state and its armies increased, as the survival of the Republic was slowly transformed into the creation of a Napoleonic empire, so it became less necessary to satisfy the social demands of the *classes populaires*. The Jourdan law of 19 Fructidor Year VI (5 September 1798), introducing universal conscription, would finally give the state the mass armies it required without the need for a social *quid pro quo*. By this time, the surviving, revolutionary bourgeoisie had learned that if they were to retain their revolutionary gains intact, they would have to dissociate the interests of an educated, propertied elite from an ill-educated, often property-less mass. The broad universalism of the radical-liberal, bourgeois revolution of 1789 and been transformed into the narrow particularism of the conservative-liberal, bourgeois revolution of 1795 to 1799. The French *notable* of the nineteenth century, politically liberal but socially conservative, was emerging, somewhat fearfully, from the Revolution.

The immediate problem for many Jacobins in the aftermath of the mass arrest and execution of over seventy *Robespierristes* in the summer of 1794, however, was survival. Some, like Tallien and Fouché, had a considerable amount of blood on their hands: the shift to the political centre, already marked out by Robespierre, would have to be made, but it would have to be very gradual. After all, the war was by no means over; even the counter-revolution had been scotched but not killed; the *sections* and their revolutionary committees still existed in Paris and the provinces and were still armed. Moving too far to the Right might endanger the political power and economic acquisitions, above all the massive transfer of church and *émigré* property, of the revolutionary elite. It would also create a window of opportunity for royalist nobles and priests who now began to filter home from exile. So, in the autumn of 1794 the infamous Law of Prairial would be repealed but the Revolutionary Tribunal and the Law of Suspects retained; the *sections* would be purged, but the revolutionary committees allowed to operate, albeit with limited powers; the General Maximum of prices reduced in scope, but again not repealed. The Terror was dying, but the *étatiste*, Jacobin Republic, relieved of its sansculotte incubus, was still very much alive.

On the political front, the return to the pre-Terror period was pursued with the recall of the seventy-five Girondins who had opposed the purge of their colleagues after the invasion of the Convention in June 1793. On the economic front, the most severe blow to the poor was the repeal of trade controls and the final abolition of the General Maximum, the latter on Christmas Eve. For the mass of consumers, the ending of price and trade controls happened to coincide with the worst winter of the eighteenth century. By the spring of 1795, the threat of starvation would push the dying Parisian Popular Movement into its last insurrectionary convulsions. The *journées* of 12–13 Germinal Year 111 (1–2 April 1795) and 1–2 Prairial (20–21 May) were poorly organised and succeeded only in providing the government with an opportunity to destroy what was left of the Popular Movement. The handful of Jacobins who had supported the insurrections either attempted suicide or were arrested; the *sections* were purged and disarmed. However, the slogans carried by the insurgents, 'Bread and the Constitution of 1793', revealed that the Jacobin 'social republic', however frail, remained an unfulfilled dream for the poorer sections of French society.

The government's repression promoted a royalist, or counter-terrorist, backlash in Paris and the provinces. In the south, a 'White Terror' swept through those regions that had been most severely affected by the Terror, with macabre and bloody reprises of the September massacres in the prisons of Tarascon, Nîmes, Marseilles and Lyon. On 13 Vendémiaire Year IV (5 October 1795), a royalist insurrection in Paris, whose main purpose was to protest against the provision whereby two-thirds of the deputies of the Convention would sit in the legislature of the new Directory, was crushed with considerable loss of life. A certain Napoleon Bonaparte led the government's troops! The Left, however, was still active, though in a less public manner. In the autumn of 1795, Gracchus Babeuf, a former land-clerk who had already played an active role in the Revolution, began to publish his *Tribun du Peuple*, the opening shot in a campaign that would lead to what has been hailed as the first communist uprising in modern history – the Conspiracy of the Equals. Pre-Marxist in its programme of distributive communism, pre-Leninist in its conspiratorial, elitist theory of action, Babouvism represented the theoretical and ideological response of those popular militants who now understood the fraudulent character of the Jacobin-sansculotte 'alliance' of the Year II.

The movement, infiltrated by spies, was easily crushed, the Directory exploiting the threat to frighten wavering ex-Jacobins from any dalliance with 'the forces of anarchy'. Babeuf was executed, leaving a loyal wife in abject poverty, but with a rich historiographical legacy.[14]

The Directory

The fundamental objective of the third Constitution of the Revolution, that of 1795, which would guide the misfortunes of the Revolution to Napoleon's *coup d'état* of 18 Brumaire Year VIII (9 November 1799), would be the exclusion of the poor – republican or royalist – from political power, or, as the former Girondin, Lanjuinais, put it: 'The time for toadying to the people is past.'[15] The Terror had excluded any possibility of moving to the Left; Louis XVIII's Declaration of Verona in June 1795, which demanded the return of national lands to their rightful owners as well as the restoration of the Catholic Church as the religion of the state, blocked off the road back to the Right. Learning from experience, the deputies framed a new Constitution that imitated the bicameral legislative systems of America and Britain, with important qualifications. At the top, five 'Directors', not a President, would execute the legislative power emanating from two councils – the Council of 500 and the Council of Elders. Although in theory between five and six million French males were given the vote, the system of indirect elections ensured that effective power was now in the hands of no more than 30,000 electors, the great, the not-so-good and the rich of post-Terror France. There would be no universalism, no political pluralism, but there were fortunes to be made in currency and land speculation as well as in supplying the bloated armies of the Republic. For a while, the exigencies of war and the fear of a return to the Terror, or to the *ancien régime*, would keep most property-owners on board.

However, from the beginning, the Directors were little more than pensioners of the military, sustained primarily by military success and the massive indemnities extorted from the 'liberated' territories abroad. It was during the period of the Directory that a war of survival was transformed into a war of French imperialism: the ghost of Louis XIV had donned the 'the red cap of liberty'! Belgium was incorporated into France in October 1795; the following spring Napoleon swept all before him in Italy, knocking out Piedmont then the Austrians after the battle of Lodi (10 May 1797). The Treaty of Campo Formio with Austria on 18 October 1797 led to recognition of the satellite republics that had been created (occasionally against the wishes of the Directory!) in Italy, Holland, Germany and Switzerland. These were the glory days of the Directory, the time when the future Napoleonic empire was being founded. It was only with the creation of the Second Coalition of England, Austria and Russia in the autumn of 1798, as well as Napoleon's ill-fated Egyptian campaign, that reversals abroad began to unmask the collapse of civil society at home.

In political terms, the Directory had failed to effect a compromise between the decentralisation of the early years of the Revolution and the centralisation of the Terror, despite the appointment of its *commissaires de la République* to departmental and local councils. The unfortunate *commissaires* became primary targets for the political and criminal murder gangs that flourished in many parts of the country, particularly in the old counter-revolutionary regions of the west and the south-east. The social and economic causes behind what the authorities dismissed as 'anarchy' and 'brigandage' are revealing. In the south-east, the disinherited of the Revolution, victims of the bourgeois economic policies of the Directory and encouraged by returning nobles and/or priests, supported the activities of the Catholic royalist guerrillas (the *égorgeurs du Midi* or the *enfants de Jésus*) adding the names of ex-terrorists, priests who had supported the Revolution and purchasers of national lands to their death-lists. In the west of France, guerrilla bands called *chouans* had detached themselves from royalist, army commanders like Puisaye by the spring of 1796 to conduct a similar reign of terror against *patriotes*. The already shaky support of the wealthier sections of the population was further compromised by the economic and fiscal policies of the Directory. Although the abolition of the *assignats* and the return of hard currency in 1796 would assist a partial, economic recovery, the arbitrary decision to balance the state's books by writing off two-thirds of the debt it owed its creditors in September 1797 deprived the Directory of support from its natural constituency. The Revolution, conceived in a state of bankruptcy, was doomed to die in a similar condition. Napoleon's *coup* of November 1799 was simply a historical accident waiting to happen, the direct consequence of seven years of war with the European powers and of the related failure of the Revolution to produce a stable political settlement.

Conclusion

The Directory lasted for four years, long enough to reveal something of the ultimate shape and meaning of the Revolution. By 1799 it was clear that 'the rule of the Lords' was over; a post-feudal, privileged, seigneurial system had been virtually swept away, although there was to be no immediate or revolutionary shift to a modern, industrial society. The Revolution had strengthened the socio-economic and socio-cultural importance of landed wealth, increasing the number of small and middle-sized farms. As for industrial production, the lion's share – particularly textiles and luxury goods – continued to be based in 'proto-industrial' towns, villages and cottages; in other words, the skilled and semi-skilled artisan, not the factory worker, still dominated the industrial workforce. The political hegemony of the nobility had declined, but its socio-economic and socio-cultural influence would continue to be evident well into the twentieth century. If, by the 1830s, the nobility owned approximately 10 per cent of the land – as opposed to around 25 per cent in the 1780s – 266 of the 357 richest men in France were nobles.[16]

Nonetheless, the undoubted victors of the Revolution, in terms of landowning and, in particular, political power were the wealthy bourgeoisie. It was the bourgeoisie and the richer peasantry who had gained most from the sale of national lands, representing, when linked to the end of the seigneurial system, a real social revolution. As for political power, the introduction of electoral democracy meant that, henceforth, it would be money and not birth that would secure a share in power, although a franchise based primarily on land would ensure a revival of influence of those nobles who survived the Revolution (and most did). In the Revolutionary interim, however, an early form of 'National Liberalism' dashed the more exaggerated hopes of the patriots of 1789. Some Jews would be enfranchised, but obliged to become 'Frenchmen'; some blacks in the colonies would also – temporarily – be given a stake in the Revolution, but only if they were property-owners. The real losers in the Revolution were the poor, in town and country. The death of the Popular Movement and the ill-fated Conspiracy of the Equals had marked the end of an attempt to create a more egalitarian society. Plans for the extension of education and the introduction of poor relief were shelved; publishers and theatre managers rediscovered the classics, or went in for popular melodrama; urban craftsmen and factory workers arguably entered the most exploitative period in modern history as the guilds were abolished and anti-coalition legislation was introduced. Women, too, lost out, confirmed now – as Rousseau had wanted – as inhabitants of the private rather than the public sphere.

However, during the troublesome period of the late 1790s, the rich, male, landed and capitalist elite exhibited distinct signs of schizophrenia when discussing the future. As we have seen, it was obviously wise to avoid 'anarchy' on the Left and 'feudal privilege' on the Right, both of which threatened their property-rights. The majority would therefore seek security, and social status, in land; a minority would take the riskier option and involve themselves in the nascent industrial capitalist economy or speculate in the spoils of war. For the Revolution had unquestionably done something to assist the more enterprising section of the bourgeoisie. It is surely foolish to deny, as followers of the Alfred Cobban line often do, that the end of feudal and church dues, the abolition of the guilds and internal customs barriers, anti-coalition laws like the Chapelier law of 1791, the introduction of a national system of weights and measures and the metric system did not favour the development of a modern capitalism system.

All this, however, was not evident to the bourgeoisie on the eve of Napoleon's *coup d'état* in 1799. For a generation, France would be run as a war economy, bringing fortune for some and ruin for others. The ultimate cost of the revolutionary and Napoleonic wars – an overseas empire lost, over a million lives sacrificed to personal and national ambition – would have to be paid by future generations. For Isser Woloch, one of the saddest ironies of the history of the French Revolution is that a movement which began with universal hopes of democracy and peace concluded with dictatorship and a generation of war. The Napoleonic conscription machine, Woloch writes, 'arguably produced the most disastrous result of the French Revolution by virtue of the mass slaughter it facilitated through the disease, privation, and battle casualties of the Empire's extravagant military campaigns'.[17] Theda Skocpol, in her comparative study of modern revolutions, reaches a different but related conclusion, arguing, first, that two of the major developments of the French Revolution – state centralisation and war – are defining characteristics of the revolutions in Russia and China; second, that revolutionary states, whether in late eighteenth-century France or late twentieth-century Iran, are best at mobilising popular support for international warfare. We should recall that the French national anthem is a hymn of praise to war.

There are two related issues that disturbed the sleep of the republican bourgeoisie in 1799, issues that explain the failure of the Revolution to achieve a stable political settlement. They concern the spiritual and social lives of the vast majority of the population. We have seen that the Civil Constitution of the Clergy was the most divisive piece of legislation passed during the 1790s. However, during the Directory, politicians continued to pursue a profoundly anti-clerical policy, imprisoning and executing hundreds of priests, attacking private catholic schools, insisting on the observance of the ten-day Revolutionary Calendar. Not one of the religious substitutes introduced by successive regimes ever came close to winning the hearts and minds of the majority of the French population. The search for *l'homme nouveau* – a new Adam relocated in a secularised, rationalised Garden of Eden, to be followed, eventually, by Eve – was pursued relentlessly by Robespierre and other virtuous republicans, but he only turned out to be the rich, often corrupt bourgeois of the Directory, shaped by a conscious policy of social and cultural apartheid from the masses.

Why was anti-clericalism of such concern throughout the Revolution? In the first place, it was, of course, one of those threads that tied the Enlightenment to the Revolution. From Condorcet in the 1780s to the *idéologue* Cabanis in the 1790s, the scientific and rationalist strain of the Enlightenment continued to fashion a new, anti-clerical intellectual elite. However, the real driving force behind the anti-clerical policy of the Directory was the fear that haunted the victors of '1789', those who had made fortunes from the purchase and resale of Church lands, or from speculation in banking, commercial or industrial ventures, and who feared any return to the past, monarchist or terrorist. When dealing with the eighteenth century in general, and with the revolutionary bourgeoisie in particular, we should never divorce the religious from the social. We have seen that, under the *ancien régime*, the Church had performed the function of an early 'Welfare State'; Robespierre's 'social republic' of the Year 11, starved of commitment, money and time, failed to replace it. The emerging liberal and capitalist ethic of the free market and individualism also offered little to the poor and the property-less. As Hannah Arendt concluded: 'Who would deny the momentous role the social problem has come to play in all revolutions.'[18] The *Enragé* leader, Jacques Roux – an ex-priest, it should be noted – had realised how momentous this issue was when he warned Robespierre during a speech in the National Convention on 25 June 1793: 'Liberty is a mere illusion when one class of men can allow the other to starve with impunity. Equality is a mere illusion when through economic monopolies the rich hold the power of life and death over their fellow men.' Arendt's observation and Roux's prescience help to explain why, *pace* François Furet and Francis Fukuyama, the Revolution is still not over.

Notes

1 E. Le Roy Ladurie, *Saint-Simon, ou le système de la Cour*, Paris, 1997, pp. 509–10; E. Hobsbawm, *Echoes of the Marseillaise*, London, 1990, p. xiv.
2 D. Outram, *The Enlightenment*, Cambridge, 1975, pp. 9–10.
3 M-H. Huet, *Mourning Glory: The Will of the French Revolution*, Philadelphia, PA, 1997, p. 22.
4 P. Campbell, *Power and Politics in Old Regime France, 1720–1745*, London, 1996; D. Van Kley, *The Religious Origins of the French Revolution from Calvin to the Civil Constitution*, New Haven, 1996.
5 P. Joly, *Du Pont de Nemours: Apostle of Liberty and the Promised Land*, Delaware, 1977, p. 94.
6 B. Baczko, 'Enlightenment', in F. Furet and M. Ozouf, eds, *A Critical Dictionary of the French Revolution*, Cambridge, MA, 1989, p. 661.
7 D. Parker, *Class and State in Ancien Regime France: The Road to Modernity?*, London, 1996, p. 27.
8 W. Doyle, *The Oxford History of the French Revolution*, Oxford, 1989, p.68.
9 K. Baker, 'The Idea of a Declaration of Rights', in D. Van Kley, ed., *The French Idea of Freedom: The Old Regime and the Declaration of Rights of 1789*, Stanford, CA, 1994, p. 196.
10 G. Lewis, *The French Revolution: Rethinking the Debate*, London, 1993, p. 61.
11 H. Arendt, *On Revolution*, London, 1990 (first published New York, 1963), p. 61.
12 A. Ado, *Paysans en Révolution: terre, pouvoir et jacquerie, 1789–1794*, Paris, 1996; and J. Markoff, *The Abolition of Feudalism: Peasants, Lords, and Legislators in the French Revolution*, Pennsylvania, PA, 1996.
13 D. Godineau, *Citoyennes tricoteuses: les femmes du peuple à Paris pendant la Révolution française*, Aix-en-Provence, 1988.
14 A. Maillard, C. Mazauric and E. Walter, eds, *Présence de Babeuf: lumières, révolution, communisme*, Paris, 1994.
15 M. Crook, *Elections in the French Revolution: An Apprenticeship in Democracy*, Cambridge, 1996, p. 116.
16 P. McPhee, *A Social History of France, 1780–1880*, London, 1992, p. 119.
17 I. Woloch, *The New Regime: Transformations of the New Civic Order, 1789–1820s*, New York, 1994, p. 432.
18 Arendt, *On Revolution*, p. 21.

Further reading

H. Arendt, *On Revolution*, London, 1990 (first printed New York, 1963).

A. Cobban, *The Social Interpretation of the French Revolution*, 2nd edn, Cambridge, 1999.

W. Doyle, *The Oxford History of the French Revolution*, Oxford, 1989.

G. Lewis, *The French Revolution: Rethinking the Debate*, London, 1993.

J. Markoff, *The Abolition of Feudalism: Peasants, Lords and Legislators in the French Revolution*, Pennsylvania, 1996.

D. Outram, *The Enlightenment*, Cambridge, 1995.

T. Skocpol, *Social Revolutions in the Modern World*, Cambridge, 1994.

I. Woloch, *The New Regime: Transformations of the New Civic Order, 1789–1820s*, New York, 1994.

7   The revolutions of 1848

John Breuilly

Introduction

By comparison with the 'great' revolutions such as those of 1789 or 1917, the revolutions of 1848 exhibit at least four peculiar features. First, the revolutionary outbreak was not preceded by political crisis triggered by conflict within the ruling order (1789) or failure in war (1917). Europe was at peace – there was no major war between 1815 and 1854. The ruling order did not appear to be badly split. There were tensions and disputes but nothing like political crisis.

Second, revolution spread rapidly across Europe. Revolution extended beyond France in the 1790s and Russia after 1917 but principally promoted by the original revolutionary regime. In 1848 there was no national centre; virtually every part of Europe between Britain and Russia experienced revolution 'from within'.

Third, the revolutionary situation lasted for a comparatively short time. By the summer of 1849 counter-revolution had triumphed. The 'great' revolutions lasted, in terms of regime instability and civil war, at least until 1795 in France and 1921 in the USSR. Finally, in the judgement of many contemporaries and historians, the 1848 revolutions 'failed'. Although the revolutions of 1789 and 1917 did not realise their proclaimed ideals, few would deny that they transformed both society and state and that the post-revolutionary world is unimaginable without them. It is more difficult to argue that case for 1848.

These four distinguishing features provide keys to understanding the revolutions of 1848. First, I outline and analyse the initial revolutionary outbreak and ask why so many governments collapsed so quickly. Second, I characterise the new revolutionary situation and ask how this could lead on to further political conflict. Third, I consider three broad political strands – radicalism, liberalism and conservatism – and how these combined to enable rapid counter-revolution. Finally, I link these arguments to broader comparative historical treatments of the revolutions and suggest how one should evaluate their significance.

Outbreak

The rapid spread of revolution

Historians in thrall to the calendar date the start of the 1848 revolutions to the January disturbances in Palermo in Sicily. However, most historians see the revolutions as beginning in Paris in February, because revolution in Paris triggered revolution elsewhere in a way which events in Sicily could never have done.

In Paris the banning of a reform banquet[1] led to mounting demonstrations on 22, 23 and 24 February, culminating in the erection of street barricades and fighting. After a brief attempt at military repression which only escalated the crisis, Louis Philippe (reign 1830–48) abdicated. A short-lived project to create a regency failed. A republic was proclaimed and a provisional government established by prominent opposition politicians, grouped around two newspapers.

There was acceptance – enthusiastic or resigned – of this Parisian achievement throughout France. In some places the news led to the planting of liberty trees, changes in municipal government and peasant defiance of unpopular laws. The provisional government set about securing its hold on power and setting in hand preparations for the election of a National Assembly on the basis of universal manhood suffrage.

News from Paris had an electrifying effect beyond France. On 26 February Heinrich von Gagern proposed in the Parliament of Hesse-Darmstadt that there be national representation and a provisional German head of government. (In referring to Germany, Gagern meant the German Confederation established in 1814–15 and which consisted of thirty-nine states of differing size, dominated by the two major powers of Austria and Prussia.) The following day there were demonstrations in the Baden city of Mannheim demanding reform, including national representation. The following two weeks saw many urban demonstrations in south-west Germany. These were accompanied by rural disturbances. Already by 29 February there were peasant actions in Odenwald and the Black Forest. On 4 March 30,000 peasants invaded the town of Wiesbaden. Two days later there were serious disturbances in the state of Württemberg. Sometimes peasants stormed the residence of the lord and destroyed it, along with records of dues and services owed. The smaller states turned to Prussia and Austria for help but they were preoccupied with their own problems. Consequently the smaller states gave way, proclaiming press and other freedoms, appointing opposition liberals to the ministry, promising to convene constituent assemblies.

Next came the Habsburg Empire. There were initially fewer rural disturbances, but news of events in France and Germany sparked off urban demonstrations. On 3 March in Buda the Magyar radical journalist Kossuth spoke out against Vienna in the name of greater Hungarian autonomy. Within a week there were demonstrations in Vienna demanding reforms. By 12 March these had enlisted student support. These peaceful

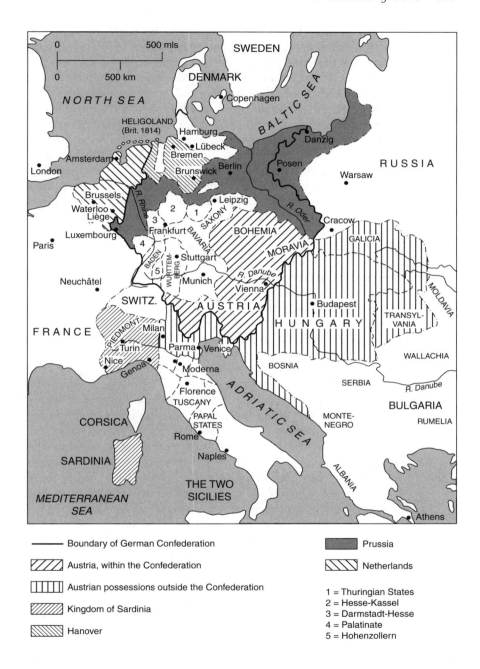

Map 7.1 The 1848 revolutions in Europe

demonstrations affected the working-class suburbs of the city where violence broke out on 13 March. The government responded with concessions – above all the dismissal of the Austrian Chancellor Metternich – and military action. Within days the government concluded the situation was beyond control, called off military action and promised many reforms.

News of Metternich's fall had a dramatic effect elsewhere; more than any other individual, he symbolised the old order. In the Polish parts of the empire and in Bohemia and Moravia there were demonstrations and reform demands. In parts of Transylvania groups took over local government. More serious were the repercussions in Italy. Already in February the King of Piedmont and the Grand Duke of Tuscany had granted constitutions. Austria directly controlled Lombardy and Venetia with their regional capitals of Milan and Venice. When news of Metternich's dismissal reached Milan there was a rising in the city. The Austrian commander Radetzsky had to retreat from the city on 22 March after five days of bitter fighting. Popular risings in Venetia, especially Venice, led to the expulsion of Austrian troops from the city on 21 March. Radetzky withdrew his troops to a secure mountain region of northern Italy. Without Habsburg support the remaining Italian states were vulnerable.

In Prussia in early March there had been rural unrest in Silesia and demonstrations in some cities. Disturbances in Berlin led to the shooting of civilians on 14 March. By 16 March news of Metternich's dismissal reached the city. A large demonstration on 18 March before the royal palace heard the announcement of concessions such as press freedom but reacted hostiley to the presence of troops. Unrest led to firing upon the crowd which retreated from the palace square to surrounding streets, where barricades were built and buildings taken over. After a night's hard fighting the King decided to withdraw troops from the city. The victory of the crowd was symbolised by the parading of the corpses of those killed during the fighting in carts before the palace where the King was compelled to stand on his balcony, bareheaded, and to bow in repentance before these victims of his army. Within the next three days Prussia announced the calling of a constituent assembly along with a range of freedoms.

In four weeks the political situation in France, Germany, Italy and the Habsburg Empire had been transformed. There was a republic in France; the Habsburg Emperor no longer controlled Hungary or northern Italy and was barely master in Vienna; the King of Prussia had been humiliated by crowd action in his capital; most of the smaller German and Italian states had promised new constitutions and appointed new ministers. Freedom of publication, assembly, association and speech had generally been achieved.

Analysis of the outbreak

One can distinguish three elements: popular action, oppositional politics and governmental responses. By the standards of other revolutions or even later in 1848 popular action was limited in size, demands and behaviour. Most crowds numbered hundreds rather than thousands. Eyewitnesses remarked upon the respectable appearance and peaceful character of most demonstrations. Demands were usually confined to constitutional reform or the removal of burdens upon landed peasants. With the crucial exception of capital cities, there was little violence, much of that symbolic, such as the destruction of records of seigneurial privilege, or unfocused, as with working-class rampages in the suburbs of Vienna. Insurrections in Paris, Vienna, Milan and Berlin were crucial to the breakdown of authority in those cities and beyond. However, with the exception of Milan, these disturbances lasted for only a day or two and troops were withdrawn before there were many casualties.

Established political opposition – whether moderate or radical – was surprised by the dramatic success of these popular actions. Street leadership, in erecting barricades and organising fighting, was provided by largely anonymous figures. Opposition politicians had to act quickly to assert their authority, presenting themselves ambiguously as both popular leaders and people who could be coopted to government. Governments responded with an injudicious mixture of concession and repression followed by panic and a rapid capitulation to small protest movements. Only in Milan was repression given a serious try, although its escalation and eventual failure could be used as an argument against that policy.

Why did government prove so inept and weak? There are specific reasons to do with the machinery of law and order. None of the capital cities had a regular, uniformed police force with experience in crowd control. Where there was dependence on civilian militias, such as the National Guard in Paris, these forces failed to rally to the government. Soldiers, trained in conventional battle methods, were a blunt instrument, escalating violence and failing to clear streets of barricades and insurgents. This compares markedly with the response of the British government to the mass demonstration called by Chartist leaders in London for 10 April. Uniformed police, good intelligence (easier when dealing with massive but organised popular movements compared to smaller scale but unorganised popular action), the swearing in of special constables, ostentatious security measures, well-publicised holding in reserve of large bodies of troops: all this stopped the challenge in its tracks. By contrast, continental governments feared revolution inexorably escalating in and beyond their capitals. They felt that middle-class opinion did not support them. Beyond France other governments were worried that a French republic might provoke a crisis, even war, for which soldiers had to be held ready. Some rulers – certainly Louis Philippe and Frederick William IV – had scruples about shooting down their subjects on the streets of their capital. For all these reasons, governments gave way to limited popular movements and brought established opponents into government to fill the power vacuum.

Central to understanding this is the 'myth' of revolution founded by 1789. Revolution in France had led to war and revolution throughout Europe between 1793 and 1815. The peace settlement of 1814–15 was not simply about creating diplomatic stability and rewarding the victors; it was also about restoring and supporting 'legitimate' government. Governments should support one another against the potentially dangerous movements of liberalism, nationalism, radicalism and republicanism. France was regarded as the centre for such movements. In 1815 Napoleon's escape and return to power caused panic. In 1830 revolution in Paris stimulated uprisings and unrest in German and Italian states and was linked to the Polish rising of 1831. Political exiles congregated in Paris where they formed international networks and plotted the next revolution. That in turn spawned a minor industry in police spying. When Louis Philippe was overthrown in February 1848 many people saw this as the start of 'revolution'. Such hopes or fears helped produce the deed. Accounts of the early stages of revolution frequently deploy the conceit of events following a script, of participants acting out the parts allotted to them by 'revolution'.

Thus it was 'natural' in France that a republic be declared. It was 'natural' that French radicals proclaim the need to restore an independent Poland and that liberals and radicals throughout Europe support that demand. Frederick William IV found it 'natural' to write to Queen Victoria describing revolution as a rising tide which had submerged smaller thrones and was lapping at the feet of mightier ones. One cannot shoot a flood. The constant resort to terms like 'flood' or 'avalanche' is testimony to fatalism. The myth of revolution produced unities of action which turned revolution into fact. This disabling/enabling myth acted as a substitute for the politico-military crises which more normally furnish the immediate conditions for revolution.

The initial impetus came from the towns, especially capital cities. Rural protests followed urban leads once peasants were confident that they could act without risk. Most demonstrations remained moderate and limited. The shift to violent conflict brought in larger and more lower-class participation about which we have some evidence from those killed or injured. Artisans, especially building workers, carpenters, shoemakers, tailors, seem to have been disproportionately involved. This can be linked to structural changes in such trades, less the cause of new technology or factory competition and more due to deskilling, penetration by merchant capital, and increasing use of domestic and female rather than workshop and male labour. Urban unemployment had sharply increased as rising food prices due to poor harvests in 1845 and 1846 reduced disposable income available for non-food purchases. Some of the initial 'social' demands were for 'organisation of work' and the right to work or at least some kind of unemployment support. One should distinguish between artisanal response to structural change and that of the unemployed to a cyclical crisis.

The centrality of urban movements can be linked to the relatively good harvests of 1847 which meant that the agrarian crisis had already passed its high point by the time revolution began. Food riots, a central feature of popular protest in 1846 and 1847, were less important in 1848. Rural movements were initially focused on issues that concerned peasants with some land – the end of remaining seigneurial privilege and more locally responsive government – although other issues like free access to the forests had a wide appeal and brought demonstrators directly into conflict with the state. However, these years of hardship had also alienated and even radicalised middling opinion, fatal for governments which had not provided institutional channels for the expression of such opinion.

The new situation

Many contemporaries felt that the world had been turned upside down. With the benefit of hindsight one can see that this was not so. Many regions – 'silent zones' is a phrase used by one historian – saw no popular movements at all. How they would respond to news of revolution made elsewhere remained to be seen. The very rapidity of governmental collapse meant it was superficial. With the exception of Louis Philippe and Ludwig of Bavaria, existing princes remained on their thrones (and Ludwig only abdicated in favour of his son). Armies withdrew resentfully from capital cities to barracks but remained intact, under their regular officers, loyal to their rulers. Government officials continued to administer, collect taxes, enforce laws. The popular movement was small and unorganised, uncertain of where to go having achieved the initial objective of governmental surrender. The new political leaders had no close connections either to these movements or the routine levers of power, and would face the dilemma of whether to focus their attention on securing and extending a popular base or extending their control over the apparatus of government.

However, this initial revolutionary step set up a dynamic. The granting of basic political freedoms stimulated an explosion in publishing, associating, assembling and talking. People who had played no part in the initial phase came forward to form organisations, found newspapers, express demands. There was an immediate focus for this new activity: the elections to be held to many different constituent assemblies – above all, those for France, Prussia and Germany in April. (Austria and Hungary had elections in June. There were elections in the Papal States and mainland Sicily in April and plebiscites in Lombardy and Venetia in May.) New and complex levels of action opened up which could maintain this dynamic: popular movements, associations and communication, elected assemblies, newly constituted governments, the old order.[2]

The multiple centres and levels of action and the inability of any one centre to impose its will upon others is arguably what defines a 'revolutionary situation'. In some cases this situation characterised a particular place. For example, in Paris there developed power centres around political clubs, militias, the public works, as well as the government (Ledru-Rollin organised his own military force at the Ministry of Interior) and the

National Assembly. The situation uncannily resembles that in Paris in the 1790s with its sansculotte *sections* and clubs, or Petrograd in 1917 with its provisional government and soviets. One power centre usually controlled affairs in a particular locality, but this varied from locality to locality within the country as a whole. Counter-revolution is the process of closing down multiple power centres and re-concentrating power into one centre.

The dynamic established through fragmentation of power and the scope it offered for hitherto unorganised groups to enter the world of politics had an ambivalent character. It mobilised new groups with new demands which could push the revolutionary process further. Conversely, it revealed contradictions between different groups and demands and increased anxiety and concern for an end to the revolutionary situation. How political forces formed and responded to this dynamic and its inherent tensions and how they interacted with one another now need to be considered.[3]

Radicalism

Before 1848

If radicalism had a buzz-word it was 'the people'. The people, sometimes understood as those who had to work to live; sometimes, more narrowly, as those who worked by the sweat of their brow, and were oppressed by a system which kept power in the hands of parasites. When Georg Büchner wanted a vivid image for propaganda purposes he used the state budget of a small German state. Each item of the budget, for the royal family, the army, the civil service, represented one group of parasites living off the people. Auguste Blanqui, the French revolutionary, constantly contrasted thirty million French 'people' (or 'proletarians') with thirty thousand parasites.

Büchner fled Hesse after peasants handed in copies of his pamphlet to the police; Blanqui spent much of his life in prison. The parasites were adept at protecting their privileges. Radicals envisaged change in two contrasted ways. One was education; once the people understood their situation the sheer weight of numbers would ensure an end to injustice. The other was conspiracy; precise blows at state power would break the hold of the small elite of parasites.

During 1848

Radicals were surprised by a revolutionary outbreak which was the result neither of conspiracy nor enlightenment. They had to think anew about how to act in a revolutionary situation. They began with certain advantages, especially in Paris and a few other cities with a lively tradition of radical organisation. Radicals with their 'power to the people' approach were quick to get on the streets, form newspapers, put up placards, organise political clubs.

The decision to hold elections presented new challenges. In France radicals like Blanqui and Louis Blanc opposed early elections, arguing that the indoctrination of centuries could not be removed in weeks. They feared that existing power-holders would exploit their control over the minds and bodies of the people to get them to vote the wrong way. The provisional republic should rule until the situation had been sufficiently altered to enable people to vote in an informed and enlightened way. There were radical efforts to mobilise crowds in Paris to delay elections. However, the concern to legitimise the republic quickly, the easy exposure to a charge of hypocrisy, even the feeling of many radicals that they could not stand in the way of early elections, help to explain why such reservations were overruled and the decision taken to hold elections to a National Assembly in April.

Radical fears proved well founded. The elections returned a more conservative assembly than that of the Chamber of Deputies elected on the narrow franchise of the July monarchy. The influence of Catholic priests, local notables and Legitimist nobles, as well as peasant indignation at additional taxation to support the Parisian unemployed – all this and more explains conservative success. Beyond France the lack of a developed radical movement and therefore a strong anti-radical reaction meant that liberals did better in elections, though radicals were in a distinct minority.

Radicals had to rethink their politics. 'The people' was a slogan, not a real category; it dissolved into groups with different, even conflicting interests. Radicals had to take note of these different interests and decide where to pitch their appeal, while emergent collective organisation among hitherto poorly organised groups could push radicalism in socially responsive directions. Work had to be done to develop appropriate organisation for an era of mass, open political organisation and regular elections. The process of relearning went furthest in France where radical and republican ideas were most developed and where the setback of electoral defeat was most keenly felt.

This was not a sudden or unified change of direction. Many radicals still hankered after simpler notions of direct action. There were attempts at *coups* or insurrections through the summer and autumn of 1848 but these failed. Many radicals distanced themselves from what they now regarded as obsolete and wrong-headed politics. However, one effect of these failed uprisings was to scare off moderates.

Radicals were tied to existing constituencies. This was especially true in France where the main base of urban radicalism in Paris was torn apart by the growing polarisation between popular institutions (above all, public works projects) and the National Assembly. The crisis came to a head in June after the issuing of a decree ordering public works employees out of Paris to remote areas. Protest led to barricade-building and the taking over by insurgents of working-class sections of eastern Paris. Republicans were split between those wishing to defend the legitimacy of the new republic and those arguing for a move forward to the 'social republic', that is, one which sought to provide jobs or benefits for unemployed urban workers. The army and other paramilitary units remained loyal to the 'legitimate republic' position. There was no panic as in February. The republican general Cavaignac allowed the insurrection to develop to its full extent and then systematically repressed it.

The repression of the insurrection emboldened regimes elsewhere to take tough action in their capital cities. Insurrection was put down in Prague in June; Vienna followed in October. By November the Berlin population had no stomach to resist the expulsion of the Prussian National Assembly and the introduction of more troops.

This loss of capital cities hastened the reorientation of radicalism to more patient and extensive political activity. (Where it did not happen, for instance, in Venice and Rome, radicalism continued along a more traditional path.) The tragedy was that this major setback also accelerated counter-revolution so that even as radicals extended their support, demonstrated by success in parliamentary elections in France and Prussia in early 1849, so their enemies built up strength even more quickly for a final confrontation which came with the 'second revolutions' of 1849. This new type of social radicalism was repressed almost as soon as it took shape. Radicals were killed, imprisoned, exiled or withdrew from active political life. Only from the 1860s, with the formation of socialist and labour parties, did this kind of radicalism re-emerge, though it was utterly changed.

Nevertheless, those second revolutions revealed the strength of radicalism even in the face of a triumphal counter-revolution. In Italy, Rome and Venice had to be retaken by force. In some of the smaller German states such as Baden, radicals put armies into the field and briefly held power. In Hungary, a movement forced reluctantly into rebellion, with a significant element of existing elite leadership, could only be suppressed by Habsburg and Russian armies, aided by Croatian troops and Rumanian guerrillas.

Liberalism

Before 1848

For liberals the buzz-word was 'constitution'. Liberals sought rule of law, government subject to impersonal constraints imposed by a constitution. They wanted a greater role for elected parliaments but, unlike radicals, were prepared to see that as one element in a constitutional monarchy, rather than the sovereign institution. They were not enamoured of universal suffrage, believing that most men lacked the education or 'stake' (i.e. property) necessary to play a constructive role.

Liberal nationalists had little time for 'small nation' nationalism. Liberals – educated people used to exercising authority in government bureaucracy, university, private enterprise and the professions – thought of the nation in terms of established political institutions and a dominant public culture. Magyar speakers of the eastern Habsburg Empire, German speakers in the western half, Polish elites of the territories of partitioned Poland, Italian speakers: these all represented 'nations'. By contrast, Slavs or Rumanians were at best regarded as groups whose identity required limited recognition in cultural terms. However, at the level of politics liberals considered that members of such groups would advance by assimilating into the dominant national culture. This was understandable, as these non-dominant cultural groups[4] had little in the way of political organisation and consciousness by 1848. This was not a view exclusive to liberals in the dominant cultural groups of East-Central Europe but was shared by others in those groups and public opinion in Western Europe.

During 1848

Liberals had been catapulted into apparent power through the capacity of limited popular movements in early 1848 to bring about governmental collapse. Governments had called liberals into ministries; they dominated many of the early parliaments outside France. Their task now was to use these positions to liberalise state institutions and policies and to enact constitutions. In Germany and Hungary these were seen as national constitutions, although this was complicated in the case of Germany by parallel attempts to enact constitutions for individual states. The more localised and uncoordinated movements of Italy meant that this did not take a national form. Poles failed to act effectively as a national movement in 1848.

However, liberals were handicapped. They were beneficiaries of revolutions they had not provoked, did not want, and often denied. Many were unhappy about the continuing dynamism of the revolutionary process. Liberals saw their task not to build a popular base for the future but to deliver the right policies and institutional reforms, in the hope that this would secure a new and stable political system. Often the best way to achieve this was seen as through agreement with the princes who still wielded great power through their control of the civil service and army. Liberals, therefore, often delayed any decisive action before they could be clear as to where such authority lay. In Germany, for example, the German National Assembly was reluctant to take a lead until it was clear whether those in power in Prussia or Austria (prince or parliament) offered the best prospect for cooperation.

Liberals, like radicals, were discovering that actual politics were more complicated than their programmes and plans had allowed. In Germany, there were divisions between Catholics and Protestants over whether Austrian or Prussian pre-eminence was to be preferred, as well as between the liberals of Prussia, Austria and the 'third Germany' (that is, the other German states apart from Austria and Prussia). Liberals in government in individual states were unwilling to cede leadership to liberals at a national level. (There were key exceptions, for example, the willingness of Lombard liberals to accept the lead of Piedmont as the only way to acquire military power against Austria while marginalising radicalism.)

Liberals found that many of their policies were unpopular. There was antipathy to liberal measures such as dismantling guilds. The principle of free movement alienated communities cherishing the power to block settlement of outsiders. Liberals were unsympathetic to interventionist measures such as the establishment of public works. All this pushed liberals towards princely authority as a bulwark against popular opposition. By September 1848 liberals were welcoming the use of troops to deal with popular opposition. If princes made concessions, this could lead to abandonment of revolution. It would be wrong to portray this as betrayal of the Revolution or class cowardice because liberals had never wanted revolution in the first place.

The 'springtime of peoples' was soon replaced by the 'nightmare of nations'. Dominant national movements came into conflict, as is shown by the German reaction against Polish nationalism in the Prussian province of Posen. More significantly, the revolution accelerated organisation and consciousness among the non-dominant cultural groups. Nationalists insisted on recognition of their cultural identity and political interests. Czechs could not accept that Bohemia and Moravia belonged to 'Germany'; Rumanians that Transylvania belonged to 'Hungary'. German and Magyar liberal nationalists found their nationalism challenged and their liberalism questioned. In response, the Habsburgs could dangle the prospects of federalism before these smaller national movements as the best way to secure their own autonomy.

All this explains why, by early 1849, liberals had been removed from power by radicals or conservatives. Liberals would only make gains from now on by acting as subordinate partners to conservatives.

Conservatism

Conservatism before 1848

So long as those who hold power are not challenged in terms of a different way of holding and using power, they have no need to elaborate arguments and actions in explicit defence of their power. Revolutions create conservatism. Modern conservative ideas were born in reaction to the French Revolution, most famously Burke's *Reflections on the French Revolution*. Conservative defences of church and monarchy were elaborated by exiles from the French Revolution and animated Bourbon policies after 1815. Legitimate government was an explicit ideological creed for Metternich, Tsar Nicholas I and Frederick William IV of Prussia.

However, this did not produce conservative *movements*. Restoration regimes were suspicious of popular appeal, even if it worked in their favour. A church-and-king mob was still a mob. It was better to work against liberals and radicals with repressive laws and police spies than arguments. Furthermore, restoration regimes had gravely compromised conservative values. The Bourbons had accepted a constitution, and when Charles X offended against it he was ejected from power in 1830 and replaced by Louis Philippe, acceptable because he was not Bourbon, republican or Bonapartist and therefore represented no principle at all. Metternich was a man of the Enlightenment who defended monarchy and religion in functional, not sentimental terms. The secular bureaucrats who ruled in central Europe had displaced localised aristocratic and church power and could hardly appeal to such traditions. Many principled conservatives found the existing order scarcely preferable to the schemes of liberals and radicals. Occasionally there was a hint of populist conservatism in regime actions but such measures were half-hearted, usually forced by events and soon abandoned.

This helps to explain the impotence of the ruling order in the spring of 1848. There was no strong sense that the form of the regime was really *worth* defending or might have any hold upon popular affection. At local level, expressed vividly in the *Verzichtsbriefe* (literally, resignation letters) drawn up by some Badenese noble landowners surrendering their privileges, there was a genuine sense of resignation. Arguably the most important political feature of the revolutions was the emergence of strong, effective forms of conservatism.

The conservative response to revolution

One can distinguish four modes of conservative response: exercise of traditional authority to mobilise segments of the population against the revolution; making of timely concessions to neutralise potential revolutionary forces; use of established institutions of authority, above all the army, to repress revolution; and construction of an innovative popular politics.

Traditional populism occupied a role in the early elections, and areas untouched by revolution could now play a part. This is clearest in the April 1848 elections in France. Legitimist elites did better in these elections than under the restricted franchise of the July monarchy. This conservatism was especially important in France because Legitimists had opposed the July monarchy and were not compromised by the overthrow of the regime. This was not the case elsewhere, where peasants had grievances against privileged landowners, who in turn were linked to the established monarchy. In Austria, slightly later elections could exploit a backlash against revolution, with areas like the Tyrol and rural Austria following a conservative lead.

However, traditional populism proved inadequate. With elections and liberties people became aware of interests and values against established authority. One response was to make concessions in order to rally certain groups to the restoration of the old order. The key group was the peasantry.

Beyond France, early 1848 witnessed widespread rural disturbances aimed at the removal of existing burdens upon peasant proprietors such as seigneurial dues, unpopular taxes and exclusion from forests. Once these achievements were legalised by new governments and accepted by princes, such peasants had little further interest in revolution. On 26 July 1848 in the newly elected Austrian Reichstag, Hans Kudlich, a peasant's son, proposed the abolition of 'all servile relationships together with rights and obligations coming therefrom'. Ninety-two of the 383 deputies were peasants. The only contentious issue concerned indemnification of the seigneurs. After debate a principle of indemnification was accepted. The Emperor signed the law as 'constitutional Emperor of Austria' on 7 September. By the time of the Vienna insurrection the peasant population of Austria had been neutralised.

A similar policy of concessions to peasants by the existing princes can be observed in other German states. Elsewhere it was less important. In Hungary, peasant emancipation was granted, but by the Magyar leaders acting in the name of the fictive King of Hungary rather than the Emperor of Austria. The effect was to mobilise Magyar peasant support behind that leadership, itself drawn largely from the landowning aristocracy. In Italy, land reform was occasionally taken up by radicals as in the Roman Republic. It has been argued that Radetzky appealed to northern Italian peasants and set them against their nationalist lords, though he did not follow a pro-peasant policy after the restoration of Habsburg rule. Finally, in France the revolutionary settlement had already created a conservatively minded smallholding peasantry whose interests were not threatened by any kind of regime except a 'social republic', and so was available for a variety of political appeals.

A less important area of concessions concerned artisans. A number of German princes opposed the extension of occupational freedom, and supported guilds and the authority of the master. A law to this effect was passed in Prussia in early 1849. However, it was more the insistence of liberals on *laissez-faire* principles which alienated artisans, and such artisans could as easily move towards illiberal radicalism. Political opinion in artisan circles varied with trade, position and region.

Concessions to artisans were inhibited and undermined by concessions to liberals. Although he dissolved the constituent assembly, the Prussian King issued his own constitution a month later. The Austrian Reichstag was moved out of Vienna before the end of 1848, but allowed to continue work on a federalist constitution until March 1849. Even when that had been rejected the government decreed its own constitution. In France, Louis-Napoleon came to the fore as constitutionally elected President of the Republic.

However, there were limits to these constitutional concessions. The Prussian constitution was revised unconstitutionally in an authoritarian direction in 1850. The Habsburg government immediately suspended the constitution it had decreed and later returned to unconstitutional rule. Louis-Napoleon abrogated the republican constitution by a *coup* in December 1851 and decreed his own imperial constitution in 1852. However, in the short term conservatives had felt obliged to make these concessions.

Things were different where counter-revolution was simply repressed. In Hungary and northern Italy, and smaller German states like Baden and Saxony, the army restored the old order without benefit of constitutions. Yet in less polarised situations the combination of conservative concession and liberal fear of radical revolution helped produce a pragmatic conservatism which embraced a wide range of social groups and political opinions. Most of France rallied behind the repression of the June insurrection. In Berlin and other German cities, businessmen who had supported liberal ministries in the spring welcomed back troops in the summer, even if accompanied by the removal of liberal ministries. There was a national dimension to this, illustrated by the approval by German liberal opinion of the crushing of the Prague insurrection by Windischgrätz who, having done the same in Vienna, ordered the execution of two deputies from the German National Assembly.

This repression came in two phases: the battle for the capital cities in 1848, and the crushing of 'second' revolutions in 1849.

The first phase can be linked to traditional and pragmatic conservatism. Traditional conservatism helped return a conservative French National Assembly which in turn provoked the June insurrection and the broad alliance against it. Something similar was at work in the restoration of order in Vienna and Berlin. When conservatives felt confident about support outside the capital city they could take their time systematically repressing opposition in the capital. This does not apply to the Hungarian and Italian cases where the whole country had to be pacified, along with capital cities. That pacification occurred later, in 1849.

Repression in the capital stimulated the redeployment of radicalism to a broader stage, taking up social questions and building support in both town and countryside. Where parliaments and elections continued to matter, radicalism could appear more threatening. Repression had to be organised on a more widespread basis. The key to this was the regular army. Most armies remained intact and loyal to established authority. In France, this meant the moderate republic. In the Habsburg army, this meant continued loyalty of German and Slav soldiers. The Habsburgs also drew upon the semi-autonomous Croatian army and Russian soldiers. In Italy, the Roman Republic was crushed by the armies of Austria, France and the Kingdom of the two Sicilies.

It is instructive to see what happened when such armed support was not forthcoming. In northern Italy the revolution could call upon the Piedmontese army. After its second defeat by Radetzky in the summer of 1849, that effectively ended resistance in Lombardy. Elsewhere in Italy, revolutionaries formed military forces out of militias, volunteers and deserters. Such forces proved adept at defending certain towns but less effective at mobile warfare and open battle. In Baden some of the army abandoned their prince and put up stiff resistance. Above all, in Hungary regular officers and military units came over to the Revolution, and there the Revolution proved hardest of all to repress.

Once soldiers had established authority, this was reinforced through political and police measures. Constitutional concessions were withdrawn or limited. Restrictive laws on association and freedom of speech were introduced. New types of policing were established to carry out surveillance on suspect individuals and organisations. Show trials were held. Radicals fled abroad, were executed, imprisoned or forced underground. The restored order was more systematically and effectively repressive than the states of the pre-1848 era.

Yet astute conservatives realised it was impossible to return to the old ways, even if more efficiently. The outbreak of revolution and rapid expansion of popular organisation, especially in France and parts of Germany, made that clear. Concessions to peasants and liberals ensured there could be no simple restoration. The realisation that many elements of radicalism and liberalism were unpopular suggested possibilities for a new kind of conservatism.

The most dramatic and puzzling example of this was Bonapartism. It was difficult to accept that Bonapartism was 'conservative', so novel was it. Louis-Napoleon came from virtually nowhere to win the Presidential election of December 1848 with a massive majority which represented substantial support across society and the political spectrum. In part, this revealed the bankruptcy of conservatism. No monarchical candidacy could be launched in 1848. Apart from Louis-Napoleon and Cavaignac, there stood only radical candidates. Anyone wanting to vote against the republic had only Louis-Napoleon. Yet many republicans also found in his favour the myth of his uncle and that he had no political record, and therefore, no political profile which identified him against the republic. The lack of a mass political culture meant there were no established parties or political positions associated with regions or classes, and Louis-Napoleon provided a weak filling for this vacuum. In the period 1848 to 1850 he took a conservative direction, supporting Papal restoration, cracking down on radicalism and making an alliance with the Catholic Church. However, in 1851 he appeared to be moving in a radical direction, opposing franchise restrictions proposed by Parliament. The December *coup* was aimed against the conservative assembly and included an appeal to the people. However, popular and radical resistance re-routed the *coup* in a conservative direction. Although there was some reshuffling of elite control in such matters as prefectural appointments in the 1850s, in the political sphere the tendency was conservative. However, support for popular social associations, a more forward foreign policy and liberal economic policy made this a complex kind of conservatism.

There was nothing like Bonapartism outside France. Nevertheless, there were more limited kinds of popular conservatism. In Prussia, an assembly of landowners unconvincingly claimed a popular mandate. The newspaper *Kreuzzeitung* sought popular legitimacy for conservative principles. Many people joined the newly formed war veterans' associations, indicating potential for linking Prussian patriotism to royalism. By the early 1850s such political auguries were supported by the pioneering sociology of Wilhelm Riehl, who argued that peasants and artisans were rooted in tradition and wedded to conservative principles, while revolution was the work of rootless groups such as the modern intelligentsia.

In the field of secular politics these were but straws in the wind, marginalised by the return to straightforwardly restrictive and bureaucratic methods. They anticipated a later politics, above all those of Bismarck. More important was how conservative politics and the churches combined. Before 1848 and in the early stages of the Revolution, it was not apparent that organised religion would buttress a conservative political order. The Catholic Church was suspicious of secular, religiously indifferent, even anti-clerical governments, even in Catholic-majority countries like France and Bavaria. Where Catholics were in a minority, the Church supported demands for state/church separation, although this meant something different to bishops than to liberals. Religious reform movements meant potential support for liberal, radical, even socialist ideas. Denominational conflict aligned with political conflict.

When the threats posed by radicalism and liberalism became apparent, this changed. The Catholic Church in France played a major role in the April 1848 elections, the priest often leading his congregation to the polling stations immediately after service. Churchmen denounced radicalism as godless. The Pope moved in a conservative and anti-liberal direction. By 1850 the French government had abandoned its anti-clericalism and granted extra support to the Catholic Church in the field of education. In the German states liberal and radical forms of Christianity were repressed. The Papacy was restored. Catholic and Protestant clerics took up social measures as alternatives to political reform, creating the basis for a new kind of populist religion.

Historiography

Revolutions are about more than politics, but as revolution is the breakdown of order and ending revolution the reassertion of order, the focus of a short treatment must be on the conflicts which produced, deepened and finally liquidated revolution. I have sketched out an argument organised around the concepts of radicalism, liberalism and conservatism.

This could mislead if it made the various revolutions appear essentially similar. Although closely connected in the opening stages, the revolutions later drew further apart. As they entered uncharted waters with the peculiar combination of apparent collapse but underlying survival of the old order, people referred less to the 'script' of revolution and instead sought novel solutions to novel challenges, paying less attention to what was happening elsewhere.

This fragmentation favoured conservative counter-revolution as liberals and radicals failed to act together. If the Hungarian army had crossed the internal Austrian/Hungarian border in support of the Viennese insurgents in October 1848, it is difficult to see how the Habsburgs could have prevailed. However, the Hungarians were defending a constitutional achievement in Hungary, not promoting revolution throughout the empire. Radical Italians in Rome, Milan and Venice hardly cooperated until the counter-revolution was on the verge of triumph. National antagonisms could be exploited by conservative forces which later repressed all national movements.

If the revolutions became increasingly disconnected (but counter-revolution increasingly connected), were they nevertheless similar? One difficulty is that historians have written about the revolutions in different ways. Writing on the French Revolution sets it in a sequence of revolutions starting in 1789. The focus is on political ideologies and movements and the social bases of such politics treated as a self-contained national event. By contrast, revolution in Italy and the Habsburg Empire is studied in terms of national rather than social movements and seen as crucially dependent upon external forces. Historiography of the German revolutions falls in between. The national question looms large but is one of unification rather than separation from or conflict with other nationalities, and is related to social and political differences between Germans. All this makes a comparative history of the revolutions difficult to write.

The best comparisons are in the social history of the revolutions, comparing peasant or artisan actions, and linking these to economic contexts. These comparisons are best developed for France and the German lands where the social history of revolutions is most advanced. However, new developments in revolutionary historiography insist that we take politics more seriously (rather than seeing these as reflexes of socio-economic forces) and pay more attention to cultural aspects.

A longer account could explore the connections of politics to social history, for instance, considering conservative concessions to peasant interests and radical cultivation of agrarian grievances. The balance and nature of such interests and grievances varied from country to country, even region to region, as did the capacities of different political movements to mobilise them. Exploring these could lead to an integrated comparative political and social history.

Political capacities were culturally informed. Political activists deployed existing rhetorics and rituals, like those associated with carnivals and festivals, to tap support. How a hitherto non-political popular culture could be politicised during revolution remains largely unresearched. Some historians refer to an 'elementary revolution', meaning actions which were never taken up by any political movement, such as land occupations and machine destructions and which were consigned to the condescension not only of posterity but their own time.[5]

Significance

The revolutions of 1848 are frequently described as failures. This implies that revolutions have purposes. Marxists see revolutions as motors of change. Ruling classes will not give up power without a fight and only after that fight can other classes reorder society and economy in their own interest. This answers the objection that revolutions cannot have purposes; it is classes which produce revolution to realise their purposes. From this perspective an unsuccessful revolution is not a revolution at all. Yet the term 'failed revolution' implies that revolution is a type of event which can be identified, irrespective of whether it produces revolutionary change.

In 1848, revolution was identified with the purposes of certain groups but these were not usually understood as classes, at least in Marxist terms. For conservative enemies revolution meant an overthrow of monarchy, family, private property and Christianity. For its supporters it meant something less hair-raising: constitutional government, equality before the law, democratically elected parliaments, shifts of power and wealth away from elites and towards the 'the people', the liberation of nations. From all these perspectives 1848 can be seen as a failure. However, this also indicates that there were different even conflicting views of whose and what purposes were to be advanced or thwarted by revolution. That makes the question of 'failure' a complex one.

One can draw up balance sheets. Who won and who lost? In social terms the most important winner was the peasantry, especially where emancipation had not yet fully applied to peasants with some hereditary title to land. Conversely, a certain kind of privileged landowner lost, although more in terms of authority and prestige than financially. Wage-labourers lost. Public works and other concessions to the unemployed were liquidated and never revived. A doctrinaire economic liberalism, along with political repression, deprived workers of state aid and suppressed their self-help organisations. In the countryside the settlement of propertied peasant grievances left smallholders and landless labourers more impotent than before. Conversely, such policies helped entrepreneurs. It is no coincidence that the first important bout of industrialisation, under free-market conditions, took place in continental Europe in the 1850s and 1860s.

A political balance sheet can also be drawn up. The losers were radicals; 1848 liquidated not only pre-1848 radicalism, it also nipped in the bud the emergence of a more socially responsive radicalism. Along with repression of free-thinking Nonconformist religion, this undermined the potential for the type of populist liberalism which developed in England

and the USA. Liberalism and nationalism were defeated, although their reorientation in authoritarian and pro-state directions laid the basis for nationalist success a decade or so later. The clear winner was the authoritarian state which entrenched itself in a much tougher and more effective way than before 1848.

This balance sheet exercise is crude. It cannot easily discriminate between short- and long-term effects, ascribes an unchanging identity to the groups (peasant, liberal, etc.) which 'win' or 'lose', and assumes a zero-sum outcome. One must also try to understand the difference which revolution made.

It altered political values. Belief in secular ideals such as 'the people', 'constitution' or 'crown' was undermined, and people turned to more 'realistic' politics. Marx insisted that radicalism, like all political values, could only be understood in relation to class interests. August Rochau[6] argued that liberalism could advance only in tandem with economic interests and must make pragmatic alliances with current power-holders. Bismarck believed that conservatism was a matter of interests and power. All three dismissed as utopian blatherings the idealism of the 1848ers. Increasingly their realistic views came to prevail.

The revolutions ended a pattern of revolutions. There was only one more classical revolution in regions affected by revolution in 1848 – the Paris Commune – and that was confined to one city. The repression of revolutionary radicalism and the toughening of the existing state with bureaucratic and populist measures placed massive obstacles in the path of such revolution. Industrialisation and the emergence of a settled, increasingly organised working class had similar tendencies. By the end of his life Friedrich Engels, Marx's closest collaborator, concluded that fundamental change did not require revolution. When the next revolution came it would be in a backward country, in Russia, the bulwark of the counter-revolution in 1848.

Chronology

1848

January   Italy: Insurrection in Sicily; King of Two Sicilies grants constitution.

February   Italy: Constitutions granted in Piedmont and Tuscany. France: Revolution in Paris leads to proclamation of provisional republic.

March   Italy: Habsburg troops driven out of Lombardy and Venetia and Piedmontese troops move in; Pius IX grants constitution in Papal States.

Germany: Demonstrations; concessions by smaller states; insurrections in Vienna and Berlin lead to new ministries; preparations for German Parliament.

Hungary: Demonstrations, new ministry appointed.

April   Britain: Mass Chartist meeting disperses peacefully.

France: Elections to National Assembly.

Italy: Elections in Papal States and mainland of Kingdom of Two Sicilies.

Germany: Suppression of radical insurrection in Baden; war between Prussia and Denmark.

Hungary: Emperor recognises autonomy with 'April Laws'.

May   France: Failure of radical demonstrations in Paris; Luxembourg Commission (to consider labour problems) dissolved.

Italy: Plebiscites in Lombardy and Venetia vote overwhelmingly for fusion with Piedmont.

Germany: A National Parliament elected and meets in Frankfurt; a Prussian Parliament meets in Berlin; elections called for Austria and court flees Vienna.

June   France: Insurrection crushed in Paris.

Italy: Austrian military success in Venetia; elections in Tuscany.

Germany: National Assembly creates provisional government and Archduke Johann of Austria elected imperial regent. Elections for Austrian Reichstag. Slav congress in Prague followed by suppression of street action.

July   Italy: Radetzky defeats Piedmont at Custozza.

Germany: Artisan congress; Austrian Reichstag meets.

Hungary: National Assembly meets.

August   Italy: Radetzky occupies most of Lombardy and Venetia.

Germany: Prussian government signs Malmö armistice with Denmark.

Austria: Court returns to Vienna.

September   Germany: Disturbances in Frankfurt after Parliament accepts Malmö armistice; Austrian Reichstag votes to abolish serfdom.

Hungary: Croatian leader Jelacic invades; war with imperial government; Rumanians prepare to take action against Hungarian government.

October	Hungary: Military success against Jelacic. Germany: insurrection in Vienna.
November	France: Constitution finalised. Italy: Democrats take power in Rome. Germany: Conservative ministry appointed in Berlin and Parliament moved out of city; insurrection in Vienna crushed and Schwarzenberg appointed prime minister.
December	France: Louis Napoleon elected President. Germany: Prussian government dissolves Parliament and issues own constitution; Franz Joseph becomes Austrian Emperor and imperial army invades Hungary.

1849

January	Italy: Democrats winning elections in Piedmont and Papal States. Germany: National Parliament issues Declaration of Basic Rights.
February	Italy: Republic declared in Rome; a revolutionary government in Tuscany.
March	Italy: Piedmont at war with Austria and defeated at Novarra; King of Two Sicilies dissolves Parliament. Germany: National Parliament completes constitution and offers imperial Crown to King Frederick William IV of Prussia; Austrian Constituent Assembly dissolved. Hungary: Its forces conquer most of Transylvania.
April	France: Soldiers sent to aid Pope in Papal States. Italy: Grand Duke of Tuscany regains power; Austrian troops besiege Venice. Germany: Twenty-eight states accept constitution but rejected by Frederick William IV. Hungary: Austrian troops defeated; declaration of independence; Emperor asks Tsar for help.
May	France: Radical successes in elections. Italy: Austria bombards Venice; Neapolitan troops reconquer Sicily. Germany: Revolutions in south-western states in support of imperial constitution.
June	France: Radical demonstrations against intervention in Rome defeated. Germany: Revolution crushed; National Parliament dissolved.

> Hungary: New assault by imperial troops and entry of Russian troops.
>
> *July*   Germany: Prussia suppresses last resistance in Baden.
>
> *August*   Italy: French troops conquer Roman Republic; Austrian troops occupy Venice.
> Hungary: Conquered by Habsburg and Russian troops, Kossuth flees country.
> By August 1849 the revolutions were effectively over although the business of repression went on for some time.

Notes

1 The established political opposition had instituted a series of these banquets where prominent political figures gave speeches and which were attended by a large audience beyond those who had subscribed to the actual meal.
2 I derive these ideas of 'levels' from Wolfram Siemann, *The German Revolution of 1848–49*, London, 1998.
3 In the section on radicalism I will pay particular attention to France, as radical movements were most developed there. In the section on liberalism I will pay particular attention to areas beyond France, as issues of constitutionalism and national government were not as important in France. By this means, and with a more balanced treatment of conservatism, I hope to combine thematic with geographical coverage.
4 This rather clumsy phraseology is now the accepted alternative to the unacceptable contemporary notions of 'historical' and 'non-historical' peoples and is more precise than that of 'large' and 'small' nations.
5 For the idea of an 'elementary revolution', see Siemann, ibid. A good example of how to relate politicisation to pre-political popular culture is Jonathan Sperber, *Rhineland Radicals: The Democratic Movement and the Revolution of 1848–1849*, New Jersey, 1991.
6 A German liberal who coined the term *Realpolitik*.

Further reading

Maurice Agulhon, *The Republican Experiment, 1848–1852*, Cambridge, 1983.
John Breuilly, *Mass Politics and the Revolutions of 1848*, part of *Core Resources for Historians: A Multimedia CD-Rom*, a 'learning package' produced by TLTP History Courseware Consortium, University of Glasgow, 1998.
Ivstan Deak, *The Lawful Revolution: Louis Kossuth and the Hungarians, 1848–1849*, New York, 1979.
Stanley Pech, *The Czech Revolution of 1848*, Chapel Hill, NC, 1969.
Roger Price, *The French Second Republic: A Social History*, London, 1972.
John Rath, *The Viennese Revolution of 1848*, Austin, TX, 1957.
Wolfram Siemann, *The German Revolution of 1848–49*, London, 1998.
Jonathan Sperber, *The European Revolutions, 1848–1851*, Cambridge, 1994.
Stuart Woolf, *A History of Italy, 1700–1860*, London, 1979.

8 The revolutionary tradition in the nineteenth and early twentieth centuries

Dick Geary

Introduction

A revolutionary tradition was created by the great French Revolution of 1789–95. Only thereafter did a class of professional revolutionaries emerge, devoting their whole existence not simply to critical thought but to analysing the revolutions of the past in order to bring about the revolutions of the future. The revolutionary tradition has expressed itself partly in revolutionary political theory, which forms the major part of this chapter. However, we will also examine the existence of revolutionary traditions of a different kind: traditions embedded in the sentiments and actions of the masses, whose dynamism and originality have usually taken the revolutionary intelligentsia by surprise and whose behaviour has been largely unscripted.

Revolutionary theory

There have been theories of rebellion against established authority since time immemorial, drawing inspiration from either a particular reading of God's will and its transgression or claims that authority was trampling upon traditional rights. Revolutions and revolutionaries of the nineteenth century were engaged in a different project: the attempt to create new worlds through a strategy, derived at least in part from the experience of past revolutions. Of course, thinkers had long imagined societies more just and less repressive than their own. In certain respects the Enlightenment paved the way for both the American and the French revolutions in its emphasis on man's ability to transform the world according to the dictates of reason and in advocating his liberation from tradition and religious superstition; though the politics of the *philosophes* were often elitist and authoritarian. In more radical mode, Rousseau had realised that large inequalities in the distribution of goods constituted a major source of social corruption and a threat to the democratic polity. De Mably and Morelly, his contemporaries, took this critique of inequality further and advocated a form of primitive (albeit agrarian) communism. The principles of religious and political liberty, adumbrated in the historic Declaration of the Rights of Man and the Citizen of 24 August 1789, did not espouse these more radical social aims but were clearly influenced by the thoughts of some of the *philosophes*, just as the founders of the American Republic put into effect Montesquieu's theory of the separation of powers (a separation copied in no European revolution). Yet these thinkers were not revolutionaries in the modern sense: they had little idea of precisely how more democratic and egalitarian societies could be created, except through the education of virtuous citizens. The mechanics of revolution remained a mystery to them, and were beyond their experience. When the American revolt against Britain began and when the Tennis Court Oath was taken in the early days of the French Revolution, the protagonists had little idea that they were embarking upon a revolution. After 1789, however, such innocence was dead.

The claim that it was the French Revolution which created the European revolutionary tradition may seem ungracious to the founders of the American Republic; for did not the Declaration of Independence in the New World impact upon the Old? It is certainly true that a transatlantic community of enlightened thinkers existed and that the revolutionaries of 1789 knew of an American precedent, as R.R. Palmer has made clear. The American Revolution had, after all, created a new, national state, founded upon the principle of liberty; and Condorcet was not alone in trying to assess its impact in Europe when he wrote his *Influence de la Révolution d'Amérique sur l'Europe* in 1786. Yet the American Revolution was not the point of reference for Babeuf, Buonarotti, Marx, Engels, Blanqui, Proudhon, Bakunin, Lenin, Trotsky or Kropotkin. For them the French Revolution was the mother of all revolutions.

This inescapable fact can be explained not only by the aquatic divide that separates the New from the Old World. It was also because the American Revolution largely ignored the social question and the imperatives of poverty, at least in comparison with the later events in France. It left large areas of life untouched. It was not followed by fratricide of monstrous dimensions; and it never equated the people with the sans-culottes, with the poor and dispossessed. Yet it was this equation which drove on the revolutions of the future. As Hannah Arendt commented, 'It is as though the American Revolution was achieved in a kind of ivory tower into which the fearful spectre of human misery, the haunting voices of abject poverty, never penetrated.'[1] Identifying but a single source of law and government, believing in a nation undivided and a single national will, so unlike the American view of a people composed of different views and interests, the French revolutionaries found themselves engaged in a project infinitely more total than anything their American cousins had imagined or wanted. Americans, according to Aléxis de Tocqueville, had a passion for liberty, but the Europeans had a passion for revolution.

The light of the French Revolution shines out from the principal revolutionary texts of the following century. Until 1917 it was the event (or chain of events), upon which European revolutions modelled or tried to model themselves. The image of revolution as a raging torrent, unstoppable, racing through different stages, following an inner logic, moving along an ascending line (Karl Marx), we owe to reflections on the events that gripped France between 1789 and 1795. The young officers, who tried to overthrow the Tsarist autocracy in the Decembrist rising of 1825, drew their inspiration from the overthrow of the *ancien régime*. Babeuf (1760–97) and the Italian born Buonarotti found their model of social change in the Terror and the war economy of 1793–94. The radical English Chartist, Bronterre O'Brien, wrote a biography of Robespierre and was influenced by French revolutionary thought. (The internationalism of the revolutionary idea was one of its crucial aspects in the nineteenth century.) The myth of 1789, as John Breuilly has shown, both enabled and disabled the revolutionaries of 1848. Marx and Engels were absolutely clear that 1848 was history repeating itself as farce: 'from 1848 to 1851 the ghost of the old revolution walked about . . . the old dates arise again, the old chronology, the old names, the old edicts.'[2] De Tocqueville too noted of the revolutionaries of 1848 that 'the imitation was so total that it concealed the terrible originality of the facts; I continually had the impression they were engaged in play-acting the French Revolution far more than continuing it'.[3] For the Romantic historians of this great upheaval (Guizot, Thierry and Michelet), the course of the French Revolution revealed classes and class conflict; and to these historians Marx expressly acknowledged his debt. From the Revolution, however, he also drew a further conclusion, namely that political liberation alone would never constitute the world of freedom. This required the transformation of economic and social relationships too. The outcome of equality before the law and formal equality of opportunity would not solve the problems of the *menu peuple*, enslaved by the necessity of poverty. Bourgeois liberalism did not mean universal liberation. Long after this, the French upheavals of 1789–95 continued to inform revolutionary thought of virtually all kinds: in 1905, for example, the Russian anarchist Peter Kropotkin could still claim that the French Revolution was the source and origin of all the present communist, anarchist and socialist concepts.[4]

It should be noted that the French Revolution also produced the great texts of conservatism and counter-revolution in the writings of Edmund Burke, Chateaubriand, Joseph de Maistre and Friedrich Gentz. Only when the old order found itself inescapably challenged did it become necessary to theorise a defence of the established order. What is more, for Burke and de Maistre the French Revolution, revolutionary terror and subsequent (Napoleonic) dictatorship showed the way that all attempts to destroy established authority must go. In the 1848 revolutions the traditional elites learned that they had to do more than simply preserve the old. They had actively to mobilise support against the forces of change. It could be argued that the European establishment subsequently learned more from revolutions than did future generations of revolutionaries (except in Russia). The rebuilding of Paris by Hausmann during the Second Empire, for example, destroyed many of the narrow alley-ways that had rendered the erection of barricades so easy; and it did so for reasons of social and political hygiene, as well as aesthetics.

The first theory of revolution to combine social criticism with revolutionary mechanics was that of François Noël Babeuf; and it was no accident that it appeared in the wake of the revolutionary upheavals of 1793–94 and their defeat. Babeuf had experienced the popular movement of the Paris *sections* first hand; and he had been impressed by the organisation of supplies for the revolutionary armies. His view of terror as an instrument of social transformation derived directly from the Jacobin Terror, and claimed that compromise sapped revolutionary energy and only served to strengthen the forces of counter-revolution. Against royalists, papists and starvers of the people only terrorism sufficed. To ignite the revolutionary spark, dormant in the impoverished people, a small, conspiratorial group of professional revolutionaries should seize power and institute a revolutionary dictatorship, dispossess the wealthy and constitute some form of agrarian communism. Babeuf himself attempted to put this into effect in a revolutionary conspiracy, the *conspiration pour l'égalité*, together with Filipo Buonarotti, who after reprieve wrote a book about the episode in 1828. The initial conspiracy reflected the desperation of the defeated revolutionary forces in July 1794 and the realisation that bourgeois rule constituted a betrayal of the people (understood as the poor). The plot was uncovered by a police spy, and Babeuf was executed in 1797. But Buonarotti's book developed the theme of conspiratorial, violent and revolutionary dictatorship further. It claimed that the experience of the French Revolution showed that the overthrow of established authority by certain wise and courageous citizens was much more important than winning votes and that opposition was to be ruthlessly eliminated. Similar arguments – a belief in the necessity of violence and at least a temporary period of dictatorship – continued to inform revolutionary thinking. In France under the July monarchy (1830–48), for example, there sprang up a variety of revolutionary secret societies. One of their members, Auguste Blanqui, epitomised the extreme voluntarism of this kind of revolutionary theory, which held that a small, conspiratorial elite could institute social revolution. Blanqui made several abortive attempts to overthrow the French government in the 1830s and 1840s, as a result of which he spent several inglorious years in prison. He believed that an elite of professional revolutionaries could seize power, erect a revolutionary dictatorship, expropriate the owners of private capital and create some form of communist state, though he said little about the precise structures of the ideal future. His theory located this *coup d'état* at a particular historical juncture, namely economic crisis, which would arrive as a result of the mismatch of production and consumption in a capitalist economy and which would create a rebellious mood among the masses; and in reaching this conclusion Blanqui was influenced by the new political economy and French utopian socialism. More will be said of these later; but it was for his commitment to violent conspiracy and ensuing dictatorship that Blanqui was to be most important in the revolutionary tradition. His ideas played a role in the development of conspiratorial theories of revolution in Russia in the second half of the nineteenth century; and some would argue that Lenin was a Blanquist. Trotsky certainly thought that Blanqui had got some things right, namely, the belief that insurrection is an art and that its rules must be learned. Although the Russian revolutionary shared the Marxist view that conspiracy alone would not bring success, he nonetheless suggested in his *History of the Russian Revolution* that the proletariat needed more than a spontaneous insurrection to bring about social revolution and that there was a role for conspiratorial organisation.

As we have seen, the concept of revolution was increasingly hijacked by the social issue. Revolutions were no longer conceived merely as political ruptures, though these were still seen as crucial, but as the harbingers of a new society. Yet, as the social question came to dominate, so forms of social change that did not necessarily involve violent revolution also appeared on the agenda. Advocates of cooperative socialism proliferated in an increasingly industrial Britain, where a new theory of exploitation was developing. In France, utopian socialists advocated egalitarian (usually agricultural) communities, which some of their followers tried to erect on the virgin soil of North America. The fantastical nature of many of their plans should not obscure their trenchant critique of capitalism, which rested on a theory of exploitation and, in the case of both Pierre Leroux, editor of the Parisian socialist journal *Le Globe* (1842) and the utopian socialist Charles Fourier (1772–1837), on an astute identification of cyclical unemployment as a necessary consequence of capitalism. At the same time Louis Blanc proposed the creation of national workshops, initially funded by a central bank but which would subsequently become self-governing and autonomous. Wage differentials would eventually be abolished; and the new workshops would be so successful that competition from private enterprises would die out. Most of the utopians saw no need to bother about the state, which was precisely why Marx called them utopians. Blanc saw a democratic state as an instrument of social change but disavowed any need for violent revolution. Thus at the same time as an insurrectionary, Babouvist-Blanquist tradition continued to entice some revolutionary thinkers, alternative, non-violent but often utopian models of change were also developing, as was the British political economy of exploitation whose proponents – notably Robert Owen, George Mudie, Francis Bray and Thomas Hodgskin – claimed that capitalist relations necessarily involved the exploitation of workers, who did not receive the full value of their labour. In Karl Marx these different traditions came together.

There is not the space here to give an account of Marx's theories of alienation, exploitation and economic crisis. However, two important points relating to these theories do need to be stated at the outset. The humanist critique of capitalism, embraced not only in Marx's early writings but also in the *Grundrisse* of 1859 and in *Das Kapital*, revolved around the concept of commodity fetishism, the commodification of human relations. That economic laws determined the fate of men under capitalism was not a statement of timeless determinism but a critique of present social relations. Man had ceased to be the subject of history and had become its object. Revolution, therefore, was not simply about the transition from one economic system to another: it also involved the liberation of man from necessity, from economic laws. Revolution entailed man's reappropriation of his fate, his rediscovery as the subject of history. As Marx wrote in *The German Ideology*, 'this revolution is necessary, therefore, not only because the ruling class can only be overthrown in such a way but also because only in a revolution can the class overthrowing it rid itself of the muck of ages and become fitted to found society anew'.[5] The statement that the proletariat must liberate itself, therefore, is not simply based on the recognition that no other class will, but also on the idea of revolution as the *self*-liberation of the working class. This view of revolution was not only at odds with vulgar Marxism, which awaited the destruction of capitalism through impersonal economic laws (itself a form of alienated existence), but also with views which ascribe the prime revolutionary role to a vanguard of professional revolutionaries. If revolution is about self-liberation through action, then it must be workers and not their surrogates who take action. This was precisely the argument that Rosa Luxemburg (1870–1919), a Polish revolutionary active in German social democracy, deployed against Lenin in 1902.

This concept of liberation obviates the claim that economic crisis will inevitably lead to the collapse of capitalism and the triumph of socialism. There are occasions, especially in the *Communist Manifesto*, when Marx seems to suggest that the capitalist mode of production is heading for one almighty, final economic crisis. However, the later volumes of *Kapital* seem to contradict such a conclusion and envisage ways in which capitalism might reproduce itself. In any case, Marx drew an analytical distinction between the collapse of capitalism on the one hand and the creation of socialism on the other. For Marx, the latter required the intervention of the proletariat. As he stated repeatedly, it is men who make history; and his *Theses on Feuerbach* of 1844 criticised the materialist doctrine that men are the products of circumstance and upbringing and stated that it is men who change circumstances.

Deterministic elements did intrude into Marxian theory of revolution, but in two specific respects: first, to reject utopian socialism, which imagined that a socialist society could be built without preconditions, other than the goodwill of men; and second, to contest the voluntarism of Blanqui, who believed that correct insurrectionary tactics would be a sufficient guarantee of success. For Marx, men made history, but in circumstances not of their choosing. Qualitative social change, the transition from one set of social relations to another, could only be achieved through revolution, the locomotive of history; but this was only possible when the forces of production had developed to their limit within the existing mode of production. Thus socialism was to be built on the achievement of capitalism, not out of poverty or outside the capitalist system. Socialist theories, which wished to resurrect a pre-capitalist world, Marx dismissed as utopian and ahistorical. Equally, he realised that violent insurrection could only produce a qualitative change from one mode of production to another if the conditions were right. Socialist revolution required the existence of a strong, conscious and revolutionary proletariat, not simply of a conspiratorial elite. Marx discovered the proletariat during his stay in Paris in the 1840s. This class, property-less and alienated, could not help but be revolutionary. It might derive benefits from short-term concessions and become stronger to fight in the future; but such concessions as might be achieved by trade union action or state protection would never amount to liberation. Unemployment and cyclical recession could only be removed systemically, by destroying their roots in a system of production for profit. Hence a revolution was necessary to transform human relations. Such a revolution would be international and built on the massive achievements of the bourgeoisie. Marx suggested that the creation of a global economy might also mean that colonial revolts, for example, in China or Ireland, could ignite the powder-keg of world revolution in the industrial heart of capitalism. What this revolution would look like, however, was far from clear. In France in the 1840s and possibly influenced by Blanqui or the revolutionary secret societies, as well as his studies of the great French Revolution, Marx does seem to have conceived of revolution as a matter of violence. The *Address to the Central Committee of the Communist League* (1850) advocates the arming of workers and proclaims the need for permanent revolution. Two years earlier the *Communist Manifesto* had spoken of despotic inroads into the rights of property. At this time Marx also drew lessons from the June Days of 1848 when, in his opinion, the bourgeoisie had turned on its working-class allies. In future the working class needed to maintain a greater distance from the political coat-tails of the bourgeoisie; and it was to be led by a communist vanguard. Thus Marx appears in the revolutionary tradition of Babeuf, Buonarotti and Blanqui; and significantly it was these remarks which Lenin was to quote against his social-democratic opponents in the course of the Bolshevik Revolution, as in *The Proletarian Revolution and the Renegade Kautsky*. Karl Kautsky, the official theorist of the German Social Democratic Party (SPD), on the other hand, could rely on a different Marx: the Marx who lived and wrote in parliamentary England in the late 1860s and 1870s. For this Marx had written in 1869:

universal suffrage is the equivalent of political power for the working class of England, where the proletariat forms the large majority of the population, where, in a long though underground civil war, it has gained a clear consciousness of its position as a class, and where the rural districts know no longer any peasants, but only landlords, industrial capitalists (farmers) and hired labourers. The carrying of Universal Suffrage in England would, therefore, be a far more socialistic measure than anything which has been honoured with that name on the Continent.[6]

Three years later, at an international congress in the Netherlands, Marx stated that violence was certainly needed to overthrow authoritarian rule, as in the military monarchies of Germany and Austria, not to mention Russia, but that a peaceful route to socialism might conceivably be possible in Britain, the USA and possibly Holland. Hence we have two distinct models of revolution in Marx's writings. However, they are not contradictory but rather reflect different strategic possibilities in different situations. Writing in predominantly agrarian France, with an undeveloped industrial working class and a restrictive franchise, violence was the only option, as it remained a country where autocrats continued to rule. In industrial societies with a large, organised proletariat and a parliamentary system, however, revolution would not necessarily require violent insurrection. Marx demonstrated a similar strategic flexibility in his discussion of the possibility of revolution in Russia. Unlike many of his followers, he was prepared to admit the possibility of a direct transition to socialism in Russia on the basis of the peasant commune, as is clear from his correspondence with Vera Zasulich. However, this possibility was hedged with crucial qualifications: it was predicated upon social revolution in the more advanced states of Europe and limited capitalist development in Russia. Marx specifically rejected the suggestions of a Russian reviewer that *Kapital* provided a model of universal historical development; and his own discussion of the Asiatic mode of production in India and China, a mode of production doomed to immobility without external intervention, pointed to alternative historical scenarios in different societies.

That Marx could envisage both peaceful and violent roads to revolution, the replacement of the rule of one class by that of another, which then uses its political power to build a new order of property relations, prefigured later divisions between Social Democrats and Communists. Yet Marx himself was always sure that a dictatorship of the proletariat was required to bring about the expropriation of the capitalist class and create socialism. To Lenin, this infamous phrase indicated Marx's commitment to revolutionary violence and autocratic rule, at least in the early stages of revolution. For Kautsky, on the other hand, it indicated no more than the need for an exclusively working-class government but one which might embrace democratic institutions. Such contradictory interpretations were possible because Marx had said so little about this dictatorship. He disliked writing recipes for the cook-shops of the future. However, in 1871 the Paris Commune provided Marx with a model for the dictatorship of the proletariat, at least as far as his published work was concerned, for he was much more critical of the Commune in private. The Commune did not simply seize hold of the existing state but rather broke state power. It did this through the substitution of a standing army by the armed people, by removing the police, bureaucracy and all the traditional agencies of the state. This was achieved through institutions of direct, popular democracy, not party dictatorship. Municipal councillors, elected by universal suffrage but recallable at any time, were responsible to the people, as were all administrators. All public service was to be done at workmen's wages; and all areas of France were to administer their own affairs through an assembly of recallable delegates, bound by mandate. The people were not to elect a parliament every few years but to exert a permanent control over their representatives. This model of working-class, non-bureaucratic self-government was indeed the political form at last discovered under which to work out the economic emancipation of labour.[7] It came into existence by force of arms. But it was no dictatorship in the Bolshevik sense.

In the 1880s and early 1890s Marxism was adopted by various European socialist parties and in particular by the SPD. The author of the party programme was Karl Kautsky who, together with Gyorgy Plekhanov in Russia and Jules Guesde in France, became the main transmitter of Marxist theory to the international socialist movement after the deaths of Marx and Engels. Orthodox Marxism, as it came to be known, followed Marx in its criticism of capitalist exploitation and its prognosis of recurrent economic crisis. It saw the proletariat as the agency of human emancipation; and it rejected piecemeal reform as powerless to remove class antagonisms and their origin in the laws of concentration and impoverishment, though its understanding of deprivation was relative (profits rose faster than wages) rather than absolute (the idea that wages would necessarily fall in absolute terms). In his influential *Road to Power* (1910), Kautsky predicted an era of intense class conflict, imperialism and war, in which the bourgeoisie would abandon liberalism and become increasingly reactionary. This radical prognosis was much admired by Lenin and repeated in the work of Rosa Luxemburg, though Kautsky himself subsequently retreated from it. Yet even at the height of his radicalism, the SPD's chief ideologue was remarkably silent on the question of tactics. When Luxemburg advocated a mass strike, her older colleague advised caution and provided an enormously long list of preconditions before any kind of action became possible. Such passive radicalism, the combination of radical criticism with the politics of inaction, was characteristic of many Marxists of this generation; and it was partly a consequence of the absence of immediate revolutionary prospects in Western and Central Europe at the end of the nineteenth century. In Germany, for example, where a powerful military regime found considerable support not only from landowning and industrial elites but also from a numerous lower-middle class of landowning peasants and artisans, and where the labour movement was divided by religious confession and ethnic tension, this strategy of organisation and propaganda, rather than direct but doomed action, made a certain kind of sense. So autocracy and exploitation produced a Marxist labour movement, radically critical of existing social and political arrangements but incapable of action. The passivity of orthodox Marxism in the two decades before the First World War, however, was also a consequence of a particular understanding of Marx, to a large extent borrowed from Engels. I am not referring here to Engels' belief, stated more than once towards the end of his life, that the age of barricades was past and that the electoral strategy of the SPD, together with the subversion of the standing army, as more and more conscripts were Social Democrats, might be sufficient to bring the party to power. Rather I have in mind the fact that Kautsky's generation came to Marx through *Anti-Dühring*, in which Engels attempted to unite the laws of natural and social science. He translated Marx's perceptions of social development into historical laws analogous to the laws of nature; and this union made the theory all the more acceptable in an age of faith in science. Kautsky came to Marx via Darwin and saw in Marx a scientific version of human development. His work, like that of Guesde in France and Plekhanov in Russia, saw history as law-governed (as, for that matter, did Lenin) and spoke in terms of economic and natural necessity. In Russia however, the development of Marxism took a rather different turn.

Marxism had originally been received in Russia by Westernisers, critical of the Slavophile belief that Russian historical development would be different to that of Western, capitalist Europe. Slavophile revolutionaries looked to the Russian peasant commune as the basis of a future egalitarian society and did not believe that their country would have to undergo a stage of capitalist exploitation. This the early Russian Marxists disputed. Gyorgy Plekhanov and the young Lenin (in his *Development of Capitalism in Russia*) were convinced that capitalism was too far advanced in Russia to turn back the clock; and they located the source of revolution not in the Russian peasantry, which had rejected the advances of the Populists (see pp. 155–6) in the 1860s and 1870s, but in the increasingly numerous and radical working class. Plekhanov continued to see the prospects of revolution through Western spectacles: a bourgeois revolution in alliance with progressive elements of the Russian bourgeoisie was a necessary prologue to the possibility of proletarian revolution in Russia, even though such a revolution would have to be led by workers on account of the weakness of the Russian middle class. Lenin and Trotsky on the other hand had a more positive view of the revolutionary potential of the Russian peasantry; and in this they were influenced by a rather unexpected source. In 1893 Kautsky had come to the conclusion that the Russian peasantry would have a role to play in a future revolution, which would have to be led by the industrial working class, on account of the weakness of the Russian bourgeoisie. In the revolutionary journal *Iskra* in 1902, he suggested that the epicentre of revolution was moving eastwards towards Russia, a point which could find some support from isolated remarks by Marx and Engels. This perception was subsequently developed by Parvus (Israel Helphand, a Russian Jew, who had found his political home in the SPD) and Leon Trotsky. The weakness of the Russian middle class meant that revolution would bring the Social Democrats (the party of Lenin, as well as his Menshevik opponents) to power. These, however, would then find themselves obliged to push the revolutionary process yet further towards socialism. After the Russian Revolution of 1905 Trotsky took this argument a stage further: the absence of a strong bourgeoisie, a consequence of Russia's backwardness and of dependence on *foreign* capital, meant that revolution would not stop at the bourgeois stage. Supported by the peasantry during the first revolution, the proletariat would find itself isolated in a second revolution. This second revolution, however, would hit capitalism at its weakest link and thus trigger a revolution in its industrial heartland. (Until April 1917 this view of permanent revolution was not shared by Lenin.)

It was also in Russia that the theory of a vanguard party was developed further, in particular in Lenin's pamphlet *What is to be done?* of 1902. It is not surprising that this has been seen by some commentators as another version of the Babouvist–Blanquist revolutionary idea. It has also been described as a continuation of the Russian conspiratorial tradition of Nechaev and Chernyshevky (as in Maureen Perrie's contribution to this volume). I am not so sure. The argument that a party of professional revolutionaries is needed to bring revolutionary consciousness to the working class, whose sectional and economistic trade union struggles will never of themselves lead to a systemic and universal critique of capitalism, to revolutionary consciousness, does sound familiar; but its justification in *What is to be done?* is explicitly derived from Kautsky, whom Lenin actually quotes. There is considerable evidence, as Moira Donald has shown, that Lenin's model of a revolutionary party at this time was the SPD. The arguments for secrecy and conspiratorial organisation in *What is to be done?* are merely contingent upon Russian circumstance (Tsarist repression); whereas the theory of consciousness from without is based upon universal propositions about the nature of revolutionary consciousness derived from Kautsky.

In the course of the 1917 revolutions Lenin's thought underwent significant change. The *April Theses* accepted that a socialist revolution was on the immediate agenda, although its ultimate success would depend upon international revolution. Soviets were now embraced as the agencies of proletarian insurrection; land was promised to the peasants; and liberation to the national minorities of the Russian Empire. Whether this reorientation was the consequence of theoretical reflection or simple opportunism is open to question; but without it it is doubtful that the Bolsheviks could have seized or remained in power.

The political thought of socialists, concerned to overthrow the existing bourgeois state, has been the major focus of this account of the development of the revolutionary idea. There was, however, another radical tradition: that of anarchism. Anarchists believed that all political institutions, including those of a socialist state, held man in bondage. A society based on justice and cooperation could only be built where all forms of governmental authority had been removed. The first, systematic theory of anarchism was itself a product of the French Revolution, specifically, however, of the disillusionment engendered by the Terror. In 1793 the English philosopher Godwin produced *The Inquiry Concerning Politic Justice*, which advocated the abolition of all forms of authority and their replacement by small social units, in which no one man imposed his will on any other. Like the utopian socialists, Godwin had little idea of how to bring about this change. The same could be said of the French anarchist, Joseph Proudhon (1809–1865). Like his contemporary utopian socialists, he began with a critique of exploitation and advocated a system of mutualism, whereby exchange between small communities of peasants and craftsmen would destroy the need for the capitalist middleman. It was in two other respects, however, that Proudhon was most influential: namely, in his distrust of all theories that looked to the state and a strict *ouvrierisme*, a belief that the working class must liberate itself, because bourgeois politics and all political parties were corrupt and self-interested. Proudhon did not advocate any form of violent revolution; but his greatest *protégé*, the Russian anarchist Mikhael Bakunin, did.

Bakunin participated in an abortive revolution in Dresden and spent many years in Russian prisons. He was one of the founders of the International Workingmen's Association in 1864, though this organisation later fell under the control of Marx and Engels. He believed in the necessity of violence to overthrow the state and that this would be the outcome of a spontaneous rising of the rural poor in Southern and Eastern Europe. Bakunin specifically rejected Marx's advocacy of a vanguard party (another form of authoritarian bondage) and did not believe that the industrial working class constituted the main source of revolutionary energy. He inspired Russian populism in the late nineteenth century and was a significant influence on the anarchist movements of Switzerland, Italy and especially Spain. It was an influence joined in the later years of the century, however, by another variant of anarchism: anarcho-syndicalism.

The organisation of workers into unions, especially of those in small units of craft production (Parisian artisans, textile workers in Catalonia), gave rise to anarcho-syndicalism which, following Proudhon, saw parliaments and political parties as necessarily corrupt and bourgeois. As the Charter of Amiens of the French syndicalist movement stated in 1908, workers would liberate themselves, untainted by middle-class influence, at their place of work and through a revolutionary general strike, which would bring capitalist society to its knees. In the hands of the French intellectual, Georges Sorel, this model of revolutionary syndicalism took on further meanings. Sorel was of a generation that rejected theories of social development based on the natural sciences and was exasperated by the caution of orthodox Marxism. The idea of a revolutionary general strike fascinated him not so much as a means of achieving specific gains for the working class but as a prophylactic for the evils, corruption and unheroic nature of bourgeois society. Thus his *Reflections on Violence* (1908) saw the general strike as a liberating myth. The glorification of violence as a purgative, irrespective of its concrete consequences, could, however, be a tool of ideologies other than revolutionary socialism or anarchism as happened in the case of fascism.

We have thus far traced the development of revolutionary political theory from Babeuf to Lenin and its migration eastwards. It is now time to assess its significance for real revolutions and revolutionary movements.

Theory and practice: the revolutionary masses

As we have seen, Lenin argued that revolutionary consciousness was imported into the ranks of the working class by intellectuals and professional revolutionaries; and similar attitudes informed the theories of Babeuf, Buonarotti, Blanqui and even Kautsky. It should be noted that the great majority of these theorists were also active in real revolutionary movements. Babeuf, Buonarotti, Blanqui and Bakunin were all involved in insurrections. Marx and Engels attempted to mobilise radicals in the Rhineland between 1848 and 1849 and subsequently helped to establish the First International in 1864. Kautsky was the theorist of a political party, the SPD, which had a Marxist programme and could boast over one million members on the eve of the First World War; while Lenin and Trotsky played vital roles in the Bolshevik Revolution of 1917. There can be no doubt that gifted agitators, intellectuals and their ideas have helped to politicise and radicalise workers, as in Paris in the 1830s and 1840s where, for example, Cabet's *Voyage en Icarie* was widely read, or in the case of Germany in the 1880s, when Engels, Kautsky and others propagated Marxist ideas. These informed the party programmes of Austrian, German, Russian and Scandinavian Social Democracy; while a revolutionary intelligentsia played a significant role in the Russian revolutions of 1905 and 1917. However, the fate of radical ideologies and revolutions depended upon far more than the persuasive powers of intellectuals or their theories.

First, the development of all revolutions (with the possible exception of the American) outran the expectations and understanding of the original revolutionaries. As the French Revolution unleashed the potential of the Parisian sansculottes, so ideas of constitutional reform receded into the background and the Revolution became ever more total in its demands. However much all revolutionary sects (Girondins, Jacobins, the *Enragés* and Hébertists) were led by men of the middle class, they were increasingly obliged to keep their eyes and ears attuned to the demands of the *menu peuple* and to instrumentalise them. As Hannah Arendt commented, an element of novelty was present in all revolutions. John Breuilly demonstrates how the revolutions of 1848 called new groups with new demands on to the revolutionary stage, that is, groups which had not previously been privy to a revolutionary tradition; and their aims (for example, in the case of German artisans) were often at odds with those of bourgeois liberalism. The division between master craftsmen and their journeymen, which gave rise to the Brotherhood of German Workers in Berlin at the end of the year, was articulated in the course of the revolution and not before. Thus revolutionary traditions, like all traditions, had to be invented and reinvented. De Tocqueville made much the same point about the French upheavals of the same year:

> from the twenty-fifth of February onwards, a thousand strange systems came issuing pell-mell from the minds of innovators, and spread among the troubled minds of the crowd . . . it seemed as though the shock of the revolution had reduced society itself to dust, and as though a competition had been opened for the form that was to be given to the edifice about to be erected in its place. Everyone came forward with a plan of his own.[8]

The 1905 Revolution in Russia began as a peaceful and loyalist demonstration, led by a priest, which was transformed into Bloody Sunday by the reaction of troops. This revolution also saw the quite unexpected eruption of workers' councils or soviets, uncontrolled by any political faction. These were the most direct expression of workers' desires for liberation, which Trotsky subsequently embedded in his understanding of permanent revolution (though Lenin only took this step in April 1917). This is not surprising; for, as revolutionary strategies were usually built on an understanding of past revolutions (as Marx complained), so theory was bound to follow practice rather than create it.

Second, the development and reception of revolutionary theory did not take place in a historical vacuum. Cooperative socialism in Britain and utopian socialism in France in the 1830s and 1840s not only reflected the development of a theory of capitalist exploitation but articulated the real grievances of craftsmen who were becoming increasingly dependent on the power of merchant capitalists. That solutions were seen in small-scale communities expressed the fact that factory production was as yet far from dominant, even in Britain, and that France was still largely agrarian. Marxism was adopted by the German Social Democratic Party at a time of rapid industrialisation, economic crisis and political repression. Thereafter it was much more likely to be embraced by labour in states that were illiberal and non-parliamentary (Austria, Germany and Russia), and where liberalism was weak, than in liberal democracies such as the United Kingdom. The caution and passivity of orthodox Marxism can be explained, at least in part, by the absence of real revolutionary opportunities in Western and Central Europe before 1914. Conversely, revolutionary practice in Russia generated a Marxism concerned with tactics and action. What is more, Lenin's triumph in October 1917 depended upon considerable tactical and theoretical flexibility, on what might be described as deviations from the tradition.

Third, not only was the relative reception of revolutionary ideologies dependent upon specific economic and political structures, as well as economic and political conjunctures, but the significance of these ideologies for the members of the movements which ostensibly adopted them was far from clear. Although some Marxist texts (August Bebel's *Woman and Socialism* and Karl Kautsky's *Economic Doctrines of Karl Marx*, for example) were widely read, most Social Democrats preferred craft manuals, works of evolutionary biology and historical fiction. When the French syndicalist leader Griffuehles was asked if he had read Sorel, he replied that he only read Alexandre Dumas. Many of the Russian workers who participated in the 1905 Revolution did not recognise any difference between Bolsheviks and Mensheviks; while in July 1917 Menshevik workers were seen carrying placards bearing Bolshevik slogans! It might also be suggested that the Russian working class would have undergone a process of radicalisation between February and October 1917 without Bolshevik propaganda or Lenin's arrival at the Finland station. The ending of the war, which generated massive material deprivation, required the removal first of the Tsarist and then of Kerensky's Provisional Government. This is not to say that revolutionary success – the actual seizure of power – in October would have been possible without the Bolsheviks; but rather that radicalisation was built into this particular situation.

What this means is first, that it is no easy matter to determine the ideological persuasions of individuals caught up in revolutionary events, not least because the very process of revolution unleashed hitherto unimagined possibilities. For example, many of those who participated in revolutionary upheavals not only in Russia but also in Germany and Austria at the end of the First World War were previously unorganised and immune to socialist mobilisation. This was especially true in the case of women, whose role in 1789 and 1917 was massive, despite the fact that they had usually been ignored by the (male) theorists of change and revolution and had been under-represented in formal organisations. Second, it suggests that ideological influence was far from the determining factor in patterns of political radicalism on the part of the populace at large. However, this must not be interpreted as a statement to the effect that workers could never be radical or revolutionary; or that workers are only ever interested in wages and working conditions. There are situations in absolutist states where any form of grievance and protest takes on political tones. As Maureen Perrie points out, the Tsarist states' reactions to strikes, even where these were initially driven by purely material concerns, made them political. In the course of revolution, with rising expectations and a world of promised freedom, the previously unthinkable could be thought and the previously quiescent could revolt. What is more, ideology or culture, not in the sense of a received intellectual theory, but as a system of beliefs and values, did play a major role in the (self-)mobilisation of the masses. Arguably these only become visible in the course of upheaval, when the shackles of liberty are – normally temporarily – removed, as in the case of the Paris *sections* and the St Petersburg soviets. The role of group norms and values in linking revolutionary theory to revolutionary practice can be seen in the circumstances described below.

Between 1750 and 1850 there was a proliferation of forms of popular protest in the shape of food, taxation and conscription riots, machine-breaking (Luddism) and strikes. In themselves these did not constitute a revolution or lead to that political rupture central to the concept of revolution; but the great revolutions often involved an escalation of these more limited forms of action. These protests, although often seen as backward-looking in the case of riots (they aimed at the restitution of infringed rights, the protection of traditional structures against both a centralising state and a changing economy) and machine-breaking, were no simple knee-jerk reactions to poverty. They rested on what E.P. Thompson has described as the moral economy of the crowd, on a set of expectations of a fair price and the belief that the state should protect its subjects against the ravages of poor harvests or unemployment. It was no accident that these riots escalated at a time when European states abandoned paternalism and adopted *laissez-faire* economic policies, i.e. ironically those policies advocated by the physiocrats of the Enlightenment. The riots were not directed against scarcity but against artificial scarcity (hoarding, the transportation of grain through or out of an area); hence food riots targeted merchants suspected of speculation and hoarding, and were concentrated in towns that were centres of grain distribution. The inner rationality of these forms of action and belief informed the actions of peasants and sansculottes between 1789 and 1795; but the actuality of revolution now gave them a political meaning. In 1848 the demands of artisans reflected values that had also informed Luddite action: merchant capitalism was parasitical, and the competition of sweated, unskilled and often female labour, as well as machines, was unfair and transgressed established norms of production. However, 1848 in Germany also revealed something else: even if artisans began by criticising unfettered market forces, some of them also became interested in the representation of the interests of journeymen against their masters; thus what began as backward-looking protest ended in the separate organisation of journeymen into a Brotherhood of *workers*, something that clearly pointed towards the future. As Marx and de Tocqueville noted, the issue of class was placed on the agenda in 1848.

Degraded artisan trades in England facing similar threats also played a role in radical Chartism and the development of cooperative socialism. The ambivalent face of protest was exhibited in quite a different way in Britain during the First World War. Skilled engineering workers, initially concerned to protect their skills and status not only against employers but also against less skilled workers and especially women, came to form the nucleus of a small, unsuccessful but revolutionary shop stewards' movement, demanding socialisation and workers' control. Once again, therefore, backward-looking motives led in concrete historical circumstances to radical, forward-looking demands.

The connection between culture and revolution is perhaps demonstrated further by the case of the peasantry in Russia. Russian peasants were dissatisfied with the terms of their emancipation in 1861 not only because they had been led to expect more, but also because their communal traditions of landownership and working, embodied in the institution of the *mir*, told them that the land was theirs. Chris Reed has argued that these collective traditions were also carried from the countryside into the factories by those seeking work in the new industrial centres.

The case of workers who joined socialist parties in ever-increasing numbers after the turn of the century shows how radical values and a consciousness of class can coexist with a disinterest in formal theory. First, the kinds of workers who joined these parties were not the most impoverished: the unskilled and women were largely notable by their absence from formal organisations before 1914. Rather they were skilled workers with relatively secure employment and – by working-class standards – relatively high wages. Their mobilisation rested not only on sophisticated electoral propaganda on the part of the socialist parties but also on a set of values bred by lengthy apprenticeship. Such workers (like earlier generations of artisans) had an idea of the dignity of their labour and the value of their work. They wished to be treated decently, as human beings; and they possessed the resources – time, money, energy – to invest in union and party membership. It was their expectations, not their misery, which facilitated their involvement in radical politics; just as the solidarities of the workplace and of the densely housed working-class neighbourhood bred a sense of collective identity beyond and outside formal organisation in socialist parties. That they did not read Marx, therefore, was in a sense of no consequence. The daily discourse of local social-democratic organisations revealed the centrality of class and solidarity to their perceptions of the world; and many of them did mount the barricades in Berlin not only in November 1918 but also in March 1919 (a much larger insurrection than the better known Spartacist rising of January). Radical continuities in Berlin, Remscheid, Solingen, Dresden and Leipzig, which subsequently produced in Germany between the wars the largest communist party outside the Soviet Union, were deeply rooted in the working-class milieu and were arguably much more important than formal party organisation or ideology.

I accept that such workers were not necessarily revolutionary. All European socialist parties possessed radical and reformist wings before the First World War. What I do not accept, however, is that their relative affluence and status as aristocrats of labour made them less revolutionary than the utterly dispossessed and impoverished. For the revolutions in St Petersburg and Moscow in 1917, in Vienna and Berlin in 1918, and in Budapest in 1919 were, on the ground and in the first instance, led by skilled engineering workers, i.e. labour aristocrats, the best-paid and most secure group of workers. It was precisely their culture and resources that enabled their action.

Whether or not the aspirations of industrial workers around the turn of the century or of artisans in 1848 resulted in revolutionary ideas, movements and insurrections, or alternatively espoused reformist, non-violent politics, depended at least as much on the political context as on differences in the nature of their aims and culture. Whether workers were reformist or revolutionary more often than not depended upon whether they could express their grievances through legal or parliamentary channels (Britain after 1850) or whether virtually all forms of protest were repressed (Russia). It was no accident that the semi-autocratic states (Austria, Germany) produced labour movements that contained both revolutionary and reformist elements. Changing political conjunctures could also transform behaviour and values. As Adrian Shubert has shown, the Asturian miners of northern Spain were largely committed to reformist politics until the 1920s, when governmental repression produced waves of insurrectionary violence. Workers who were intimidated by powerful employers and authoritarian policemen in peaceful times could suddenly enter the historical scene with an elemental violence when the forces of social and political control broke down, as in the case of German steel and chemical workers at the end of the First World War.

One should also beware of assuming unbroken lines of a revolutionary tradition on the part of large groups of people. That Parisian artisans found themselves on the barricades in 1789, 1830 and 1848 certainly suggests continuities, a tradition; and I suppose it is true that it is easier to conceive of overthrowing regimes when it has been done before and especially if it has been done often. However, the Parisian crowds of the June Days in 1848 were not the same as those of 1793. Socialism in the rural French *midi* in the Third Republic was not a simple continuation of a radical tradition: it was located in different places and among a different constituency, as Tony Judt has shown. Above all we should guard against the facile assumption that revolution was successful in one country and not in another because of a revolutionary tradition or its absence. For the success or failure of revolutions has had much more to do with the power and cohesion of existing regimes than with revolutionaries.

Notes

1 Hannah Arendt, *On Revolution*, London, 1990 (first published New York 1963), p. 90.
2 Karl Marx and Friedrich Engels, *Selected Works*, Moscow, 1962, vol. 1, p. 247.
3 Alexi de Tocqueville, *Recollections*, London, 1948, pp. 9–13.
4 Peter Kropotkin, *The Great French Revolution, 1789–1793*, London, 1909, pp. 581ff.
5 Karl Marx and Friedrich Engels, *The German Ideology*, London, 1965, p. 56.
6 Karl Marx and Friedrich Engels, *On Britain*, Moscow, 1962, p. 361.
7 Marx and Engels, *Selected Works*, vol. 1, pp. 516–22.
8 De Tocqueville, pp. 81–5.

Further reading

Hannah Arendt, *On Revolution*, London, 1990 (first published New York, 1963).

Moira Donald, *Marxism and Revolution*, New Haven, 1993.

Dick Geary, *European Labour Protest, 1848–1939*, London, 1981.

Leszek Kolakowski, *Main Currents of Marxism* (3 vols), Oxford, 1978.

George Lichtheim, *The Origins of Socialism*, London, 1969.

James Joll, *The Second International*, London, 1969.

J.R. Talmon, *The Origins of Totalitarian Democracy*, London, 1970.

Charles, Louise and Richard Tilly, *The Rebellious Century*, London, 1975.

9 The Russian Revolution

Maureen Perrie

'The Russian Revolution' may be defined as a process that began in the early twentieth century and continued into the 1930s – or even to the end of the Soviet Union in 1991. In this chapter, however, I shall take a narrower approach, focusing on the three discrete political revolutions of the first two decades of the century: the events of 1905 and those of February and October 1917. Insofar as all three revolutions had their roots in the same crisis of the old regime, and in the same intellectual revolutionary tradition, I shall begin by examining these common factors before proceeding to consider and compare the specific features of each individual revolution.

'Reform from above' and economic development

Although Robert V. Daniels has recently tried to fit Russia into a pattern in which 'all the great revolutions of history . . . break out when the tension between a changing, modernising society and a rigid traditional government can no longer be contained',[1] Crane Brinton rightly noted, in his classic comparative study, that an 'effort . . . to reform the machinery of government' was an important common feature of the four societies he examined (England, America, France and Russia). He added:

> Nothing can be more erroneous than the picture of the old regime as an unregenerate tyranny, sweeping to its end in a climax of despotic indifference to the clamor of its abused subjects.[2]

Indeed, an interaction between 'reform from above' and 'revolution from below' was a major feature of the last decades of Tsarist Russia. The old regime was unable to sustain the impetus of reform, or to satisfy the expectations of further amelioration that it raised – and thereby it increased the dissatisfaction of oppositional elements in society rather than appeasing it.

The main 'reforms from above' in nineteenth-century Russia were implemented in the reign of Tsar Alexander II (1855–81). These reforms were introduced in the aftermath of Russia's defeat by Britain and France in the Crimean War of 1854–56. The Crimean fiasco highlighted Russia's military inferiority to the major European powers of the day, and punctured the complacency about the virtues of the Tsarist system which had characterised the reactionary reign of Nicholas I (1825–55). Liberal statesmen assumed that Russia's military defeat reflected her social and economic backwardness; and they advised the new Tsar to take advantage of the situation in order to introduce reforms. Although Soviet historians believed that any significant reform must have been the product of a 'revolutionary situation', and therefore argued that such a situation already existed between 1859 and 1861 (in the form of peasant unrest and criticism from the revolutionary intelligentsia), the 'Great Reforms' of Alexander II were in reality a rare example of a government voluntarily embarking on a programme of changes which were designed to strengthen the state both externally and internally. Great power status, however, required economic modernisation; but economic modernisation threatened to undermine social and political stability. This dilemma was to plague Tsarist governments for the next half-century.

Alexander's reforms sought to strengthen the state by modernising its institutions and making them more efficient. Serfdom had long been recognised as the most anachronistic element in the Tsarist system, but previous rulers had been reluctant to tamper with it, because its abolition would have required reforms in virtually all other areas. The nobles not only had economic powers over their serfs; they also performed administrative, judicial and tax-collecting functions, and new arrangements would have to be made to replace these. Having decided to abolish serfdom for reasons of state, Alexander II was obliged to carry out a far-reaching programme of reform which, under the influence of some of his more enlightened advisers, came to incorporate elements of Westernising liberalism.

The Emancipation of the Serfs in 1861 granted the peasants of noble landowners their personal freedom, together with a share of the estate land, for which they had to pay through 'redemption dues' (a form of mortgage). The land allocated to the peasants was held not by individuals, but collectively by the village commune, which periodically redistributed it among the households in proportion to their size. The other major reform of the 1860s and 1870s affected the system of local government: it introduced the principle of elections for the new provincial zemstvos and municipal Dumas, with a property qualification that guaranteed majorities to the nobles in the countryside and to the richer businessmen in the towns.

Radical opponents of the government criticised its reform programme as inadequate. Many liberal nobles had wanted to see the introduction of an elected representative assembly at national level, but Alexander II insisted that his powers as autocratic ruler should remain unrestricted. The peasants too were dissatisfied, feeling that a 'true' Emancipation would have given them all of the land, and not just a share of it. The democrats' demands for a national elected assembly would not be met until the 1905 Revolution; peasant aspirations for the land of the large estates were satisfied only in 1917.

But conservatives too were unhappy with the reforms. Some felt that conceding the principle of representative government, if only at local level, marked the introduction of alien and potentially destabilising Western institutions into the autocratic system. Their misgivings seemed to be confirmed when symptoms of social and political unrest began to appear from the early 1860s: peasant protests against the terms of the Emancipation; a nationalist uprising in Russian Poland; student demonstrations; and the emergence of revolutionary organisations which in the late 1870s adopted terrorist tactics. These manifestations provoked harsh responses by the government; and the assassination of Alexander II led to further repression. The reign of the new Tsar, Alexander III (1881–94), and the first part of the reign of his successor, Nicholas II (1894–1917) were marked by policies which Soviet historians characterised as 'counter-reforms'. The term is something of a misnomer, however: the main framework of the 'Great Reforms' remained intact, although restrictions were applied in various spheres. Certainly no further reforms were implemented before 1905 in the spirit of liberalisation that had characterised some of the measures of Alexander II; but the Russian economy continued to modernise, and the greatest advances in economic development in the late imperial period took place in the politically repressive decades of the 1880s and 1890s.

Although the Russian economy had not been entirely stagnant in the final decades of serfdom, industry developed slowly in the first half of the nineteenth century, and Emancipation did not immediately accelerate this process. The inadequate infrastructure of transport and communications was a major obstacle to economic growth. The government actively promoted railway-building from the 1860s and 1870s; and in the 1880s and 1890s state intervention became increasingly important for the expansion of heavy industry more generally. Strong mining and metallurgical sectors were essential underpinnings for the armaments production on which Russia's great power status largely depended. The industrial boom of the 1890s is generally associated with the name of Count Sergei Witte, Minister of Finance from 1892 to 1902, but Witte was continuing and building upon the policies of his two immediate predecessors in the Ministry of Finance, Vyshnegradskii and Bunge, who had encouraged foreign investment in key sectors. Industrial production expanded at the average rate of 8 per cent per annum in the 1890s, before succumbing to the effects of the international depression of the turn of the century.

By the beginning of the twentieth century a new industrial labour force had been created, numbering around two million people. In many areas this new social group still retained close ties with the peasantry from which it was recruited; and contemporary intellectuals debated the extent to which it was a true 'industrial proletariat' of the type identified by Marx as the bearer of revolutionary socialism in Western Europe. The living and working conditions of Russia's urban industrial workers were as harsh as those elsewhere in Europe in the early stages of industrialisation. Like all other groups in Russia they had no civil rights, and workers' organisations such as trade unions were illegal. Strikes too were prohibited, and those which occurred often led to confrontations with police or troops, so that even primarily economic disputes with employers turned into actions with political ramifications. Not surprisingly, the industrial workers were to play an important part in the revolutions of 1905 and 1917.

Agricultural production had also grown, although more slowly than industrial output, in the second half of the nineteenth century. After the initial wave of peasant protests against the terms of the Emancipation settlement, the countryside was relatively peaceful until the early twentieth century. Contrary to some assertions concerning the emergence of an 'agrarian crisis' by the turn of the century, it has now been indisputably established that agricultural production expanded more rapidly than population, and that there was an increase in the available food supply per capita even after Russia's substantial grain exports are taken into account. The generally positive overall picture of post-Emancipation agriculture, however, concealed significant regional differences. The Central Black Earth area (a wide agricultural belt south of Moscow, stretching from the Ukraine to the Volga) contained many pockets of peasant poverty and pauperisation. The Volga region was badly affected by famine in 1891; and the Ukrainian provinces of Poltava and Khar'kov were the scene of extensive peasant unrest between 1902 and 1903.

The underlying problem in the countryside was that neither noble landowners nor peasants were satisfied with the Emancipation settlement. Most nobles felt that they had been inadequately compensated for the loss of their lands; many failed to make a satisfactory adjustment to the new conditions, and some – particularly the owners of smaller and medium-sized estates – sold up and moved to the towns. Those who remained were antagonised by government policies that favoured industry in the 1890s; and the oppositional stance adopted by many zemstvo assemblies in the late nineteenth century reflected the economic plight of the nobles who dominated them. As for the peasants, especially in those areas where the pressure of population growth had created 'land hunger' (the shrinking of the average size of communal land allotments), hopes of a new 'second Emancipation' settlement, involving the compulsory redistribution of all the land of the large estates, had not entirely disappeared. Noble property rights to land were never recognised as entirely legitimate by Russian peasants; and whenever the Tsarist state was demonstrably weakened, as it was in 1905, they sought to take advantage of this in order to assert and implement their claims to the land.

By the turn of the century, the combined effects of government reform policies and of economic development had brought about a marked modernisation of the Russian social structure. The traditional agrarian classes – the landed nobility and the communal peasantry – were being supplemented by growing urban groups. The urban population of European Russia almost doubled between 1867 and 1897, increasing from 10 per cent to 13 per cent of the total. A new bourgeoisie was beginning to emerge, formed both from the older merchantry and from nobles who had realised capital from land sales. The urban population was swelled not only by industrial workers but also by a growing army of domestic servants, shop assistants, tradespeople and clerical workers. And the expansion of education, which contributed to the growing ranks of the state bureaucracy, also created a new stratum of members of the free professions (doctors, lawyers, teachers and so on). The 1897 census indicates that the 'intelligentsia' in the broad sense (including both officials and professionals) numbered almost 800,000 people, of whom over 100,000 had higher education.[3] Although peasants still constituted more than 80 per cent of the population, Russian social structure – and the structure of urban society, in particular – seemed to be developing along Western lines. As society became 'modernised' and 'Westernised', most contemporaries assumed that political change – in the form of some kind of democratisation of the autocratic system – would follow. But it was also widely assumed that – as in Western Europe – the old regime would not surrender its prerogatives without a struggle, and that a revolution would be required before political freedom could be obtained in Russia.

The Russian revolutionary tradition

The idea that Russia might follow the example of France in throwing off the shackles of absolutism was first introduced into the Tsarist Empire by groups of young officers who had taken part in the Napoleonic wars and sympathised with the ideas of the French revolutionaries. A number of secret societies were formed in the reign of Tsar Alexander I (1801–25); but their attempt to stage an uprising in December 1825 proved unsuccessful. The 'Decembrists', as they became known, were regarded as the first Russian revolutionaries, and their martyrdom (the leaders were executed) served as an example and inspiration for future generations.

In the reign of Nicholas I, however, it was not universally accepted that Russia was destined to follow the same path of evolution as her Western European neighbours. Educated public opinion divided into two camps, the 'Slavophiles' and the 'Westernisers'. If the latter believed that Russia was essentially a backward variant of a common European developmental model, the former preferred to stress the distinctiveness or even uniqueness of Russian social and political structures. A similar fault-line was later to divide Russian revolutionary socialists into two camps: the Populists, who believed that Russia would find her own path to socialism; and the Marxists, who thought that Russia would follow the same route as Western

Europe, first experiencing a bourgeois-democratic revolution directed against feudalism and absolutism, and then progressing through capitalism to socialism via a proletarian revolution.

Revolutionary Populism developed in the 1860s and 1870s, largely as a critique of the Great Reforms. Although it is conventionally seen as a native Russian form of socialism, Populism owed much to Western intellectual currents such as Romanticism, nationalism, anarchism and cooperative socialism, while the conspiratorial and insurrectionist tactics advocated by Nechaev and Tkachev had their roots in the revolutionary tradition of Babeuf and Blanqui. Populism was a broad and contradictory movement rather than a single ideology or organisation, but all Populists assumed that Russian socialism would be a predominantly agrarian system, based on the peasant commune, which they idealised as a proto-socialist institution which embodied the principles of equality and social justice. Populists believed that Russia could and should avoid capitalism in industry and agriculture, and that a socialist revolution was both possible and desirable in the immediate future. Attempts by Populist intellectuals in the mid-1870s to 'go to the people' and rouse them for revolution foundered on the incomprehension of the peasantry, however, and in the late 1870s the Populist 'People's Will' party resorted to political terrorism. Their murder of Alexander II in March 1881 failed to trigger the revolution from below that they had hoped for; the ensuing repression virtually destroyed Populism as an organised movement, and the failure of its terrorist tactics, following the failure of the earlier campaign of popular propaganda in the countryside, caused a major ideological crisis for the survivors in emigration and the underground. Populism was to revive in the early twentieth century in the form of the neo-Populist Socialist-Revolutionary (SR) Party, but 'classical' Populism bequeathed a legacy to Russian Marxism too, in the form of Lenin's concept of the revolutionary party, which had much in common with the organisational ideas of the terrorists of the 1870s.

Marxism as a distinctive variant of Russian socialism emerged in the 1880s. Marx's ideas had been known in Russia from an earlier date (a translation of *Das Kapital* was published legally in Russia in 1872), but they were not considered to have much relevance in a predominantly agrarian empire. The discrediting of Populism after 1881, however, together with irrefutable signs of capitalist industrialisation in the 1880s and 1890s, strengthened the appeal of Marxism. There were however undeniable problems for Russian socialists who wished to take Marxism as a guide to action. Russia had not yet undergone a bourgeois-democratic revolution; and although industry, and the industrial proletariat, were growing rapidly, it would be decades, if not generations, before they outweighed agriculture and the peasantry. The absence of political freedom, moreover, meant that it was impossible for a mass labour movement to develop on the Western model: disagreements on the implications of this for the nature of a Marxist revolutionary party were to lead to the historic split between

Bolsheviks and Mensheviks at the Second Congress of the Russian Social Democratic Labour Party (RSDLP) in 1903. The Mensheviks held to the ideal of recruiting party members from the mass of workers, while Lenin's Bolsheviks preferred a narrower concept of the party as an elite of professional revolutionaries bearing socialist consciousness to the proletariat from outside.

The question of the role that a socialist party ought to play in the bourgeois-democratic revolution also divided Russian Marxists. The Mensheviks concluded that the socialists should act as leftist allies of the bourgeois liberals; but the Bolsheviks were sceptical about the revolutionary potential of the Russian bourgeoisie. In the course of the 1905 Revolution, Lenin was to identify the mass of the anti-feudal 'petty-bourgeois' peasants, rather than the bourgeoisie proper, as appropriate allies for the proletariat. He argued that the Revolution would create a 'provisional revolutionary-democratic dictatorship of the proletariat and peasantry' rather than 'bourgeois democracy' on the Western model.

At the same time as Lenin was attempting to adjust classical Marxism to the reality of Russia's still predominantly peasant society, the SR leader Viktor Chernov was endeavouring to modify classical Populism to the context of Russia's emerging industrial capitalism. Chernov developed the concept of a broad category of 'working people' (*trudyashchiesya*) which included the mass of the peasantry as well as the urban and rural proletariat in the narrower Marxist sense of wage-labourers. But although the 'working people' comprised the overwhelming majority of the Russian population, Chernov did not believe that the forthcoming revolution would be a socialist one. By 'socialising' the land through transferring the large estates to the peasant communes, the impending transformation would go further than a 'bourgeois-democratic' revolution; but the socialisation of agricultural production – like the socialisation of industrial production – would have to await a second, socialist stage of revolution.

Logically, in a society which had not yet undergone a bourgeois-democratic revolution, liberalism should still have been a revolutionary ideology. But liberal ideas, which had been adopted from the West in the mid-nineteenth century at more or less the same time as socialism, were never a significant force in Russia. The social base of liberalism lay in the professional classes, and in the disaffected nobles in the zemstvos who wished to see the extension of the representative principle from local to national level. Before 1905 it lacked support from the industrial and commercial bourgeoisie, who were a relatively small and insecure group, conventionally divided between the Moscow and St Petersburg entrepreneurs. The Moscow merchants were traditional, Slavophile and patriarchal in their attitudes, and hence generally supportive of the autocracy; St Petersburg's industrialists were more Westernised and cosmopolitan, but they were involved in sectors that were highly dependent on state orders and hence on government patronage. These bourgeois groups were to be among the beneficiaries of the 1905 Revolution, but it was a revolution that was not of their own making.

The 1905 Revolution

By 1902 to 1903 the government of Nicholas II was confronting a range of challenges that posed a greater threat to social and political stability than anything it had faced in the nineteenth century. Peasant unrest was spreading from the Ukraine towards the Volga; and workers' strikes, especially in the south of Russia, paralysed wide sectors of industry. Organised political opposition to Tsarism had also begun to emerge, in the form of the SR and SD parties, and also of various liberal groups. The SRs embarked on a terrorist campaign, claiming the life of Minister of Internal Affairs D.S. Sipyagin in 1902, and of N.M. Bogdanovich, the governor of Ufa, in 1903. Neither the SRs nor the SDs, however, achieved any significant success in organising peasants and workers before the 1905 Revolution.

It was against the background of these various manifestations of discontent that V.K. Plehve, the Minister of Internal Affairs, is alleged to have made the fateful remark that, 'In order to hold back revolution, we need a small victorious war'.[4] Although Japan was technically the aggressor, attacking the Russian fleet at Port Arthur in January 1904 without making a formal declaration of war, the Russian government had been pursuing a reckless policy of provocation in the Far East since the end of the 1890s. In the only previous test of her military might since the Crimean War, Russia had defeated Turkey in 1878; but Japan, contrary to Russian expectations, proved to be a much harder nut to crack. In spite of the near-completion of the trans-Siberian railway, communications between European Russia and the theatres of war in Manchuria were inefficient, and Russia suffered a series of humiliating defeats both on land and at sea.

As in 1856, and foreshadowing 1917, military reverses served to trigger major domestic upheaval. In the case of the Russo-Japanese War, the effects were primarily political: the fighting was remote from the main centres of population in European Russia, and the economy was not affected to the same extent as in the First World War. But the military defeats served further to discredit the regime in the eyes of its many critics: for the socialists it had become embroiled in an imperialist adventure; in the eyes of the liberals it had failed to defend Russian national interests against a foreign threat. Thus in 1904 to 1905, as subsequently during the First World War, the liberals were able to provide a patriotic justification for their critique of autocracy, advancing their claims for representative government as a potentially more effective alternative to bureaucratic rule.

When SR terrorists killed Plehve on 15 July 1904, the government already felt itself so undermined by military failure that it responded by appointing the relatively liberal Prince Svyatopolk-Mirskii as his successor. Mirskii offered a number of minor concessions to the liberals; the latter, however, interpreted concessions as a sign of weakness, and stepped up their attacks on autocracy. The liberals by themselves, however, had little leverage on the government, as they voluntarily limited themselves to the use of non-violent means such as meetings and petitions. The main trigger for the revolutionary events of 1905 was provided by 'Bloody Sunday', when government troops opened fire on an unarmed workers' demonstration in St Petersburg on 9 January 1905. Empire-wide protests against the shootings escalated into a wave of revolutionary violence. The SRs' assassination of the Tsar's uncle, Grand Duke Sergei Aleksandrovich, on 4 February was justified by the party as revenge for Bloody Sunday; and other forms of revolutionary violence, too, claimed legitimacy as responses to the unprovoked action of the authorities on 9 January.

Between January and October 1905 all groups of society joined in the attack on the Tsarist government. The strike movement involved not only industrial workers but also various professional groups; and the strikers' demands were political as well as economic. Peasant attacks on noble estates began in the spring of 1905, and continued into 1907. Mutinies took place in the army and the navy, both at the front and in the rear. The government responded with a series of political concessions from February 1905. Only in October, however, did the Tsar, on the advice of Witte, offer a package of reforms sufficiently radical to split the opposition. The Imperial Manifesto of 17 October 1905 promised full civil liberties, and the convocation of a national representative assembly, the State Duma, which would have legislative powers and a broad franchise. This was enough to satisfy most of the liberals; and even some of the socialists were prepared to give the promised reforms a chance. The more extreme revolutionaries, however, wanted to press on for a democratic republic and a constituent assembly, and for social reforms such as the eight-hour day and the expropriation of the large estates. These radicals organised a workers' insurrection in Moscow in December 1905 which was brutally crushed by government troops in the most violent episode of the year. Thereafter the regime contained the Revolution by a judicious combination of repression and reform.

It is often asked whether the events of 1905 justify their conventional description as a 'revolution'. In terms of outcome it can be argued that little changed. The autocracy survived, modified only slightly by the existence of the State Duma. Social changes too were minimal: the main reform package, Stolypin's agrarian legislation of 1906 onwards, which encouraged the breakup of the peasant commune, may even be regarded as counter-revolutionary, insofar as the measures which it introduced corresponded more to the interests of the government than to the demands of the peasants. Even viewed as a bourgeois-democratic revolution, 1905 was abortive and incomplete. Yet the nature of the events of 1905 must be regarded as revolutionary, with widespread resort to violence on both sides. Contemporaries had little doubt that what they were experiencing was the long-awaited revolution, even if they were eventually to conclude that its relative lack of success made it Russia's 1848 rather than her 1789.

The failure of the revolutionaries to achieve their aims has often been blamed on the weakness and divisions of the opposition to Tsarism, and especially on the inability of the socialist parties to organise and coordinate their actions and those of their supporters. While these criticisms are undoubtedly valid, a comparison with the next round of the assault on Tsarism suggests that they were not the most crucial factors. The socialist parties were little stronger during the First World War than they were in 1905, yet Tsarism was to collapse in a matter of days from the start of the first strikes and demonstrations in February 1917. This indicates that the significant difference lay not so much in the strength of the revolutionary movement as in the weakness of the state. In particular, Tsarism in 1905 retained the loyalty of sufficient troops to suppress the Revolution, and the support of senior officials and generals with the will to use them. In February 1917, as we shall see below, neither of these conditions prevailed.

After 1905, a similar pattern of events unfolded to that of the post-Crimean period. The unsuccessful war was followed by a series of 'reforms from above' (although the post-1905 reforms, unlike those of the 1860s and 1870s, were forced from the government by a real revolutionary situation) and by a new wave of economic expansion: there was a marked revival of industrial growth from about 1908, largely stimulated by the demands of rearmament. Symptoms of a renewed and potentially revolutionary crisis appeared between 1912 and 1914, even before Russia's disastrous involvement in another war led to a new attack on Tsarism in February 1917.

War and revolution, 1904 to 1914

Questions have often been raised about the importance of war as a cause of the Russian revolutions of the early twentieth century. As we have seen, revolution was already brewing before the outbreak of the Russo-Japanese war, and we may legitimately ask, therefore, whether the war might not have postponed revolution for a year, rather than accelerating it, as is more conventionally assumed. How likely was revolution in the hypothetical case that Japan had not attacked Port Arthur in January 1904? While we cannot entirely rule out the possibility that an incident such as 'Bloody Sunday' might have occurred in peacetime, it is improbable that it would have had the impact that it had in 1905 if the legitimacy and authority of the autocratic system had not been undermined by military reverses. In addition, the war, as a national disaster, created problems for all sectors of society simultaneously, thereby guaranteeing a temporal coincidence of discontent that weakened the state even though the opposition parties were unable to organise and coordinate their supporters effectively.

Similar questions have been raised about the significance of the First World War for the events of 1917. Some historians take a positive view of developments in Russia between 1906 and 1914. They are optimistic about the prospects for evolution towards a Western-style parliamentary democracy, and towards market-led capitalism in agriculture as well as industry, on the basis of Stolypin's reforms. For these 'optimists', the First World War was the major cause of the February revolution: the unfortunate timing of the outbreak of hostilities, before the reforms of 1906 onwards had fully taken root, diverted Russia from the path of peaceful evolution which she might otherwise have followed. Other historians are more pessimistic about the chances of non-revolutionary development: they see the changes introduced after 1905 as belated and inadequate responses to the deep systemic faults highlighted by the Revolution. The 'pessimists' believe that a new revolutionary crisis was inevitable, even in peacetime, and they identify symptoms of this new crisis on the eve of the war, when a wave of industrial unrest, triggered in February 1912 by the shooting of striking gold miners on the River Lena in Siberia culminated in a general strike in St Petersburg in July 1914. Most pessimists see the war as only the final straw that broke the autocratic camel's back; but some believe that the Balkan crisis may actually have delayed the Revolution by three years.[5]

Plehve's supposed comment about the 'small victorious war' has suggested to some historians that the Russian government, in both 1904 and 1914, may actually have welcomed foreign war – or even deliberately courted it – as a diversion from internal discontent. There is little evidence for such a machiavellian interpretation, even for the Japanese war. For 1914, the evidence all points in the opposite direction: Russian statesmen were highly reluctant to go to war over Serbia, some foreseeing all too clearly the domestic consequences of defeat. It was only when they realised that Russia's national interests and international prestige would be irreparably damaged if she backed down in the face of the Austrian ultimatum that they regretfully ordered mobilisation of the army.

The First World War and the February Revolution

Once the war began, it contributed to the events of the February Revolution through its impact on both the economy and politics. By 1915 an extensive system of national mobilisation was in place: priority was given to heavy industry, which expanded to meet the demands of the army, but the production of consumer goods was adversely affected. Although harvests remained good, the peasants reduced the amount of grain they marketed: faced with growing inflation and shortages of consumer goods, they preferred to retain their produce in the village. This, together with the disruption of transport systems, affected food supply, especially to the northerly capital city (which had been patriotically renamed Petrograd – a Russified form of the Germanic-sounding Petersburg – on the outbreak of war). By the beginning of 1917, workers' strikes in protest against a decline in real wages were supplemented by women's demonstrations against the inefficient food-supply system and rumours about the introduction of bread rationing.

After an initial display of support for the war, the liberals in the Duma became increasingly critical of the government's incompetent conduct of military affairs. A 'Progressive Bloc' was formed of opposition deputies who put forward demands for a ministry accountable to the Duma rather than to the Tsar. In August 1915 Nicholas II left Petrograd to take up personal command of the army at Mogilev. The Empress remained in the capital as virtual regent; she was increasingly influenced by the disreputable 'holy man' Rasputin, who had a mysterious ability to control the bleeding of her young son, the haemophiliac Tsarevich Aleksei. Rumours about Rasputin's influence over the Empress, and over ministerial appointments and government policy, served to undermine the authority of the regime, even among traditional elites who had previously been the staunchest supporters of the autocratic principle. By the end of 1916 many generals in the army high command had come to sympathise with the Progressive Bloc's demand for a 'responsible ministry', and regarded the Tsar's intransigence as the chief impediment to the formation of a competent government.

When strikes and demonstrations broke out in the capital in February 1917, it was the mutiny of the troops of the Petrograd garrison, who refused to obey orders to fire on unarmed civilians, that began the process of turning what had at first seemed to be just another street protest into a revolution. Even then, the Tsar favoured the option of sending military forces from outside Petrograd to suppress the unrest. The high command, however, advised Nicholas to call off the punitive expedition and to agree to the Duma's demand for a constitutional monarchy. Subsequently the generals concurred in Nicholas' abdication and in the formation of a Provisional Government comprised largely of Duma liberals. When Nicholas' younger brother, Grand Duke Michael, refused to accept the throne, the monarchy effectively came to an end. The speed of events indicates the extent to which Tsarist authority and the social base of support for the autocracy had been eroded in the course of the war.

The rapid collapse of Tsarism, and the role of the workers and soldiers on the streets of Petrograd, meant that the outcome of the February Revolution was much more radical than the constitutional monarchy that the liberals had advocated. The disappearance of the autocracy created a kind of power vacuum, in which the Provisional Government competed with the Petrograd Soviet – the representative body of the revolutionary workers and soldiers – for influence over the future course of events.

1917: from February to October

The period of the First Provisional Government (March to April 1917) is conventionally characterised as one of 'dual power', when the predominantly liberal government was offered qualified support by the moderate socialist parties (the Mensheviks and SRs) which held the majority in the Petrograd Soviet. Although the programme of the moderate socialists for the first (bourgeois-democratic) stage of the Revolution had much in common with that of the liberals, their tactical alliance soon foundered on the question of war aims. The leaders of the Soviet supported the continuation of the war only for the purposes of national and revolutionary defence; the liberals, by contrast, believed that the February Revolution had given them a mandate to continue the war more effectively than the Tsarist government had done. When Foreign Minister P.N. Milyukov sent a Note to the Allies on 18 April, hinting that the Provisional Government shared the expansionist war aims of Tsarism, street protests in Petrograd led to Milyukov's resignation and the formation of a new government in which the Mensheviks and SRs were formally represented.

By the time of the creation of the coalition government at the beginning of May, the position of the Bolsheviks was already sharply distinguished from that of the moderate socialists. Since the outbreak of war in July 1914 Lenin had adopted an extreme 'internationalist' position. He denounced the imperialist war as a symptom of the final crisis of European capitalism and advocated turning it into an international civil war for socialism. Lenin welcomed the February Revolution as the first battle of the European revolution. His 'April Theses', issued on his return to Russia from Switzerland, condemned the Provisional Government for its continuation of the war, and called for the transition to the second stage of the Revolution, which would transfer power to the soviets, as democratic institutions of the workers and poorest peasants. On the basis of this interpretation, Lenin refused to participate in the May coalition (or its successors); thenceforth, as the only significant political party untainted by a role in government, the Bolsheviks served as a vehicle for protest votes in the soviets. They attracted support from workers and soldiers who were increasingly dissatisfied with the policies of the Provisional Government, for which the Mensheviks and SRs now shared responsibility.

Between May and October the Provisional Government suffered attacks first from the left and then from the right. In the 'July Days', Bolshevised workers and soldiers in Petrograd protested against the hardships caused by the war, and called for the overthrow of the Provisional Government. But the Petrograd Soviet was still dominated by moderate socialists who rejected the idea of soviet power; and the Bolsheviks themselves were divided on tactics, with Lenin feeling that a seizure of power was premature. The government met violence with violence, using troops to suppress armed demonstrations on the streets, and thereby exposing itself to Bolshevik charges that it had already become counter-revolutionary.

The moderate SR politician Alexander Kerensky became Prime Minister in the second coalition government, formed in the aftermath of the July Days. Following the failure of the summer military offensive, General Kornilov, the new Supreme Commander of the army, was widely seen by right-wing forces as the only man who could restore order and prevent the spread of anarchy in town and countryside. Kerensky himself may have briefly colluded with Kornilov, but Kornilov's demands for dictatorial powers were too extreme; Kerensky dismissed him, and the ensuing attempt at a military *coup* fizzled out before it had really got off the ground. A third coalition government was cobbled together in September, with the prospect of having to hold out for only a few weeks until the much-delayed elections to the Constituent Assembly took place in November. But before the elections were held, the Bolsheviks overthrew the Provisional Government, in the name of the soviets of workers' and soldiers' deputies, on the night of 25 October.

A major question which arises in relation to the Bolshevik seizure of power concerns the extent to which it can be seen as a minority *coup d'état* rather than a revolution. Insofar as the overthrow of the Provisional Government was planned and organised in advance by the Bolshevik Party, the October Revolution contrasts markedly with the February Revolution, which is generally depicted as a 'spontaneous' or unplanned revolution. The term '*coup d'état*', however, implies not only an armed insurrection, but also the imposition of a minority dictatorship. How much popular support did the Bolsheviks have in October 1917? The party had undergone a great expansion after February, its membership growing from perhaps 20,000 to around 250,000 by October. The new members were mostly workers, and Bolshevik support in the soviets came primarily from workers and soldiers. Although they had a majority in the Second All-Russia Congress of Soviets of Workers' and Soldiers' Deputies, which opened on the night of 25 October and approved the overthrow of the Provisional Government, the Bolshevik Party lacked support from the peasant mass of the population. In the elections to the Constituent Assembly, held in November 1917 on the basis of universal suffrage, the Bolsheviks gained only 25 per cent of the vote, while the SRs obtained an overall majority. The Constituent Assembly met for only one day, in January 1918, before being forcibly dispersed by the Bolsheviks. The Bolsheviks' short-lived governmental coalition with the Left SRs, in the winter of 1917 to 1918, gave way to a single-party dictatorship from March 1918.

In spite of this evidence of the undemocratic nature of Bolshevik rule, some 'revisionist' historians have argued that October was nonetheless a popular revolution, insofar as the Bolsheviks associated themselves with the grievances and aspirations not only of the workers and soldiers but also of the rural masses. The Bolsheviks' 'Decree on Land' of October

1917 permitted the peasants immediately to take over the large estates, and thereby legitimised the land seizures which had begun soon after the February Revolution. The Bolsheviks, therefore – the revisionists imply – provided a more valid expression of peasant interests than the SRs, whose spokesmen in the Provisional Government had condemned land seizures, arguing that the agrarian question had to be solved not 'from below' by direct action, but by legislation by the Constituent Assembly.[6]

Revisionists have also questioned the idea that the Bolsheviks were able to seize power in October because they were a highly centralised, organised and disciplined conspiratorial party. They point out that with the influx of a mass membership in 1917, Lenin's earlier concept of the party as an elite organisation of professional revolutionaries was tacitly abandoned. The American historian Alexander Rabinowitch has argued that in 1917 the Bolsheviks were a relatively democratic and decentralised party, whose flexible structure enabled the leadership to listen and respond to the aspirations of the masses.[7]

Some of the most recent interpretations of 1917 have moved away from Marxist-inspired emphasis on social revolution and class struggle, in order to examine the deeper political dimensions of events.[8] Stress has been placed on the extent to which the collapse of the repressive Tsarist state in February 1917 led to the disintegration of authoritarian and hierarchical power relations at lower levels too: in the factories, in the armed forces, in the countryside, and even in the patriarchal family. The proliferation of new mass organisations, such as soviets, factory committees, soldiers' committees and land committees, marked a significant devolution of power away from the centralised authority of the state towards the localities and the grass-roots. This process greatly handicapped the Provisional Government in its attempts to take charge of events; the Bolsheviks, by contrast, had already come to control many of these lower-level locations of power before they seized what remained of the state in October. After October, however, and particularly during the civil war, the Bolsheviks succeeded in rebuilding the state as a centralised and authoritarian regime to which the popular democratic institutions of 1917 were soon subordinated and sacrificed.

Lenin's ideological flexibility played a major role in enabling the Bolsheviks to gain support in the mass organisations of 1917. Not only did he put forward effective popular slogans such as 'bread, peace, land and freedom', but he was eclectic in his programme, promising 'workers' control', with its anarcho-syndicalist connotations; borrowing the SR policy of 'socialisation of the land', and competing with the non-Russian parties by offering self-determination to the nationalities. Yet at the same time Lenin continued to offer an overarching Marxist justification for the seizure of power by a socialist party in backward Russia, by stressing the international character of the crisis of capitalism represented by the First World War. Although in this respect Lenin's ideology of 1917 was consistent with the ideas of the most radical wing of European social democracy, it also had much in common with Populism and anarchism, neither of which stressed 'objective' factors such as the level of capitalist development and the extent of proletarianisation as prerequisites for socialist revolution in Russia. Like certain Populists and anarchists, too, the Bolsheviks of 1917 advocated the notion of a direct transition from feudalism to socialism; and had a robust disregard for bourgeois liberal notions of constitutionalism, civil rights and the rule of law.

Just as questions have been raised about the connection between the 1905 Revolution and that of February 1917, so historians have asked whether the February Revolution led inevitably to October. There were undoubtedly major structural problems in the Tsarist regime – such as the weakness of the bourgeoisie and the unsatisfied nature of peasant aspirations for the land – that made a moderate democratic outcome to a revolutionary overthrow of the monarchy unlikely, even in peacetime. With the social and economic dislocations caused by a world war, the possibility of a new authoritarian solution was correspondingly greater. The availability of Lenin's Bolshevik Party, with its commitment to the idea of the dictatorship of the proletariat, further increased that probability.

But 'accidental' factors, such as the errors and misjudgements of the Bolsheviks' main socialist rivals, also played their part. Ironically, many of the tactical mistakes of the Mensheviks and SRs derived from the lessons they drew from previous revolutions, and especially from the French Revolution. It was axiomatic for the moderate socialists of 1917 that revolutionary extremism was likely to be self-defeating and to play into the hands of counter-revolutionaries (the experience of 1905 seemed to confirm this pattern). Thus the Mensheviks and SRs were anxious to preserve their alliance with the liberals, first in the form of the 'dual power' relationship of March and April, and subsequently in the coalition governments of May to October. Right up until its overthrow, the Provisional Government expected the greater danger to come from the right rather than the left. The Bolsheviks too raised the spectre of counter-revolution, depicting not only Kornilov but also Kerensky as would-be Bonapartes; but they used the perceived threat from the right in order to justify their seizure of power in October as a pre-emptive strike to defend the gains of the Revolution. In reality, of course, it was the Bolsheviks' action that was to lead to armed mobilisation by their opponents, and to the outbreak of civil war.

The results of October

Unlike moderate socialist leaders such as Kerensky, who advocated class conciliation at home for the duration of the foreign war, Lenin was not afraid of revolutionary violence. Although he condemned the sacrifice of workers' lives in the First World War, he advocated civil war as a means to the establishment of socialism; and he also justified the use of revolutionary terror against his opponents. The number of deaths in 1917 attributable to the events of the revolutions, as opposed to those of the First World War, was relatively small; but the loss of life resulting from the Russian civil war was of catastrophic proportions. Evan Mawdsley has estimated that the total number of deaths caused directly or indirectly by the civil war may have been as high as ten million, four times the number of Russian victims of the First World War.[9] The horrific experience of the civil war undoubtedly had a brutalising effect on the nature of the Soviet system which emerged from it.

Lenin continued to hope for the outbreak of fraternal socialist revolutions elsewhere in Europe. He had no clear plan of action to deal with the situation he faced by 1921, when the Reds had proved victorious over the Whites in the civil war: the foreign intervention forces had withdrawn, but European capitalism had stabilised and the Bolsheviks faced the challenge of building socialism in a backward country whose economic and social structure had been ravaged by seven continuous years of war, revolution and civil war. After the end of the civil war, the radical forms of socio-economic organisation known as 'War Communism' were relaxed: under the New Economic Policy (NEP) of 1921 onwards, small-scale capitalism was permitted in some sectors of light industry as well as in domestic trade and agriculture. In many respects this was a strategic retreat; but the main socio-economic changes of 1917 to 1918 – the abolition of large-scale private agriculture and the nationalisation of heavy industry – were preserved. NEP in its turn proved to be only a temporary breathing space, before Stalin's 'revolution from above', during the period of the First Five-Year Plan (1928–32), re-established state control over all sectors of the economy for a breakneck industrialisation drive, accompanied by the forced collectivisation of peasant agriculture. From the mid-1930s, while pressing on with economic modernisation, Stalin presided over changes, involving a reversion to certain more traditional social and cultural forms, which have been described as a 'Great Retreat'.

Comparative historians who claim to detect a common pattern in revolutionary processes have found evidence of a Soviet 'Thermidor' in both NEP and the Stalinist system of the late 1930s onwards. But the political continuity of the Bolshevik dictatorship from October 1917 right through to the end of the Soviet Union, and the persistence of the centrally planned economy from 1928 to 1991, make it difficult to speak of any kind of restoration of the pre-October regime within the Soviet period. The system retained its anti-capitalist and anti-democratic character for more than seventy years. To that extent, interpretations which try to fit Russia into a pattern that takes the French Revolution as its archetype are somewhat artificial.

The outcome of the Russian Revolution was very different both from the Western-style bourgeois democracy aspired to by the liberal leaders of the first Provisional Government, and from the democratic socialism which was the objective of the Mensheviks and SRs. Those who supported the Bolsheviks in 1917 in the hope of implementing 'soviet power' in the form of decentralised popular democracy were soon bitterly disillusioned. The Bolshevik leaders' expectations that their revolution would develop in the context of a Europe-wide overthrow of capitalism were also unrealised. Yet the profound and persistent changes in economic and social structures which the Bolsheviks implemented fully justify the description of the events of October 1917 as a revolution: one which was to cast as long a shadow over the history of the twentieth century as the French Revolution had over the nineteenth.

Notes

1 Robert V. Daniels, *The End of the Communist Revolution*, London, 1993, p. 101.
2 Crane Brinton, *The Anatomy of Revolution*, revised and expanded edition, New York, 1965, p. 39.
3 For a discussion of the problems involved in a statistical analysis of the social structure of late imperial Russia, see Maureen Perrie and R.W. Davies, 'The social context', in R.W. Davies, ed., *From Tsarism to the New Economic Policy*, Basingstoke, 1990, pp. 29–46.
4 S. Yu. Vitte, *Vospominaniya. Tsarstvovanie Nikolaya II* (2 vols), Berlin, 1922, vol. 1, p. 262.
5 For the terms 'optimist' and 'pessimist' see A. Mendel, 'On interpreting the fate of imperial Russia', in T.G. Stavrou, ed., *Russia under the Last Tsar*, Minneapolis, 1969, pp. 13–41.
6 For a sympathetic summary of the 'revisionist' position see Edward Acton, *Rethinking the Russian Revolution*, London, 1990.
7 Alexander Rabinowitch, *The Bolsheviks Come to Power*, London, 1979, pp. 311–13.
8 For this approach see those contributions to Edward Acton, Vladimir Iu. Cherniaev and William G. Rosenberg, eds, *Critical Companion to the Russian Revolution 1914–1921*, London, 1997, which are summarised in William G. Rosenberg's Introduction, pp. 22–5.
9 Evan Mawdsley, *The Russian Civil War*, Boston, 1987, p. 287.

Further reading

Edward Acton, *Rethinking the Russian Revolution*, London, 1990.
Edward Acton, Vladimir Iu. Cherniaev and William G. Rosenberg (eds), *Critical Companion to the Russian Revolution 1914–1921*, London, 1997.
Orlando Figes, *A People's Tragedy. The Russian Revolution 1891–1924*, London, 1996.
Christopher Read, *From Tsar to Soviets: The Russian People and their Revolution, 1917–21*, London, 1996.

10 Counter-revolution and the 'failure' of revolution in interwar Europe

C.J. Wrigley

Revolutions have been very effective mobilisers of support for the defence of property and the 'restoration of order'. From the time of the great French Revolution, the experience of revolutionary upheaval has brought together motley alliances – often including erstwhile enemies – to resist revolutionary change and oppose its proponents. Revolution was not only threatening to many of the inhabitants of the country concerned but also to the interests of investors from abroad, an increasingly sizeable and vocal force within the international economy after 1870. Hence external intervention against revolution was not only intended to overthrow what were deemed to be alien systems of government but also to restore the sanctity of contracts on which the workings of capitalism within the international economy depended.

Counter-revolution occurs in societies in major crisis, whether political, economic or social (or a combination of them). It is marked by coalitions which wish to overthrow the new political order and either restore the old order or, as in Italy and Germany, to create a new order which includes many traditional values, some of which are endowed with heightened respect, but which goes well beyond former conservatism. Arno J. Mayer has commented that 'counter-revolution is a product and stimulant of instability, cleavages and disorders. It thrives when normally conflictual but accommodating forces begin to abandon the policies of compromise'.[1]

The two world wars of the twentieth century caused massive disruption to the established order in many countries and, in some cases, even more so to their imperial territories. As well as the often drastic direct effects of the wars, including military occupation, military defeat and economic privation, there were indirect effects such as inflation and other adverse change in the international economy which also affected the older patterns of power. By 1945, the old aristocratic and military elites, still politically strong in Europe other than Britain and France in 1914, had been replaced by newer coalitions of conservatism. The post-First World War years were notable for effective counter-revolutionary mobilisations against various 'red perils'.[2]

Lenin had great expectations that revolution in Russia in October 1917 would soon be followed by the spread of revolution to more advanced industrial countries, notably Germany. Germany had seen the greatest ostensibly Marxist party, the SPD, in the pre-1914 period and Lenin expected Berlin to be the centre of world communism and German its first language. In early 1919 he even had hopes that England would not be 'the centre of reaction' but was on the eve of a revolution, telling the writer and journalist Arthur Ransome,

> you cannot stop a revolution, although Ramsay MacDonald will try to at the last minute. Strikes and Soviets. If these two habits once get hold, nothing will keep the workmen from them. And Soviets, once started, must sooner or later come to supreme power. But certainly it would be much more difficult in England. Your big clerk and shop-keeping class would oppose it, until the workmen broke them.[3]

However, the opposition of shopkeepers, clerks and many other groups in advanced capitalist countries was among the reasons why Lenin's hopes of international revolution were dashed within a few years of the end of the First World War.

Outside intervention and counter-revolutionary force

A feature of the immediate post-Armistice period, as in the 1790s and 1848, was outside intervention against revolutionary governments. Intervention was decisive in Hungary, unsuccessful in Russia and a powerful threat in Germany. In the case of Bela Kun's 133-day communist-socialist coalition regime in Hungary, its existence so near to Austria provoked a *frisson* of fear among the Austrian and other nearby propertied classes. The *Neue Freie Press* warned, in ominous words given the Turkish siege of 1683, 'Bolshevism is at the gates of Vienna'.[4] The Big Four at the Paris Peace Conference supported Rumanian and Czech forces invading Hungary, the Rumanians making a successful, final offensive on Budapest between 24 July and 4 August 1919. Rumanian anti-Bolshevik terror and looting was followed by White terror organised by Julius Gömbös and Tibor Eckhardt, in which Jews as well as socialists were murdered, and by the counter-revolutionary regime under Admiral Miklos Horthy (in effect established in November 1919 and lasting until October 1944).

The threat (or actuality) of Allied intervention in Central and Eastern Europe was backed until mid-1919 by the continuance of the blockade. This was used not only as an instrument to force the defeated countries to agree to peace terms but also as a means of removing leftist governments. The blockade section of the Allies' Supreme Economic Council was explicit that even after Germany had made peace, a blockade would be used against Bolshevik Russia and Hungary until 'steady' governments were in power which offered 'satisfactory guarantees of liberty and stability'.[5]

In Russia, counter-revolution failed between 1917 and 1920. The Bolsheviks had seized power in the midst of war when the appeal of their slogan 'Peace, Land, Bread' was paramount and when the Western Allies were too embroiled with the Central Powers to intervene. In contrast, in Germany between 1919 and 1923 it was the SPD which had brought about peace by accepting the Armistice of 11 November 1918 and, in 1919 at least, it was the revolutionary Left which was likely to precipitate a renewal of warfare by advancing Allied intervention in Germany. In Russia, when the Allies did intervene, they did so half-heartedly, incurring hostility as foreign invaders without providing decisive support for the Whites.

In Russia, the counter-revolutionary military forces were divided and were operating on the peripheries of a huge country whereas the Bolsheviks controlled the state and the central communications system. For much of the agrarian population (some four-fifths of the whole) the Whites represented a greater evil than the Bolsheviks, even with their grain seizures and committees of the poor. Savage reprisals against dissident peasants had been a feature of Tsarist Russia, especially since the late eighteenth century, and the White forces did nothing to allay expectations of severe brutality in the areas they came to control. Above all, the Whites represented the restoration of land to the old landlord class, a direct threat to the main aspirations of the peasants to continue to own the land they worked and, for many, had newly acquired in the upheavals of the war and the revolutions. This fear of a return of the old order was illustrated in the Moscow area when, in October 1919, Denikin, the White Commander of South Russia, reached Orel, under 200 miles from Moscow, and a quarter of a million peasants returned to fight in the Red Army, having deserted earlier.[6]

This was a contrast with Germany, where counter-revolutionary forces were in a much stronger position. Faced with an uncoordinated series of Red uprisings in Berlin, Munich, the Ruhr, the Halle-Merseburg region and the ports of Bremen and Hamburg, the forces of law and order (whether army, police or the *Freikorps*) were able to mobilise effectively against them, one by one. The size of the *Freikorps*, right-wing paramilitary units led by ex-army officers, and the rapidity of its mobilisation at the turn of 1918 was indicative of the strength of anti-Left forces in Germany. Such forces operated in early Weimar Germany with the SPD leaders' blessings. The pact between Friedrich Ebert (German Chancellor, 10 November 1918 to 1925) and General Wilhelm Groener, in November 1918, ensured army support for the SPD government in its suppression of risings by the revolutionary Left while maintaining the dominance of the traditional German officer corps in the army. In Germany, the radical soldiers and sailors who had been at the heart of the November 1918 Revolution and the councils movements, were the most eager to leave the services, and by Christmas 1918, or shortly after, most had been demobilised.[7] In addition, the much smaller German agrarian population (roughly one-fifth of the whole) already owned the land and was vehemently hostile to urban Reds and, indeed, to Berlin. They were reliable supporters of counter-revolution and many served readily in the army and the *Freikorps*. Thus, unlike Russia, major revolutionary support – with the exception of a period in Bavaria – did not extend beyond the industrial and urban areas.

The role of the middle classes

In Russia, there was not a sizeable middle class which could have resisted and then played a major role in overthrowing the Bolsheviks, unlike Germany and other Western European countries. In addition, most of the railway network was owned by the state and much of the investment in substantial sectors of the industrial economy came from abroad. The business elite comprised only about 200,000 individuals, according to one estimate for 1910 to 1912. As for the size of the bourgeoisie as a whole, one recent assessment for mid-1914 suggests a total of about two million people.[8] Some industrialists had even discredited themselves after the February 1917 Revolution by closing down their factories in Petrograd and removing some of their capital equipment by rail to Finland. As a whole, the Russian middle classes were weak compared with the powerful, anti-socialist middle classes of Germany.

After a brief period of shock in late 1918, when the believed-to-be invincible German army retreated beaten, the German middle classes were quick to mobilise against revolutionary socialism. Middle-class women's sense of outrage was well expressed by leaders of the German Protestant Women's League (*Deutsch-Evangelischer Frauenbund*, or DEF) who, as Nancy R. Reagin has commented,

> chose words that would have been applicable to a betrayed woman, which reflected their own identification with the nation: Germany's defeat represented her 'defilement' and 'shame', while the Treaty of Versailles was seen as a 'rape', entailing a loss of 'honour'. More generally, the 1918 military defeat and the subsequent peace treaty affronted the heightened sense of patriotism and nationalism widespread among the old Imperial classes and the middle classes – and the Weimar regime rekindled anti-socialist and even anti-semitic hatreds.[9]

Many were ready and eager to believe General Hindenberg's myth that Germany had lost the war because the army had suffered 'a stab in the back' by socialists on the home front. The propagation of this myth was facilitated by the strong anti-socialist press.

The German middle classes were sizeable enough, with very substantial financial resources, to make a very effective contribution to the prevention of the 1918 German Revolution being extended more radically in a Marxist direction. There were much larger industrial managerial and professional classes than in Russia, and these were strong in their own political and social culture. There was also the sizeable and vigorous *Mittelstand*, comprising small shopkeepers, tradesmen, artisans and craftsmen plus the 'newer' group of white-collar workers (which even in 1907 were estimated to number some two million private and one-and-a-half million state employees).[10] The German propertied classes had generally done well under the Kaiser, with the great burden of taxation being indirect (the tariffs) and falling disproportionately on the working class. Socialist change, let alone Bolshevism, alarmed them. Although the propertied groups were usually politically fragmented, they united with speed against the Red menace in late 1918 and afterwards.

Divisions of the Left

The success of the counter-revolutionary forces was greatly assisted by the substantial divisions within German socialism. The SPD leadership, much of the SPD membership and most probably a large section of the German working class (given the SPD's 11.5 million votes, 37.9 per cent of the vote in the January 1919 constituent assembly election even allowing for others who voted for them as a party of order), aspired in the short term to establish a democratic system of government at all levels, substantial social welfare provision and a far more labour-friendly system of industrial relations. These aspirations were achieved by the SPD in office (mostly in coalition governments) and defended. For them, Bolshevik rule in Russia was a warning, not an inspiration. In contrast this programme was insufficient, indeed held in contempt, by many in the rival USPD, and especially by Rosa Luxemburg and the Spartacists, who wished through mass agitation to foster continuing revolution in Germany. Faced with mass demonstrations and Red risings, the SPD leadership put themselves firmly on the side of 'Order'. They gave tacit, and later explicit, support to the right-wing bands which crushed the mass demonstrations in Berlin in January 1919 and murdered Rosa Luxemburg and Karl Liebknecht. Thereafter, the SPD in office used the *Freikorps* and the army not only to repress revolutionary uprisings but also strikes.

Thus in Germany, unlike Britain, the socialist and labour movement was seriously divided during and after the First World War. Divisions that had long been present were made more clear-cut with the formation by the Spartacus League and the Bremen and Hamburg Left radicals of the *Kommunistische Partei Deutschlands* (KPD) on 30 December 1918.[11] The SPD in office was quite literally a counter-revolutionary body, while the KPD was involved in insurgency until 1923. However, as Dick Geary has observed, the experience of Austria in 1934, when the Viennese working-class movement was smashed by government forces, suggests that had the German Left been united, it might well have been defeated by the powerful and determined counter-revolutionary forces present in Germany.[12]

The counter-revolutionary forces, notably the *Freikorps*, displayed their loathing for their republican masters with the Kapp *putsch* of March 1920. Precipitated by the disarmament conditions of the Treaty of Versailles, rebel *Freikrops* and *Reichswehr* (army) units took control of Berlin (with Wolfgang Kapp, a leader of the right-wing wartime *Vaterlands partei*, at their head). In conditions of near full employment, the Left was very successful in bringing about the defeat of Kapp and his associates by a general strike. However, the incident clearly revealed the limited loyalty to the republic of much of the *Reichswehr* which did not support the *putsch* ('*Reichswehr* does not fire on *Reichswehr*', as the senior General von Seeckt apparently observed at a critical time). It was also followed by the *Reichswehr* demonstrating that it could and would suppress left-wing forces in the Ruhr and elsewhere, and by disbanded *Freikorps* members forming illegal paramilitary groups behind claims of being private clubs. The judiciary also showed that its loyalties remained with the old order, giving light sentences to those involved in right-wing political violence or illegal activities (including Hindenburg and Hitler in 1923) but severe ones to those of the Left. The Kapp *putsch* was also followed by the national and state governments reorganising their forces of law and order to deal with further radical strikes or other manifestations of working-class radicalism.[13]

Parliamentary democracy, as well as the Left, was also under challenge in post-First World War Italy. While Italy did not experience defeat, many Italians were disappointed with the outcome of the peace negotiations. For the propertied classes, wounded national pride was combined with fear of the flow of Red revolutions through Eastern and Central Europe. This was compounded by economic dislocation as Italy made the transition from a war to a peace economy, followed by the seizure of uncultivated land and the occupation of factories by militant factory workers during the *biennio rosso* in 1919 to 1920. In contrast, first Gabriele D'Annunzio, a well-known writer and adventurer, and then Benito Mussolini, offered nationalistic alternatives to socialism. D'Annunzio provided a vigorous example of direct action when, with a force of over a thousand volunteers, he occupied Fiume which was in dispute between Italy and Yugoslavia from September 1919 until December 1920. In so doing he repudiated the views of the Allies, the Italian government and Yugoslavia (but had the tacit support of the Italian army).

Like the counter-revolutionary forces in post-First World War Germany, Mussolini offered both patriotism and the defeat of revolutionary and non-revolutionary socialism. Against the 1919 'diplomatic defeat' of Italy, he offered to turn *Italietta* (little Italy) into a new Roman Empire. Like the German Right, the former Corporal Mussolini romanticised 'the spirit of the trenches'. While the Left lionised deserters and even deemed returning front-line troops to be class traitors, Mussolini glorified the camaraderie of the troops and blamed the Italian defeat at Caporetto in 1917 by Austria-Hungary on the old elite of politicians and the anti-war socialists.

The Fascist action squads fought the Left in the streets, murdering and terrorising on a scale even exceeding that of the German Right in 1919 to 1920; and, like Germany, their action was condoned or tacitly supported by the leadership of the army.[14] One active Fascist wrote in 1923 that the Fascists had 'freed the country from the Mongolian scourge', a view of the communists which could have been equally expressed by the German Right. Mussolini, in a 1921 election speech, told the propertied classes what they wanted to hear: 'Communism is grotesque and only worthy of uncivilised tribes' and 'it is necessary that the bourgeoisie, in whose hands is the directive power in business, should be able to continue its work in tranquillity'.[15]

Mussolini was helped by a divided but much weaker socialist and labour movement than Kapp and his associates had faced in 1920. More important, while Weimar democracy was new and still had substantial support, Italian parliamentary democracy was notable for its weakness and for a rapid turnover of premiers (five between the 1918 Armistice and October 1922). The liberals were as divided as the socialists. Moreover, the briefly strong Catholic presence in post-war Italy, in the shape of the PPI (*Partito Popolare Italiano*) which, soon after being formed, had won 20 per cent of the national vote and 100 seats in the 1919 national elections, and the Catholic trade union confederation (*Confederazione Italiana dei Lavoratori*), was weakened by the rise of Mussolini. The new Pope, Pius XI, was strongly anti-Bolshevik and was happy that Mussolini would compromise with Catholicism (having been initially hostile). Many former PPI voters turned to the firmly anti-socialist fascists and in the 1923 elections the PPI vote fell to 9 per cent of the national vote and subsequently the party was dissolved.[16]

Violence and *coups*

By 1922 fascist violence, spearheaded by the action squads, had been followed by seizure of effective power in many provincial cities. The labour movement's attempt at a general strike in July 1922 against Fascism had none of the success of the German Left against Kapp. Indeed, as the Italian strike was intended to influence parliamentary manoeuvres to form a new coalition government, Fascists could oppose it as the 'defenders of order' on the side of the propertied classes. Its failure – dubbed by a socialist leader 'the Caporetto of the workers' – accelerated the weakening of the Left.[17] In contrast, Mussolini's threatened march on Rome in October 1922 was a threat which worked. Before the march took place Mussolini was summoned to Rome to form a government. On 30 October, Mussolini announced his coalition cabinet and 70,000 blackshirts marched through Rome.

Adolf Hitler, another ultra patriot and former corporal of the First World War, was also invited to form a minority government. Like Mussolini, he went on to seize substantial power from above, having been given initial power by other politicians in a struggling democratic system. Like Mussolini, Hitler had not been part of previous coalition governments, so was a politician untarnished by the political mess that many felt needed clearing up. By the time Hitler was offered high office the Nazis, like the Italian Fascists, had carried out terror in the streets, doing their utmost to destabilise the political system during a political, economic and social crisis. In the early 1930s, unlike 1920 at the time of the Kapp *putsch*, the labour movement was weak because of mass unemployment and so strike action was an unrealistic option against the Nazi advance to power. In the case of the KPD, over two-thirds of the membership in industrial areas was unemployed or underemployed. Nevertheless, the KPD's activity on the streets, often in response to Nazi and police violence, added to many of the propertied classes' fears and their readiness to turn to the Nazis to smash communism.[18] Moreover, the German middle classes had no love of what they deemed to be the Weimar Republic's lavish social welfare provisions and too generous industrial democracy legislation for workers, especially in highly competitive and adverse economic conditions of world recession. Hitler and the Nazis could draw on strong propertied classes' fear of Red revolution and a long-established, right-wing, *völkisch* nationalism.

In Austria, Spain and Portugal in the 1930s the propertied classes and others upholding traditional values rallied with vigour against the threat of radical Left governments bringing about major social change. In Portugal, Salazar offered elite rule, with appeals to 'a consciousness of order, of justice, and of honest work' or to such keywords of his regime as 'Nation, Family, Authority and Hierarchy'.[19] Salazar's traditional rhetoric followed an earlier reaction against a discredited parliamentary democracy in Portugal: Major Sidonio Pais' military dictatorship of April to December 1918 followed the coming and going of forty-four governments in sixteen years. Salazar's regime, like that of Engelbert Dollfuss (1932–34) in Austria, was Catholic and corporatist, with the trade unions, employers' organisations and strikes banned. Under Salazar a militia used violence against displays of opposition and a secret police force operated against opponents of the government. Salazar provided a conservative, authoritarian regime to protect those who feared socialism, communism and perhaps any substantial threat to 'traditional values' of a primarily rural and Catholic country.[20]

Catholic corporatism provided a substantial block to the advance of socialism and communism beyond 'Red Vienna'. Indeed, the Dollfuss government made what many of its supporters considered to be a preemptive strike against 'Red Vienna' and the Left in 1934, suppressing the Social Democratic Party, all associated socialist bodies and the trade unions. This included artillery shelling the Goethehof, which caused massive damage as the working-class flats had very thin walls. In taking such action the Dollfuss government was supported by the nationalistic and vehemently anti-socialist paramilitary, the *Heimwehr*. Dr Jill Lewis has argued that the *Heimwehr* acted as 'the quasi-legal shock force' of the Christian Social government when it seized the weapons of the Socialists' militia.[21]

Rural–urban hostilities and politicised catholicism

Like Germany, there was great and lasting hostility to the 1919 peace settlement among some sections of the new Austria's population, given the dismemberment of the old Habsburg monarchy into nation states, yet the Allies forbade the union of the Germans in Austria with Germany. In the 1920s and after there continued to be German nationalist sentiment and some nostalgia for the 'traditional values' of the empire under Francis Joseph (1848–1916). Even more so than the hostility to Berlin shown in parts of Germany, there was a provincial distrust, even hatred for Vienna; a loathing for the social welfare and socialist culture of 'Red Vienna'.[22] This was partly a strong example of rural–urban hostilities, areas such as the Tyrol feeling that they had been plundered of their agrarian resources by Vienna and the military during and after the First World War. In Salzburg, Styria and the Tyrol peasants were the key groups which formed the *Heimwehr* after the First World War; one report in 1921 estimated the Tyrolese and Salzburg *Heimwehren* to be 22,000 and 15,000 strong respectively. A British observer in 1920 warned that 'the scene seems to be set ... for a civil war between town and country'. As well as peasants, the *Heimwehr* drew on other characteristic anti-socialist groups: nationalist students, petty-bourgeois, non-union working-class and ex-army officers. By 1927 some *Heimwehr* leaders were talking of a 'march on Red Vienna' just as Mussolini had threatened a march on Rome.[23] The Austrian internal pressures for a move of a Right group against 'Red Vienna' was greatly reinforced by the interest and intervention of both Mussolini and Hitler in Austrian affairs.

Yet, while the *Heimwehr* was a very important contributor to the smashing of the Left in 1934, it was the Catholic Centre Party under Dollfuss that replaced parliamentary democracy with the corporate state. It brought together a rural and traditional Catholicism with an urban and more radical Catholicism. The existing concerns of many Catholics with the post-1918 state, and even more with Vienna's government, was reinforced by Pope Pius XI's encyclical letter, *Quadragesimo anno*, which called for social reform but for the reorganisation of society along corporatist lines in the expectation that this would lead to greater social harmony. However, as Alfred Diamant has written, 'Catholic politicians simply picked out whatever seemed the most effective anti-republican and anti-democratic argument and were little concerned with questions of compatibility of the Romantic and Catholic ideas they used in this indiscriminate fashion'.[24] Dollfuss himself loathed 'Red Vienna' and could draw on an Austrian Catholic political tradition of corporate political aspirations. In 1933 he made his aims explicit: 'The day of the capitalist system, the era of the capitalist-liberal economic order is past. We demand a social, Christian, German Austria, on a corporate basis and under strong authoritarian leadership.'[25]

In Spain there was also a powerful politicised Catholicism and an authoritarian nationalism. Much of Spain's very strong Catholic culture was inimical to radical republicanism. As in Ireland, there was a strong bond with agrarian society, deemed to be more pious than urban society. Moreover, in Spain the old order that Catholicism supported was predominantly landed. Spanish Catholic trade unionism was more conservative than that in France, Germany or elsewhere, and was notably reticent in challenging vested interests. So much so that a more populist Catholic body, the *Sindicatos Libres* (Free Trade Unions) emerged on the Right, which for seven years was the second largest union in Spain.[26] Similarly, there was much Catholic reluctance to go beyond support for the monarchy and Church in order to appeal to electors in a parliamentary system.

In Spain, as in Portugal, there was a period of military rule before a lengthy dictatorship. Miguel Primo de Rivera overthrew a dishevelled and much discredited parliamentary democracy in 1923. While professing liberal sentiments, Primo de Rivera's government (1923–30) became increasingly authoritarian. His rule, with its 'Italianate borrowings and fascist fringes', provided a precursor for General Francisco Franco. Spain had remained neutral in 1914 to 1918, so had not suffered defeat as had Germany and Austria, nor had great nationalist aspirations and expectations been dashed as in Italy. Yet, like Italy and Austria, there was a powerful nostalgia for a golden imperial past.

The advent of the Republic in 1931, accompanied by politicians in power determined to reform and generally modernise Spain, led to a conservative backlash. Such serious determination for change was confronted by a range of vested interests, with outside supporters anxious to assist the crushing of such radicalism. This was a situation which was echoed several times in South America and elsewhere after the Second World War, with the USA (through the CIA) supporting counter-revolutionary forces.

Powerful opposition to the Republic came, as in Austria, from most Catholic bodies. In the 1933 elections their umbrella organisation, the *Confederación Española de Derechas Autonónomas* (CEDA), became the largest group in Parliament. It was committed to reversing the Republic's secular constitution and returning Spain to the old social order. In their efforts to achieve these aims, Catholics were encouraged by the success in office of Salazar and Dollfuss. With the electoral victory of the Popular Front in February 1936, political Catholicism was ready to support another military move to restore traditional values and order, this time in the face of a secular and socialist regime. Support for Franco became even stronger when large numbers of clerics were killed in mid-1936 in Republican-held areas. Catholic conservative forces were fused under Franco with the direct-action, anti-Left Falange, which grew rapidly in 1936 to 1937 and terrorised the Left in much the same way that the Fascist squads had in Italy before Mussolini took office.[27]

Fear of change and conservative responses

Those threatened by substantial social and political change in interwar Europe resisted by taking measures commensurate with the gravity of the challenge. If the challenge was primarily parliamentary, as in Britain, then anti-socialist electoral alliances in the constituencies and coalitions in Parliament were sufficient. In the wartime and immediate post-war unrest there were moves to rally patriotic or propertied groups, by such bodies as the National Party and the Middle Class Union. However, the great majority of the British Labour Movement was relentlessly moderate and the Conservative Party, free from coalition under Lloyd George after 1922, secured ample electoral support from 1922 to the Second World War to reassure the propertied classes that it alone was an adequate guarantee that no social revolution would occur in Britain.[28]

Where the challenge was revolutionary or especially menacing, the propertied and conservative groups made stronger responses. In Italy, Portugal, Germany, Austria and Spain substantial support moved further to the Right as the political situation deteriorated in terms of traditional concerns. In Spain, as Martin Blinkhorn has argued, many conservatives supported the CEDA if it could achieve a gradual and peaceful replacement of radical Republicanism. When, instead, the popular Front emerged victorious in 1936, support swung to more violent means for strategic rather than ideological reasons.[29]

While the Left often ranted on about class war, counter-revolutionary forces in Europe were ready, willing and able to practise it, or, at least, to take violent and vigorous action against socialists and communists. This was not only so in Nazi Germany, but also in Hungary, Italy, Portugal, Austria, Spain and elsewhere in interwar Europe. The Left was famously divided: whether it be the SPD and the Spartacists in early 1919, the SPD and KPD thereafter in Germany; or the anarchists, the *Partido Obero de Unificación Marxista* (POUM), socialists (PSOE) and communists (PCOE) in Spain.

Moreover, the Left's weaknesses in combating the Right were added to by ideological muddles over whether their methods were parliamentary or revolutionary and, if the latter, what strategies they envisaged as necessary. The Communist International followed what Eric Hobsbawm has described as a 'suicidal policy' not only of greatly underestimating the threat of the Nazis in Germany but of pursuing 'a policy of sectarian isolation ... deciding that its main enemy was the organised mass labour movement of social-democratic and labour parties (described as 'social-fascist')'. By 1934 the only sizeable and politically influential communist party outside of Russia was the French.[30] This did adopt a parliamentary strategy, participating in the Popular Front coalition government of Leon Blum (1936–37). This, however, did not secure a revolution such as Lenin had hoped for in advanced industrial countries.

Those mobilising against revolutionary or radical reforming governments not only vehemently opposed such governments' policies and values but also had their own revered traditions and culture. In the Weimar Republic, as Alan Steinweis has observed, 'cultural antimodernism provided a common denominator between older conservatives, conservative revolutionaries, and the *völkish* Right'. The Nazis vigorously denounced 'Art Bolshevism'.[31] There was much in the more 'advanced' modern art and writings of the interwar years to outrage Catholic and, for that matter, Protestant traditionalists. This was especially so for many women, who felt that family values were in danger of being undermined by the Left.

Alongside this, there was in most countries a clash of rural versus urban cultures and politics. This also had provincial versus capital dimensions, the rural provinces being notably hostile to 'Red Vienna', Berlin, Rome or Madrid. In Germany, other than Bavaria where for a while in 1919 there were radical peasants' councils, the post-war peasants' councils were counter-revolutionary bodies. In the Rhineland Free Peasants' groups sprang up to represent the peasants' interests as producers against the controls of the state and the demands of urban consumers. In its 1921 programme the Free Peasantry made it clear it would resist 'any immoral intervention into private enterprise' and complained of 'the helplessness of a weak peasant parliamentary representation and of the government, which cannot ward off the iron struggle of the proletariat and other consumer interests'. The Free Peasants and other such agrarian bodies in Germany found that their bargaining strength as producers, never that strong, declined quickly as food prices dropped in the late 1920s and early 1930s. Many peasants, especially males and Protestants, turned to the Nazis in elections.[32]

The Old Order took severe action against radical peasant parties, even where these had strong electoral support. The most significant Eastern European instance was Bulgaria, where the Bulgarian Agrarian Union under Alexander Stamboliski held office from 1919 to 1923. The right-wing parties united to oust this agrarian reforming government. The Bulgarian Right had the support of the Orthodox Church and King Boris. It studied Mussolini's tactics in Italy and likewise set up 'sporting clubs' and 'youth organisations' which could be used for the intimidation of opponents. In June 1923 the Bulgarian Agrarian Union leaders were ruthlessly butchered after a *coup d'état.*[33]

Those mobilising against revolutionaries or radicals could build not only on rural anti-socialists but also on the range of others to whom socialism rarely succeeded in appealing. These included the propertied classes, white-collar workers, shopkeepers and small employers, the pious and the nationalistic. Nationalism between the wars – as now – had myriad faces.

Among the more potent was xenophobia, a powerful force for dividing worker from worker. Socialism also had very mixed success, at best, in meeting women's aspirations, let alone mobilising women to play an equal part in labour movement organisations.[34]

Economic hard times often proved divisive. Younger workers were frequently alienated from older, married workers when choices were made as to who was laid off work. Youths were especially vulnerable to mass unemployment. They were the victims in Germany and elsewhere of cuts in welfare expenditure. Even middle-class youths suffered, as job opportunities evaporated when small businesses went bankrupt. Many of these drifted to the Right after 1930.[35]

Unemployment could also be used by right-wing bodies to recruit members. This was the case, for example, in Upper Styria, Austria, where Jill Lewis has commented, 'without a *Heimwehr* card it was not worth applying for a job and, as unemployment soared, this became a major incentive to join'.[36] It was an approach practised by the Nazis in Germany. Unemployment weakened trade union power, making collective defence against right-wing offensives much harder.

For success the counter-revolutionary forces needed the support, or at least the tacit support, of the forces of law and order. In the aftermath of the First World War there were many who felt that they had learned the lessons of the war and, if on the defeated side, wished for a replay in which there would be a 'patriotic' government and a united people on the home front. As well as anti-socialist military and police in many countries, there were also readily mobilisable groups of the disaffected from the lower ranks. These were willing to partake in the violent intimidation of radical agrarians, trade unionists, socialists, communists and – in the case of the Black and Tans and auxiliaries in Ireland – nationalists.

Post-war disruption or serious economic dislocation mobilised the propertied classes to defend their wealth and status by whatever means was effective. The combination of economic concern and hurt national pride experienced by many middle-class Germans in the period after the First World War was well recaptured later by Ernst Jünger. He wrote of his middle-class father:

> One morning he came to breakfast and brandished a bundle of freshly minted fifty-mark notes in his hand. 'Now's a good time to commit suicide. Your obituary could read "He could not survive his country's misfortune"'.

His mother, meanwhile, would 'sit frozen in a stare lamenting the vanished second Reich'.[37] While Weimar survived the post-war turmoil and hyper-inflation it was to fall under the pressures of economic recession and deflation, with the propertied classes hostile to high taxes and favourable welfare and working conditions for the working class. However, the anger and despair – economic and nationalistic – described by Jünger was widespread among the opponents of radical change or revolution.

Fear of revolution, or even of substantial change, was a powerful mobilising force which thwarted Lenin's hopes of a rapid spread of revolution after the October 1917 Russian Revolution. In the face of economic, social and political turmoil the established order – property-owners, persons of status, the predominant churches, the leadership of the armed forces, those who admired empire or national power roles – turned to those who might best defend them from 'red revolution'. Even those who themselves used the rhetoric of revolution could be used against the Left. When Mussolini told Gramsci he was trying to create a new ruling elite, Gramsci observed that Mussolini's 'new fascist elite was turning out to be little more than the bourgeois ruling class of pre-fascist Italy dressed in black shirts'.[38] This may be too simplistic, but there is much truth in the suggestion that many of the propertied classes in Europe turned with alacrity to the most effective bulwarks against the revolutionary Left.

When conditions were not dire, too many people in the industrialised societies of Europe felt they had something to lose. In Britain, talk of Labour taking poor people's meagre post office savings was a powerful canard. There were also non-material things which many felt to be at risk, especially when there was rampant atheism and talk of 'free love'. There was also widespread national pride, with the victor nations of 1918 less troubled by revolutionary unrest than the defeated – and many in the defeated turning to the 'patriotic Right'. The culture of family and religion, hierarchy and national pride was underlined by the powerful press of the propertied classes. The promise of a revolutionary upheaval did not have an alluring appeal to many, unless conditions were terrible through war or economic collapse; and even when conditions were truly grim, a revolution of the Left was only one drastic option. Even in dire conditions, the Left in Europe was weakened by divisions which gave counter-revolution even greater prospects of success.

Notes

1 Arno J. Mayer, *Dynamics of Counterrevolution in Europe, 1870–1956: An Analytic Framework*, New York, 1971, p. 4.
2 Major assessments include Charles S. Maier, *Recasting Bourgeois Europe: Stabilization in France, Germany and Italy in the Decade after World War I*, Princeton, NJ, 1975. For the old order, see Arno J. Mayer, *The Persistence of the Old Regime: Europe to the Great War*, New York, 1981.
3 Arthur Ransome, *Six Weeks in Russia in 1919*, London, 1919, p. 79.
4 William B. Slottman, 'Austria's *Geistesaristo Kraten* and the Hungarian Revolution of 1919', in A.C. Janos and W.B. Slottman (eds), *Revolution in Perspective: Essays on the Hungarian Soviet Republic of 1919*, Berkeley, CA, 1971, pp. 158–9.
5 S.L. Bane and R.H. Lutz, *The Blockade of Germany after the Armistice 1918–1919*, Stanford, CA, 1942, pp. 473, 489, 500–4.

6 Orlando Figes, 'The peasantry', in E. Acton, V. Cherniaev and W.G. Rosenberg (eds), *Critical Companion to the Russian Revolution 1914–21*, London, 1997, pp. 543–53, and his *Peasant Russia. Civil War: The Volga Countryside in Revolution 1917–21*, Oxford, 1989.

7 Wolfram Wette, 'Demobilisation in Germany 1918–19: the gradual erosion of the powers of the soldiers' councils', in C.J. Wrigley (ed.), *Challenges of Labour: Central and Western Europe 1917–1920*, London, 1993, pp. 176–95.

8 P. Gattrell, 'Russian industrialists and revolution', in Acton *et al.*, pp. 572–83; Maureen Perrie and R.W. Davies, 'The social context', in R.W. Davies (ed.), *From Tsarism to the New Economic Policy: Continuity Change in the Economy of the USSR*, New York, 1991, pp. 31–5.

9 Nancy R. Reagin, *A German Women's Movement: Class and Gender in Hanover, 1880–1933*, Chapel Hill, NC, 1995, pp. 203–4; Detlev J.K. Peukert, *The Weimar Republic: The Crisis of Classical Modernity*, London, 1991, pp. 66–8.

10 John Hiden, *Republican and Fascist Germany: Themes and Variations in the History of Weimar and the Third Reich, 1918–1945*, London, 1996, p. 167.

11 For a valuable recent history of the KPD see Eric D. Weitz, *Creating German Communism, 1890–1990: From Popular Protest to Socialist State*, Princeton, NJ, 1997.

12 Dick Geary, *European Labour Politics From 1900 to the Depression*, London, 1991, p. 55.

13 V.R. Berghahn, *Modern Germany*, Cambridge, 1982, pp. 75–6; Weitz, pp. 100–3.

14 On the rise of Italian Fascism, see, among many, Adrian Lyttelton, *The Seizure of Power: Fascism in Italy 1919–29* (2nd edn), Princeton, NJ, 1987; John Whittam, *Fascist Italy*, Manchester, 1995.

15 Pietro Gorgolini, *The Fascist Movement in Italian Life*, London, 1923, pp. 26, 46. Mussolini provided an enthusiastic Preface to the book. Dr Gorgolini had been one of the 'Fascists of the first hour' and condemned the excesses of the action squads (including in his book, p. 25).

16 Martin Conway, *Catholic Politics in Europe 1918–1945*, London, 1997, pp. 30–1.

17 By the reformist socialist, Filippo Turati, *Fascist Italy* (1995), p. 36.

18 Weitz, *Creating German Communism*, pp. 144–5, 185–7.

19 Tom Gallagher, 'Conservatism, dictatorship and fascism in Portugal, 1914–45', in Martin Blinkhorn (ed.), *Fascists And Conservatives: The Radical Right and the Establishment in Twentieth-century Europe*, London, 1990, pp. 157–75.

20 Jill Lewis, 'Conservatives and fascists in Austria, 1918–34', in Blinkhorn, *Fascists and Conservatives*, pp. 98–117; see also Jill Lewis, *Fascism and the Working Class in Austria, 1918–1934*, Oxford, 1991.

21 Helmut Gruber, *Red Vienna: Experiment in Working Class Culture 1919–1934*, Oxford, 1991.

22 Elisabeth Dietrich, 'The fear of revolution in rural Austria: the case of Tyrol', in Wrigley (ed.), *Challenges of Labour*, pp. 215–28; C. Earl Edmondson, 'The Heimwehr and February 1934: reflections and questions', in *The Austrian Socialist Experiment: Social Democracy and Austromarxism, 1918–1934*, Boulder, CO, 1985, pp. 39–45; F.L. Carsten, *The First Austrian Republic*, London, 1986, pp. 28, 74–8.

23 Alfred Diamant, *Austrian Catholics and the First Republic: Democracy, Capitalism and the Social Order, 1918–1934*, Princeton, NJ, 1960, p. 193.

24 Ibid., p.194.

25 Martin Blinkhorn, 'Conservatism, traditionalism and fascism in Spain, 1898–1937', in Blinkhorn (ed.), *Fascists and Conservatives*, pp. 118–37 (at p. 129).

26 Colin M. Winston, *Workers and the Right in Spain 1900–1936*, Princeton, NJ, 1985, pp. 5–9, 120–3 and 328–9.

27 Conway, *Catholic Politics*, pp. 57–8 and 67–9; Mary Vincent, *Catholicism in the Second Republic: Religion and Politics in Salamanca 1930–1936*, Oxford, 1966; Blinkhorn, 'Spain', in Blinkhorn (ed.), *Fascists and Conservatives*, pp. 133–4.

28 Bernard Waites, *A Class Society At War*, Leamington Spa, 1987; C.J. Wrigley, *Lloyd George and the Challenge of Labour*, Brighton, 1990.
29 Blinkhorn, 'Spain', in Blinkhorn (ed.), *Fascists and Conservatives*, p. 132.
30 Paul Heywood, *Marxism and the Failure of Organised Socialism in Spain, 1879–1936*, Cambridge, 1990; E.J. Hobsbawm, *Age of Extremes*, London, 1994, p. 104.
31 Alan E. Steinweis, 'Conservatism, national socialism, and the cultural crisis of the Weimar Republic' in L.E. Jones and J. Retallack (eds), *Between Reform, Reaction and Resistance: Studies in the History of German Conservatism from 1789–1945*, Oxford, 1993, pp. 329–46.
32 Jonathan Osmond, *Rural Protest in the Weimar Republic: The Free Peasantry in the Rhineland and Bavaria*, London, 1993, pp. 31–48, 139–44.
33 John D. Bell, *Peasants in Power: Alexander Stamboliski and the Bulgarian Agrarian National Union, 1899–1923*, Princeton, NJ, 1977, pp. 154–5, 211–13 and 237–42. For a more hostile view of Stamboliski, see George D. Jackson, *Comintern and Peasant in East Europe 1919–1930*, New York, 1966, pp. 161–6.
34 R. Koshar (ed.), *Splintered Classes: Politics and the Lower Middle Classes in Interwar Europe*, New York, 1990; S. Berger and A. Smith (eds), *Nationalism, Labour and Ethnicity, 1870–1939*, Manchester, 1999; H. Gruber and P. Graves (eds), *Women and Socialism – Socialism and Women: Europe Between the Two Wars*, Oxford, 1998.
35 E. Harvey [essay], in Richard J. Evans and Dick Geary (eds), *The German Unemployed*, London, 1987, p. 143; E. Harvey, *Youth and the Welfare State in Weimar Germany*, Oxford, 1993.
36 Lewis, 'Conservatives and fascists', p. 112.
37 Thomas Nevin, *Ernst Jünger and Germany: Into the Abyss, 1914–1945*, London, 1997, p. 76.
38 As expressed by Denis Mack Smith, 'Revolution and counter-revolution in modern Italian history', in E.E. Rice (ed.), *Revolution and Counter-Revolution*, Oxford, 1991, pp. 153–70.

Further reading

S. Berger and A. Smith, (eds), *Nationalism, Labour and Ethnicity, 1870–1939*, Manchester, 1999.

Martin Blinkhorn (ed.), *Fascists and Conservatives: The Radical Right and the Establishment of Twentieth Century Europe*, London, 1990.

Martin Conway, *Catholic Politics in Europe, 1918–1945*, London, 1997.

Dick Geary, *European Labour Politics From 1900 to the Depression*, London, 1991.

Helmut Gruber and P. Graves, *Women and Socialism – Socialism and Women: Europe Between the Two Wars*, Oxford, 1998.

Charles S. Maier, *Recasting Bourgeois Europe: Stabilization in France, Germany and Italy in the Decade After World War 1*, Princeton, NJ, 1975.

C.J. Wrigley (ed.), *Challenges of Labour: Central and Western Europe 1917–1920*, London, 1993.

11 Revolution from the Right

Fascism

Roger Griffin

The Marxist and liberal denial of Fascism's revolutionary credentials

'Nazism makes out it is subversive. The most terrible white terror against people and socialism the world has ever seen takes on a socialist disguise. To this end its propaganda must develop a revolutionary facade with trappings of the Paris Commune.'[1] Even today there are many for whom this pronouncement, made by the Marxist philosopher Ernst Bloch in 1933, the year in which Adolf Hitler came to power, still rings true. 'Real' revolutions, they assume, do not just replace one socio-political, economic or technological system by another, but in doing so enable humanity (or at least one part of it) to pass from a lower to a higher stage of development. The Right, however, even at its most radical, is widely seen as wanting to put a stop to such progress by creating a modern state whose real purpose is to preserve the traditional class system and its values, or even put the clock back by invoking the ancient qualities of the race as the basis of contemporary society.

Assumptions of this kind have meant that fascism's own claims to be a revolutionary force have been widely rejected by its opponents. Marxists, for example, are committed to the belief that the capitalist world order will eventually be overthrown and give way to one in which systemic inhumanity and exploitation will finally cease. They are thus predisposed to assume that anything which tends to postpone the advent of socialism is 'reactionary', while the radical transformation of society in an anti-socialist direction pursued by fascism makes it 'counter-revolutionary'. By the same logic, fascist talk of a rejuvenated national community in which class conflicts will dissolve is axiomatically treated by Marxists as an elaborate exercise in 'false consciousness', or using ideas and values which conceal the true intentions. Inter-war fascism was the product of a crisis of capitalism, threatened from within by the breakdown of the financial, social and political structures which maintained it, and from without by revolutionary socialism.

This pincer movement, so Marxists believe, caused it to drop its liberal disguise which made it appear rational and humanistic, and resort to an openly authoritarian, terroristic form of state government. Fascism was either directly generated by bourgeois elements or cynically manipulated by them to defend the capitalist state, often with the direct collaboration of residual feudal forces such as the Church and aristocracy. Its main ploy was to pretend to destroy the system so that it could divert the subversive energies of the masses into serving a belligerently nationalistic state which, despite claiming to restore dignity to the working class, in the long run could only increase its exploitation and suffering. In short, it simulated revolution for reactionary ends. True to this position the British activist Robert Palm Dutt, writing in the same year as Ernst Bloch, told his fellow Marxists that in order to preserve capitalism the ideologues of the 'Fascist Counter-Revolution' had to pretend to be enemies of capitalism: 'To prevent the working-class revolution, they are compelled to stage their masquerade revolution, and even dub it a "socialist revolution".'[2]

A bias which in some respects is even more insidious, because less easily detectable, is displayed by many 'liberal' academics. They have no qualms about using such terms as 'the American Revolution', 'the French Revolution', or even 'the 1848 Revolutions' (all of which in the short term failed in their objectives). They even concede the Russian Revolution to have been revolutionary, since, however misconceived Lenin's vision of the ideal society, he at least set out to replace 'backward' Tsarist Russia with a recognisably 'modern' industrialised state. Yet most liberals have been unable to accept that fascism was revolutionary because they do not recognise the existence of a fascist ideology, and see it as reducible to little more than a leadership cult, extreme nationalism and organised brutality. Thus for Roger Scruton, the author of *A Political Dictionary* (1982), interwar fascism was 'an amalgam of disparate conceptions, often ill-understood, often bizarre': it had 'the form of an ideology without the content'. Another reaction is to treat it as the throw-back to an age of barbarism, as when Hugh Trevor-Roper dismissed Nazi ideology as 'bestial Nordic nonsense'. Even when non-Marxist historians have recognised the modernising, revolutionary thrust of fascism, they have sometimes felt the need to qualify it by adopting a phrase which is deliberately paradoxical, such as 'a revolution of nihilism',[3] 'modernist anti-modernism'[4] or 'reactionary modernism'.[5]

This chapter flies in the face of such 'common sense' by arguing that even if the radical Right in general is 'reactionary', at least in its fascist manifestations it does indeed function as a revolutionary ideology. Or to quote the American academic Eugen Weber's thoughtful essay on this topic: 'fascism, too easily defined as counter-revolutionary, is not a counter-revolution, but a rival revolution: rival of [the communist one] which claimed to be the only one entitled to the label. . . . For the fascists, communism is not subversion attacking the established order, it is a *competitor for the foundation of power.*'[6] Before a case can be made for this approach, however, it is necessary to clarify what we mean by two keywords, both of whose meaning is strongly contested by 'experts': 'revolution' and 'fascism'.

'Revolution' and 'fascism' as ideal types

If the terms 'revolution' and 'fascism' are both conceptually fuzzy and value-laden, then any discussion of their relationship risks being so subjective as to become pointless. The solution to such dilemmas, which are a recurrent feature of the human sciences, is to create an artificially tidy definition known in the social sciences as an 'ideal type'. An ideal type has the same sort of relationship to the empirical reality being defined as a stylised underground railway (subway) map has to the actual network of rails and stations it displays.[7] It does not tell you about the characteristics of any one phenomenon, but singles out the things which all manifestations of one type of phenomenon have in common.

'Revolution' can be used as an ideal type to refer to 'a fundamental (structural) change which, while manifesting itself in a particular sphere of human activity, has radically innovative consequences for a wide nexus of social and psychological realities associated with it'. This means that, as long as the break with the past is sufficiently radical, a set of events may be revolutionary without necessarily furthering the Marxist or liberal scheme of historical progress. As for our working definition of fascism, a ready-made, off-the-shelf ideal type can be brought into service without resorting to a piece of conceptual do-it-yourself. In the course of the 1990s there was a growing consensus outside the Marxist camp that fascism is a form (or genus) of modern, mass politics which draws its ideological cohesion and mobilising force from the vision of imminent national rebirth. In other words, for fascists a period of perceived national decline and decadence is giving way to an era of renewal in a post-liberal new order.[8]

Approached from this angle, fascism is an essentially *revolutionary* form of ultra-nationalism (i.e. a highly chauvinistic and overtly anti-liberal nationalism). It is characterised by a populist dimension which involves mobilising the masses to provide authentic (and not simply engineered and manipulated) support *from below* for the drastic actions taken by the self-appointed new elite *from above* to save the nation from what it perceives as terminal decline. This suggests that we should not dismiss simply as empty rhetoric, or 'mindless Latin nonsense', a speech made by Mussolini on the eve of the march on Rome which brought him to power:

> We have created our myth. The myth is a faith, a passion. It is not necessary for it to be a reality. It is a reality in the sense that it is a stimulus, is hope, is faith, is courage. Our myth is the nation, our myth is the greatness of the nation! And to this myth, this greatness, which we want to translate into a total reality, that we subordinate everything else.
>
> For us the nation is not just territory, but something spiritual. There are States which have had immense territories and which have left no trace in human history. It is not just a question of size, because there

have been minute, microscopic States in history which have
bequeathed memorable, immortal specimens of art and philosophy.
The greatness of the nation is the totality of all these qualities, of all
these conditions. A nation is great when it translates into reality the
force of its spirit.[9]

What makes this statement symptomatic not merely of Italian Fascism but
of fascism in general ('generic fascism') is that it relates directly to the fact
that the Fascist state attempted to mobilise the people as a whole through
mass organisations, a constant stream of propaganda, and elaborate political ritual to enlist them emotionally in the epic transformation of their
country into a dynamic, modern, productive military power. Moreover,
even if it had to be seen as collaborating with traditional ruling elites –
the civil service, the monarchy, the armed forces, the Catholic Church
– it did so in a spirit far removed from that of conservative reaction: in
a *revolutionary* spirit, in fact. The Exhibition of the Fascist Revolution, which
opened in Milan in 1932 and was seen by nearly four million visitors, was
designed not as a publicity stunt, but to create a dramatic sense for the
visitor who walked through the rooms that with the advent of Fascism
Italy and all its inhabitants had literally entered a new historical era.[10]

Further implications of the ideal types

Another consequence to be drawn from the ideal types we have used is
that, when seeking to establish which inter-war movements or regimes
were fascist, our attention should focus not on external features, such as
the leader cult, anti-socialism, aggressive foreign policy or militarism, which
can be displayed by many radical Right formations. Instead the central
criterion used is the core ideology and the policies adopted to turn it into
reality, and whether they had a thrust that was ultimately reactionary in
that it wanted to restore the social structures and values of the past, or
rivalled communism in being innovative and revolutionary in wanting a
new type of society. Inter-war fascism did not want to retain a traditional
social structure in a modernised form, let alone literally return to a pre-
modern idyll. Nor did it merely pay lip-service to the notion of mass-
mobilisation. Rather, even if it was forced to secure the collusion of conservative forces on tactical grounds to ease the transition from the old society,
it aspired to create a new type of state, one based on the energies
which flowed from a rejuvenated national community bound together by
patriotic fervour.

If a number of interwar movements, other than Italian Fascism, can also
be classified as fascist, it is because, while the peculiar historical circumstances in which each one arose made it unique, they all shared a struc-
turally identical myth of national renewal through mass-mobilisation and
proposed radical policies to achieve it. They included Nazism, Falangism,

the British Union of Fascists, the Romanian Iron Guard, and Brazilian Integral Action. However, other movements often associated with fascism, such as the Irish Blue Shirts and the Rexists of interwar Belgium, can be seen on closer inspection to have lacked the *innovative* radicalism or anti-traditionalism implicit in the rebirth myth needed to qualify as fascist.

Moreover, on closer inspection, a number of authoritarian regimes often lumped together with Fascist Italy turn out to have pursued no radical plan to create a new ruling elite, but exercised power on behalf of conservative forces despite the fascist facade they created by adopting the external trappings of fascism (leader cult, mass rallies, shirted youth movements and so on). These 'parafascist' regimes include Franco's Spain (1939–75), Dollfuss' and Schuschnigg's Austria (1933–38), Antonescu's Romania (1940–44), and Pétain's Vichy France (1940–42). These were indeed 'counter-revolutionary', and tried to absorb, marginalise or eliminate not just communism, but 'real' fascism as well as a revolutionary threat to their ascendancy.[11] In Spain, for example, Franco, whose basic concern was to crush the Republican forces and restore the power of landed elites, the monarchy and the Church, was careful to absorb the genuinely fascist Falange to give his regime an aura of dynamism and appeal to the young it would otherwise have lacked. In Romania, King Carol II first tried to crush the country's extremely violent fascist movement, the Iron Guard, but its popularity led him to change tack and bring some of its leaders into government. After his abdication he was succeeded by General Antonescu who pretended to be prepared to share power with the Iron Guard, but then seized the first opportunity to liquidate it by force. These episodes reveal the fundamental antagonism between conservatism and fascism, however much practical considerations force them into partnership.

A third implication which follows from our ideal types is that only two interwar right-wing regimes were actually revolutionary and hence fascist: Fascist Italy and Nazi Germany. It is important to stress, however, that while they share an identical core myth of national rebirth, profound differences divide the concrete ways in the circumstances which brought them to power and the ways in which this myth was manifested. For one thing, the situations which allowed Fascism and Nazism to complete the transition from movement to regime were very different. Italy was extremely poorly integrated socially and economically underdeveloped compared to Germany. Moreover, it was the extreme socio-political chaos of the immediate post-war years which enabled Mussolini to threaten to carry out a *putsch* with his Blackshirts in October 1922 (the march on Rome) and so persuade King Emanuel III to make him head of a coalition government. To implement the revolution in the Italian state and society he intended, he had to wait until January 1925 after another state crisis provoked by the Fascist murder of the socialist deputy Matteotti had given him the chance to establish an authoritarian regime. Hitler's attempted *putsch* of November 1923 failed miserably, and it was the shattering impact of the world Depression on Germany's economic, political and social life that contributed to the paralysis of the state which enabled his party to win mass support at the polls. The depth of the crisis also convinced leading politicians to use Nazism to strengthen their own position, culminating in his appointment as Chancellor in January 1933.

However, there are striking parallels between the success of the two fascisms in entering the citadel of state power. As in the case of every major political revolution in Western history, the immediate context for their success was a deep-seated crisis in the Old Order. In both cases the leaders were sufficiently resourceful to take advantage of the structural flaws in a parliamentary system which had shallow roots in the national tradition and which was widely discredited, where the traditional 'conservative' Right was too weak and divided to provide an effective alternative, and where revolutionary socialism was powerful enough to cause genuine alarm while remaining a marginalised force. Furthermore, in both countries elements in the liberal and conservative establishment chose to make crucial concessions to fascism on the mistaken assumption that they could 'tame' it and dispense with its help once stability had returned to political and economic life.

In terms of actual worldview and specific policies as well, vast differences separate Fascism and Nazism, just as the personalities of Mussolini and Hitler were in many respects poles apart. Yet such contrasts merely emphasise how the same ideological myth of national renewal can assume highly diverse surface manifestations. Moreover, there was much in common in the institutional changes which the two regimes made to the state apparatus and in the social engineering they undertook to revitalise the 'national community'.[12]

The mythic core of the fascist revolution

If what we are suggesting is true, and fascism should be approached as a revolutionary form of nationalism, why does the term 'fascist' for most people now have purely negative connotations of totalitarianism, destructiveness, nihilism and inhumanity? First, it should be noted that this has not always been the case. Until Italian Fascism started forging an ever closer relationship with Nazi Germany, it was a common view in Europe and the USA that Mussolini had performed wonders for his country. A popular American love-song of the 1930s went 'You're the tops, you're the great Houdini. You're the tops, you're like Mussolini!'

The creation of the 'Axis' between Fascist Italy and Nazi Germany in 1936, the brutal involvement of both countries on the side of Franco in the Spanish Civil War, and the fact that Italy was allied to the Third Reich when it started the Second World War, and thus became linked to the unimaginable scale of atrocities committed by the Third Reich, permanently changed the image, not just of Italian Fascism, but of fascism in general.

The fact that the fascist revolution eventually came to be synonymous for most with war and calculated inhumanity is no coincidence. Rather it is implicit in the fascist vision of national rebirth itself, which is compounded of not one, but two myths which when combined can unleash enormous destructive power. The first is the concept of the nation as an organic entity, personified as the hero of an epic story which passes through moments of glory and shame, of power and weakness. An example of this myth is provided by the Italian Nationalist Association which merged with Fascism in 1923:

> The fundamental thesis of Nationalism, which places the Nationalist doctrine in a special relationship with respect to all other political doctrines, is that the various societies existing on the earth are true organisms endowed with a life which far transcends that of individuals and which is sustained for centuries and millennia. Thus the Italian nation does not only contain the 36 million Italians alive now, but all the hundreds of thousands of millions of Italians who will live in future centuries, and who are conceived as components of a single whole. In this conception each generation and every individual within a generation is but a transient and infinitesimal part of the nation, and is the cell of the national organism. Just as cells are born, live and die, while the organism remains the same, so individuals are born, live and die while the nation continues to live out its millennial existence.[13]

As can be seen from this passage, the central metaphors of ultra-nationalism are vitalistic. They frequently fuse the physical realms of biology, territory and matter with the metaphysical realms of spirit, heroism and will: the recurrent fascist images of 'blood' and 'race' combine both these dimensions. Fascist nationalism is a world of mythic imaginings where the claims of history, destiny and providence embodied in the nation over the individual are total, and where empathy with all human beings irrespective of their race and value to society is seen as a symptom of the spiritual decadence to be overcome. It is a world where utopian longings for renewal revolve around polarised opposites: health/sickness; our nation/the enemy; man/woman.

If ultra-nationalism is male chauvinist in its imagining of man – man the warrior, man the hero, man the creator – it is equally so in its fantasising of woman: woman the nurturer, woman the companion, woman the procreator. Compassion and doubt are weaknesses to be overcome, hardness and certainty virtues to foster. Under the Nazis the words 'brutal' and 'fanatical' actually acquired positive connotations. The nation, as the sum of all its fascistised individuals, must behave like a warrior-male. It must be disciplined, proud, courageous, well-equipped and trained, ready to fight, bent on conquest, and supplied with the human means to do this by the reproductive and caring qualities of woman.[14]

What of the second component myth of fascism: rebirth? The myth of rebirth or 'palingenesis' belongs to a far more ancient metaphorical universe than 'nation'. It evokes the experience of decay and death as presaging a new life, a new creation. Within the palingenetic imagination destruction is a prelude to regeneration, the death of the purest is transformed into a meaningful sacrifice by becoming part of the epic phase of history which is unfolding. Once a theory of genetic or racial purity enters this vision of future greatness it becomes logical to winnow the grain and destroy the chaff so that only the wheat is left. Or as one Nazi ideologue put it as early as 1925:

> No pity is to be shown to those who occupy the lower categories of the inferior groups: cripples, epileptics, the blind, the insane, deaf and dumb, children born in sanatoria for alcoholics or in care, orphans, criminals, whores, the sexually disturbed etc. Everything done for them not only means taking resources away from more deserving causes, but counteracts the breeding selection process. . . . This bottom category means destruction and death. Weighed and found wanting. Trees which do not bear fruit should be cut down and thrown into the fire.[15]

The totalitarian nature of the fascist revolution

Fascism emerges when ultra-nationalism becomes fused with the myth of rebirth as a response to a society in distress, thus creating an ideology whose central vision is the purging of the old society of its decadence and the rejuvenation of the nation in a new order inhabited by a new type of human being, the fascist 'new man'. Some idea of the scope of this utopian vision can be sensed in the following declaration by Robert Ley, the head of the Nazi organisation, the German Workers' Front, taken from a speech he made in 1938:

> There is one thing we must understand if we are to comprehend the greatness of this time: we are not dealing with a new state system, or a new economic system. We are not dealing with anything external like the building up of the army, or the economy, – it comes down to the renewal of man, the individual man. Human beings are undergoing a transformation.
>
> Do you believe that an idea has ever achieved this ever before? The renewal of human beings manifests itself in the fact that this idea is actually able to transform the most intimate aspects of human lives. National Socialism has the power to free the German people, the individual German, from the damage inflicted on him which has been preventing him from performing his task. That is its ultimate, its greatest achievement.[16]

To carry out the 'renewal of man' in a nationalist spirit involved in practice the coordination of all aspects of social, economic, political, cultural
and mental life within an authoritarian state. The elimination of liberal
freedoms and socialist internationalism was thus for fascists part of a healing
process. This is why the Fascists *boasted* about having turned Italy into a
'totalitarian' society,[17] and 'the total state' was an equally positive term
for the Nazis.[18] The negative connotations which these terms have acquired
for political scientists when they consider the fascist (and communist) bids
to retool society stem from the horrendous human costs of their 'total-
ising' efforts. Any revolutionary myth which attempts to eradicate the
pluralism of modern society in pursuit of the utopia of a 'totally' coordinated
society must inevitably lead to a perverse travesty of that utopia. What
results is a dystopia (or 'bad' utopia) in which the destruction and inhumanity instituted by the state are justified by reference to the ultimate
goals it is seeking to realise: the creation of a new type of state inhabited
by a new type of man.

However, the totalitarian implications of fascism's attempt to realise its
utopia depend on the particular characteristics of each movement. This
is demonstrated by the fact that Fascist Italy was much less authoritarian
than Nazi Germany. Before it came to power Fascism which, unlike the
Nazi Party, had never developed a mass electoral following, was such a
fragile concept that Mussolini was forced to compromise his radicalism
extensively. He had few scruples in doing so because he was prepared to
chop and change particular declared beliefs to meet the demands of the
moment as long as he could pursue his ultimate objective of leading
the process of Italy's transformation.

Moreover, the alienation from the state and weak socialisation of most
Italians meant that the Fascist ideals of heroism and blind faith in the
leader could not be grafted easily on to the existing political culture. This
meant that huge concessions had to be made to conservative forces and
that any radical transformation of Italian social life was out of the question.
Furthermore, the country's technological and material resources were poor
compared to those of developed nations north of the Alps, so that the
build-up of the armed forces was slow and territorial ambitions had to be
restrained: the main outlet for Italy's imperialist ambitions before the
Second World War was Ethiopia, a feudal African state without a modern
army. Nor was Fascism more destructive or inhumane in its subjugation
of Ethiopia than some nineteenth-century 'liberal' powers had been (e.g.
Belgium) in bringing their colonies to heel.

It would also be wrong to assume that Fascism developed a terror apparatus on anything like the scale of Nazism. The main enemies identified
by the regime's ideology before the passing of anti-Semitic race laws in
1938 were stridently anti-Fascist liberals and communists, who with few
exceptions were either sent into internal exile in the rural south or imprisoned without recourse to torture or executions. In fact, until Fascism

became embroiled in Hitler's schemes for a new European order, it presided over less social violence than had occurred during the near civil war conditions which prevailed in liberal Italy between 1919 and 1921, and which allowed Mussolini's Blackshirts to become a major political force. In cultural matters, too, Fascism did little to censure artistic creativity or impose a particular style (though it kept a tight rein on the content of news reporting in the press, radio and cinema). Instead, it ensured that it was seen as the patron of all cultural production, whatever the style or content, just as it used propaganda to associate itself with all Italy's technological and sporting achievements whatever the politics of the inventor or athletes responsible.[19]

The Third Reich was an altogether different proposition. Its leaders were generally ruthless in pursuit of their interpretation of Nazi ideals. Its paramilitary formations numbered hundreds of thousands of 'fanatical' followers prepared to be 'brutal' for the good of the nation. It had at its disposal a highly modernised country of immense industrial and technological resources and, compared to Italy, an educated, socialised population. Its version of ultra-nationalism pursued the goal of racial health and hygiene based on a blend of a spurious science of 'eugenics' which identified as enemies to the purity of the national community whole categories of human beings from Jews (four to six million killed) and gypsies (over 750,000 killed) to homosexuals and the physically and mentally disabled, most of whom eventually fell victim to a programme of systematic extermination: over 320,000 ethnic Germans were sterilised and as many as 150,000 murdered in order to improve the racial health of the 'national community'. This is not to mention the many millions of Polish and Russian prisoners of war and civilians who were enslaved or killed as embodiments of racial inferiority.

Meanwhile, Nazism's crusade against spiritual decadence ultimately extended beyond the persecution of ideological enemies such as Communists, Freemasons, and radical Christians such as Jehovah Witnesses, to the attempted destruction of all forms of art held to be subverting 'German values' and dismissed as 'cultural Bolshevism'. By this was meant all literature and painting which did not directly evoke Nazi ideology in an immediately recognisable way. As a result, Germany witnessed the wholesale elimination of what is known to art historians as 'modernism', along with experimental music and the products of 'racially inferior' cultures. This led to the banning of all art, literature and music by Jews, as well as the outlawing of jazz (because it was identified with Negroes). So popular was swing-jazz, however, that the directors of Nazi propaganda commissioned versions to be made of American hits sung with lyrics specially written to foster racial hatred and ridicule the enemy.

Nazi foreign policy was also vastly more ambitious and destructive than Italy's. It involved incorporating vast areas of Europe within an empire based on racial principles and the wholesale exploitation of its human, material and cultural resources for the exclusive benefit of the Greater Germany. No wonder Nazism's bid to realise its fantasies of a new order led to war, inhumanity, mass slavery, mass murder and attempted genocide on an unprecedented scale using all the material and logistical resources of the modern state.

The fascist 'permanent revolution'

The radical destructiveness implicit in the Nazi utopia was compounded by features intrinsic to fascist ideology as a whole. All revolutions are by definition destructive, and prepared, even if only in the 'transitional period', to prioritise one segment of humanity over all others which are holding back 'progress'. The liberal revolution necessitates the destruction of a feudal or communist *ancien régime*. The communist revolution in theory requires the destruction of bourgeois capitalism, and in practice has led to mass murder and terror on a vast scale in many of its national variants, for example, in Russia under Stalin, in China under Mao Tse-tung, or in Cambodia under Pol-Pot. Even the Velvet Revolutions of 1989 in Poland and Czechoslovakia destroyed a Soviet colonial system which had brought to many ordinary citizens some measure of stability, material security and social peace, all of which were quickly eradicated by the wild capitalism that ensued.

Where the fascist revolution differs significantly from liberal (bourgeois) and Marxist revolutions is that in theory these, though carried out locally, aimed to establish bridgeheads in the territorial battle against the 'old order' in a process which would one day bring benefits to humanity on a global scale. One of these benefits was to be international peace. Certainly there was talk in the interwar period of a 'universal' fascism and a number of attempts at forging international linkages with like-minded movements, linkages which post-1945 fascism has continued to cultivate and which have become truly global in the 1990s with the advent of the Internet. Moreover, both the Fascists and the Nazis saw themselves as saving not just their nation from decadence, but 'civilisation' as a whole. Nevertheless, the main focus of fascism has always been the 'home' nation, not 'humanity', and its revolution in that sense is a highly sectional one. It was Italians whom Fascists wanted to revitalise by reawakening in them the heroic qualities of the Ancient Romans, while the Nazis resorted to the most extreme measures imaginable in order to weld all healthy ethnic Germans into a unified national community, or *Volksgemeinschaft*.

Another important difference lies in the fact that, unlike the liberal or Marxist, the fascist cannot envisage a 'steady state' of society which has reached a point of social equilibrium and calm. To a fascist, stasis means not a welcome stability, but stagnation, entropy and death. Fascism is thus driven to perpetuate the dynamism of the revolutionary moment that brought it to power, to create the conditions of 'permanent revolution'.

A radical, eugenically fixated fascist regime such as the one which the Nazis actually installed (and others such as the Romanian Iron Guard or contemporary American neo-Nazis have only been able to dream of establishing) is forced by its own logic to preside over a constant process of creation and destruction: the establishment of the 'new state' must be accompanied by destroying or coordinating the old system.

For the fascist revolutionary, then, destruction of enemies is thus neither nihilistic nor inhuman, but an integral aspect of a permanent revolution. The principle which logically follows from the mythic premises of his worldview is one of destroying to build, or what one fascist thinker has called 'creative nihilism'.[20] The fascist transforms or (in the case of Nazism) surgically removes the 'unhealthy' elements of the nation so that it can be regenerated, prunes the national tree of its dead branches and excess foliage so that it can grow better, and preserves at least his segment of humanity from the ravages of decadence and the threat of being 'swamped' by 'inferior' cultures and races so that civilisation can be saved.

Fascism as a temporal revolution

The palingenetic logic of death and rebirth which underlies the fascist revolution is not rational. It is ritual. No matter how modern the bureaucratic, logistical and technological dimensions of the Holocaust, the psychological drive behind it was steeped in the ritual of purification and sacrifice: the impure had to be destroyed so that the nation might be rejuvenated, the pure had to be prepared to die so that Germany might live. The ritual dimension of fascism expresses itself most clearly in the central role played in both the Fascist and Nazi regimes by political liturgy, their 'religious' style of politics.

In practice, liberal and communist regimes have had constant recourse to the political liturgy, for example, the American primaries filled with coloured balloons or the vast Soviet May Day parades in Red Square, but inter-war fascism consciously made such rituals central to its concept of revolution. The 'oceanic assemblies' staged by Fascism whenever Mussolini spoke in public, the torchlight parades and mass rallies held at Nazi party congresses, the saturation of public space with the symbols of the regime (the fasces, the swastika), as well as the crucial role played by the leader cult, the urge to create monumental architecture, and the constant recourse to rhetoric and spectacle in both regimes, were too conspicuous not to be noticed by commentators at the time. Thus the French Ambassador to Germany witnessed the extraordinary impact which the 1937 Nuremberg Rally had on the crowds, commenting:

> The atmosphere of general enthusiasm into which the old city has been plunged is amazing and quite indescribable: the peculiar frenzy which has gripped hundreds of thousands of men and women, the romantic excitement and mystic ecstasy which has overtaken them like

a holy rapture. An effect is produced which many find irresistible. They return home seduced and taken in, ready to serve the cause, with no idea of the dangerous reality which is concealed beneath the deceptive pomp of the huge processions and parades.[21]

While modern society may have lost its unifying beliefs and rituals, there is every indication that the human beings living in it have still not become totally secularised. In particular they tend to feel deeply threatened when familiar social systems break down, not only because of the material insecurity and hardship which face them. At this point they can be gripped by what one major expert in comparative religion has called 'the terror of history'.[22] In such circumstances a new ideology, a new political, social or religious movement can offer a new framework to their lives which provides a diagnosis of the cause of the chaos, and restores a sense of effectiveness, belonging and future.

According to this line of analysis the acute social and political instability which affected Italy in the years immediately following the First World War and the collapse of Germany's Weimar Republic after 1929 created conditions in which the ritual style of politics used by both Fascism and Nazism generated a sense of enthusiasm which no conventional party could inspire in its followers, and went on to play a crucial role in the regimes which they formed in creating a sense of collective euphoria and belonging. Fascism operated as a substitute religion. What converted millions to this religion was not their reason, but rather the subjective sensation of being lifted out of a chaotic, distressing period of history into a new era imbued with a sense of harmony and destiny.

The irrational, mythic component so central to fascism should not be confused with anti-modernity. The apparent obsession which both regimes had with the past (the Roman Empire in the case of Fascism and the Aryan and Germanic past in the case of Nazism) stems from the desire, not to regress to the past, but to reawaken the *eternal* qualities of the race. Fascism was thus not *anti-modern*: it attempted to create an *alternative* modernity. Neither was it anti-capitalist in the sense of being in principle opposed to private property and privately owned business. However, contrary to what Marxists assume, fascists were radically opposed to the individualist and materialist spirit or *ethos* of capitalism, especially international capitalism. They wanted to replace it by a pervasive sense of loyalty to the nation that would imbue people's lives with a spiritual quality which they held was lacking in a consumerist society.

Fascism's objective revolution

The stress I have placed on the subjective dimension of the Fascist Revolution should not, however, detract attention from the changes which both regimes sought to bring about in external reality. For example, while neither the Fascist nor Nazi state wanted to abolish capitalist economics and private property, they had no scruples about involving themselves with the economy on a scale unprecedented in any liberal state except in wartime, whether through the corporative system as in Italy, or through cartelisation and huge state industries as in Germany. In the build-up to the Second World War both regimes also pursued the goal of self-sufficiency (autarky), the Nazis to the point of creating a vast European empire whose material and human resources (i.e. foreign workers and concentration camp inmates by the million) were ruthlessly exploited for the good of the Third Reich. When large industrial firms such as Krupp, Daimler Benz or IG Farben made high-tech products with slave labour it was hardly business as usual for capitalism.

Both regimes also indulged in a massive programme of social engineering which involved creating mass organisations for every social grouping, retooling the educational system, symbolically appropriating all aspects of leisure, sport, culture and technology, whether by associating them with the genius of the new state (as in Italy) or through enforced coordination and social control (as in Germany). The goal common to both regimes, however, was to create a thoroughly fascistised cultural habitat in which a new type of human being, the fascist 'new man' (and woman), would spontaneously emerge, instinctively and joyfully prepared to devote all their talents, idealism and energy to the cause of the nation. Vast public works such as the building of motorways and (in Italy) the draining of marshes, the Nazi plans to rebuild the centre of Berlin on a monumental scale and rename the city 'Germania', the radical overhaul of the educational system to mass-produce Fascist or Nazi values: these were hardly symptoms of a purely 'subjective' revolution. It was the sheer scale on which both regimes were prepared to mobilise the nation's human and physical resources to pursue their territorial claims on Europe, and the horrifying extent to which the Nazis carried out their scheme to create a racially pure and healthy Third Reich, which is the most eloquent testimony to the revolutionary dynamic of fascism.

Fascism was not just a revolution of values, an attempt to make a clean break with the liberal, humanist and eventually Christian traditions, but a concerted effort to deploy the unprecedented capacity of the modern state for social engineering to bring about a fundamental transformation in the way society was going to be run and every one of its inhabitants was going to live. It took a massive effort by the British, the Americans and the Russians to create a military machine sufficiently powerful to prevent the Nazis from turning even more of their utopian fantasies into grim reality.

Conclusion

Within the conceptual framework that we constructed at the outset, fascism has revealed itself to be a radical form of 'revolution from the Right' with a highly specific ideological dynamic. Not only did the two inter-war regimes based on it self-consciously attempt to create an alternative modernity which harnessed the power of a supercharged nationalism, but they deliberately operated with a ritual style of politics aimed at providing a new sense of collective belonging and meaning for populations disoriented by a profound social crisis. They aimed to produce a new type of human being, a new type of state, a new era.

This interpretation of fascism may conflict with conventional wisdom on the subject, but it is fully consistent with the conclusions which G.L. Mosse, one of the world's foremost specialists on Nazism, has drawn after more than four decades of studying the dynamics of fascism. When, in 1997, he reviewed the progress which scholars have made in understanding fascism since the war, he commented that the idea of:

> fascism as a revolution has been one of the most difficult of all the so-called revisionist theses to accept, for fascism has usually been characterised as reactionary and backward looking. Whether we accept or deny its origins in the French Revolution, fascism wanted to create new men. This was intended as a cultural and social, but not an economic revolution.[23]

Mosse went on to ascribe this blind spot to the 'amazing' extent to which models of revolution based on Marxism and on the liberalism of the French Revolution still dominate academic thinking. Once such prejudices are overcome, it becomes obvious that, though the following passage taken from a speech by Goebbels is by its nature a piece of propaganda, it is simultaneously the expression of a deep conviction: the conviction that under Hitler Germans (those deemed 'capable of community', that is) were living through a revolutionary new era.

> The revolution we have carried out is a total one. It has embraced all areas of public life and transformed them from below. It has completely changed and recast the relationship of people to each other, to the state, and to life itself. The revolution was in fact the breakthrough of a fresh world-view, which had fought for power in opposition fourteen years to provide the basis for the German people to develop a new relationship with the state. What has been happening since 30 January[24] is only the visible expression of this revolutionary process. The revolution did not begin here. It was only carried through to its final conclusion. At bottom it is the struggle for existence of a people which, left to its old forms of cultural life and played out values, was otherwise due to collapse. . . .
>
> The German people, once the most fragmented in the world, atomised into its component parts and hence condemned to impotence as a world power, and ever since 1918 lacking the arms, and, what is

worse, the will to assert its rights before other nations, has risen up in a unique demonstration of its sense of national strength.[25]

Notes

1 Ernest Bloch, 'Inventory of a revolutionary façade', in *The Heritage of our Time*, Cambridge, 1991, p. 64.
2 R. Palme Dutt, *Facism and Social Revolution*, London, 1933, p. 225.
3 Hermann Rauschning, *Germany's Revolution of Destruction*, London, 1939; the title of the US edition was *The Revolution of Nihilism*, New York, 1939.
4 Robert Soucy, 'Drieu la Rochelle and the modernist anti-modernism in French fascism', *Modern Language Notes*, vol. 95, no. 4, 1980.
5 Jeffrey Herf, *Reactionary Modernism*, London, 1984.
6 Eugen Weber, 'Revolution? Counter-revolution? What revolution?', in Walter Laqueur (ed.), *Facism: A Reader's Guide*, Harmondsworth, 1976, p. 509.
7 For further elaboration of the concept ideal type see Roger Griffin, *The Nature of Fascism*, London, 1993, pp. 8–12.
8 For a fuller account of this definition see Roger Griffin, *International Fascism*, London, 1998, p. 14.
9 Benito Mussolini, Il Discorso di Napoli [The Naples speech], 24 October 1922, *Il Popolo d'Italia*, No. 255, 25 October, 1922, *Omnia Opera di Benito Mussolini*, ibid., XVIII, pp. 453–58, in Roger Griffin, *Fascism*, Oxford, 1995, pp. 43–4.
10 Jeffrey Schnapp, 'Epic demonstrations: Fascist Modernity and the 1932 Exhibition of the Fascist Revolution', in Richard Golsan (ed.), *Fascism, Aesthetics, and Culture*, New Hampshire, 1992.
11 See Griffin, *The Nature of Fascism*, ch. 5, for an overview of interwar European authoritarianism in the light of these distinctions.
12 A convincing account of these common denominators has been given by Alexander de Grand in his *Fascist Italy and Nazi Germany. The 'Fascist' style of Rule*, London, 1995.
13 Cited in Griffin, *Fascism*, pp. 37–8.
14 For the misogynist (women-hating) dimension of fascism see Klaus Theweleit, *Male Fantasies*, Cambridge, 1989 (2 vols).
15 Cited in Griffin, *Fascism*, pp. 118–19.
16 Ibid., pp. 142–3.
17 Ibid., pp. 52–3.
18 Ibid., pp. 138–9.
19 See Marla Stone, 'The state as patron', in Matthew Affron and Mark Antliff, *Fascist Visions*, Princeton, NJ, 1997, pp. 205–38.
20 See Griffin, *Fascism*, pp. 351–4.
21 Quoted in Guido Knopp, *Hitler. Eine Bilanz*, Berlin, 1995, pp. 82–3.
22 Mircea Eliade, *The Myth of Eternal Return*, Princeton, NJ, 1971 (1st edn 1949).
23 G.L. Mosse, 'Renzo de Felice e il revisionismo storico', *Nuova Antologia*, vol. 133, 1988, p. 182.
24 i.e. 30 January 1933, when Hitler became Reich Chancellor.
25 Reproduced in Griffin, *Fascism*, p. 134.

Further reading

Alexander de Grand, *Fascist Italy and Nazi Germany. The 'Fascist' Style of Rule*, London, 1995.

Emilio Gentile, *The Sacralization of the State in Fascist Italy*, Cambridge, MA, 1996.

Roger Griffin, *The Nature of Fascism*, London, 1993.

Roger Griffin, *Fascism*, Oxford, 1995.

Stanley Payne, *A History of Fascism, 1914–45*, London, 1995.

Eugen Weber, 'Revolution? Counter-revolution? What revolution?', in Walter Laqueur (ed.), *Fascism: A Reader's Guide*, Harmondsworth, 1976.

12 The anti-Communist revolutions in the Soviet Union and Eastern Europe, 1989 to 1991

Robert V. Daniels

The collapse of Communism and the nature of revolution

Two unforgettable images bracket perceptions of the revolutionary fall of Communism: the opening of the Berlin Wall in November 1989, and Boris Yeltsin standing on a tank in Moscow to defy the hardline *coup* plotters of August 1991. Between and around these landmark events swirled a storm of defiance and rebellion that brought about one of the most spectacular developments of the twentieth century, when the old political order in the Soviet Union and its bloc of East European satellite countries came to an end. By many standards – the break in governmental continuity, the depth of change, the reversal in dominant public attitudes – this movement was one of the great revolutions of history, as its protagonists, including Soviet General Secretary Mikhail Gorbachev, believed. Yet there are peculiarities about this upheaval – the lack of violence in most places, the centrality of national independence, and the targeting of the Soviet system that was itself the product of revolution in 1917 – that raise the question whether it was a true revolution.

It is important to understand what the Soviet and East European anti-Communist revolutions were actually contending against. 'Communism' is often construed as the revolutionary doctrine of Karl Marx, implemented in Russia by Vladimir Lenin to begin a seventy-year 'utopian experiment' that ultimately 'failed'. In reality, the old regime preceding the revolutions of 1989 to 1991 was no longer an experiment, but a post-revolutionary, imperialist dictatorship dressed up in the language of Marxist ideology.

In any case, the events of 1989 to 1991 still invite analysis in the framework of the comparative history of revolution, following as they did the classic Russian revolutionary upheaval of 1917 to 1921, the pragmatic consolidation of the New Economic Policy in the 1920s, and a protracted post-revolutionary dictatorship, ushered in by Stalin's 'revolution from above' of the early 1930s and marked by imperialist expansion after the Second World War. Stalin's 'Great Retreat' back to conservative social and cultural norms in the mid-1930s, along with his purge of most of the old revolutionaries, could be considered as the functional equivalent of a monarchical restoration. Ultimately, the Stalinist post-revolutionary dictatorship gave way to a revival of the original revolutionary spirit, in a less violent and more democratic form.

This final phase of the revolutionary process, a moderate revolutionary revival, so to speak, is the setting in which the crisis of Communism can best be understood. Corresponding events resolving the revolutionary process were the Glorious Revolution of 1688 in England and the Revolution of 1830 in France, each overthrowing a restored version of the old regime and reinstating the principles of the early, moderate phase of the original revolution. In the Soviet case, return to the moderate revolution began in 1985 with *perestroika*, the attempt under Gorbachev at reform or 'restructuring' of the old system, and culminated in its complete repudiation at the hands of Yeltsin.

Ever since Stalin consolidated his post-revolutionary dictatorship into a form of nationalistic 'barracks socialism', the Soviet regime had rigidly suppressed any dissent or representation of competing social interests, both at home and in the countries of Eastern Europe under its domination. At the same time, pursuing modernisation and industrialisation as the basis of military power, Soviet rule was generating an urbanised and sophisticated populace and a revolution of rising expectations that could not be contained indefinitely by lifeless propaganda and tired coercion. Like the old regime leading up to every classic revolution, the ageing Soviet system sowed the seeds of its own destruction. Actual collapse only awaited some kind of shock such as the leadership succession difficulties of 1982 to 1985 provided.

The moderate revolutionary revival is not, of course, foreordained in any particular form. In the terminology of the European political tradition, Gorbachev's reform efforts from 1985 to 1991 represented a Left variant. Yeltsin's personal rule from 1991 to 1998 represented a Right variant. He repudiated everything associated with the Communist Revolution, and found his models, politically in the semi-reformed Tsarist regime that followed the Revolution of 1905, and economically in the anti-socialist, free-market theory favoured in the United States and Great Britain. This variant came to grief in the economic crisis of 1998, leaving Russia to work out its destiny, perhaps through democratic evolution, perhaps in a return to authoritarianism, perhaps in a new revolutionary cycle such as the one which interrupted the moderate revolutionary revival in France in 1848.

A special dimension that the anti-Communist revolutions shared with some of their predecessors was decolonisation. This was a feature of the revolutionary process in France, when Napoleon's empire collapsed between 1813 and 1814, and of the Russian Revolution in 1917, when the national minorities of the empire took advantage of turmoil at the centre to declare independence, temporary for some peoples, longer term for others. Similarly, the moderate revolutionary revival in the Soviet Union meant a widening opportunity for the Communist-ruled satellite countries in Eastern Europe to assert their independence, and then for the non-Russian minorities of the Soviet Union – half the country – to press once again for independence *vis-à-vis* this reincarnation of the Russian Empire.

The Soviet old regime

The old regime leading up to the upheaval of 1985 to 1991 was unusual in being itself the outcome of a revolution. However, it represented only the later, post-revolutionary phase of the process, a form of totalitarianism more severe for its own people than even the Nazi version. Tested by victory in the Second World War, the Stalinist system survived its founder's death in 1953, a brief succession struggle, sometimes disruptive reforms including the superficial 'de-Stalinisation' undertaken by Nikita Khrushchev between 1956 and 1964, and the reassertion of political stability and military priorities – 'neo-Stalinism' – under Leonid Brezhnev from 1964 until his death in 1982.

Economic progress in the Brezhnev era was accompanied by most of the indicators of modernisation. Becoming preponderantly urban, the Soviet Union developed a strong scientific establishment with the attainment of universal secondary education, saw the growth of a large middle class of professionals and white-collar workers, and underwent a revolution of rising expectations among all strata of the population. The country began to experience the classic pre-revolutionary condition of 'cramp', as an advancing society was frustrated by economic shortfalls and a political regime of ageing bureaucrats, who operated through the control structure of the Communist Party and the secret police and were unwilling to accommodate the new forces that their system had engendered.

Brezhnev's demise at a decrepit 77 opened the way to the determined if not much younger Yuri Andropov, a Politburo member and former head of the secret police who promised to tighten up the now creaky and corrupt machinery of the Soviet government and economy. As it turned out, Andropov was already terminally ill, and upon his death in February 1984 the office of general secretary passed to the doddering conservative Konstantin Chernenko. *De facto*, Chernenko shared his leadership role with the vigorous Gorbachev, the youngest member of the Politburo, who had worked his way up through the party apparatus with only the slightest intimation of the changes he was about to introduce. Chernenko lasted barely a year, and upon his death the party conservatives attempted to block a takeover by Gorbachev, failing by a scant four to five vote in the Politburo. Gorbachev thereupon stepped into the place of his stodgy predecessors with a vision of radical reform. Thus was born the programme of *perestroika*, and with it the beginning of the end of Communism.

The Soviet Empire

The old regime in the form of the Soviet Union held sway not just over a country but over an empire, embracing two great bands of subject peoples. One was the inner empire inherited from Tsarist days, combining Russians and a host of minority nationalities. This was the Soviet Union proper, the empire that broke apart in 1991. The other band was the outer empire, consisting of the countries of Eastern Europe that fell under Soviet domination immediately after the Second World War. Technically they remained independent states, though they were ruled by Communist dictatorships subservient to the Soviets. This was the region of anti-Communist revolution in 1989.

The origins of the Soviet Empire go back to the two world wars, the collapse of Tsarism, and the brief European hegemony of Nazi Germany. Russia had already become a multinational empire in the Tsarist era, through its gradual expansion over the centuries. Defeat in the First World War created the opportunity for the first great wave of decolonisation of the empire's minority nationalities. The peace treaty of Brest-Litovsk that the new Soviet government was forced to sign in March 1918 granted independence to the Ukraine and to the three Transcaucasian states of Georgia, Armenia and Azerbaidzhan. Poland and the Baltic states of Estonia, Latvia and Lithuania, occupied by Germany during the war, got their chance to declare independence after the Armistice in November 1918. Finland was granted independence by the new Soviet government in the mistaken expectation that it would join the cause of revolution.

The fates of these newly created countries were quite different. Poland, Finland and the Baltic States, supported by the Western powers, successfully maintained their independence throughout the interwar period. By contrast, the Ukraine and the Transcaucasian republics were forcibly Sovietised by the Red Army in the course of its victorious civil war against the 'White' counter-revolutionaries, and were then combined with Soviet Russia (along with Belorussia, carved out of Russian territory) in a federal union. This was the Union of Soviet Socialist Republics, put into effect in 1924 under the firm central control of the Communist Party. Additional Soviet republics – Kazakhstan, Kirgizia, Uzbekistan, Turkmenia and Tadzhikistan – were set up in territory that Russia had conquered during the nineteenth century.

Beyond this, actual expansion by the Soviet Union had to await the circumstances of the Second World War, by which time the Soviet Union under Stalin had become more reactionary than revolutionary – like France under Napoleon. In 1939 to 1940, pursuant to his non-aggression pact with Hitler, Stalin moved into most of the territory that Russia had lost in 1918: eastern Poland, south-eastern Finland, the three Baltic states and the region of Bessarabia (lost to Romania in 1918, annexed to the USSR as the Moldavian Soviet Republic). Thus, in the form of fourteen 'union republics' joined with the Russian Republic in the USSR, was the inner empire of Soviet rule established in the framework that would continue right up to the collapse of 1991.

The creation of the Communist outer empire was the direct consequence of Nazi Germany's brief domination of Eastern Europe before and during the Second World War. Driving the German forces back in 1944 to 1945, the Red Army occupied Hitler's satellite allies Romania, Bulgaria and Hungary, as well as his victims Poland and Czechoslovakia, and finally took over the eastern portion of Germany itself. Hardly was the war over when Stalin proceeded to cement Soviet control over the newly occupied region beyond his borders by inserting local Communists into nominally coalition governments. It was then an easy process to establish total Communist dictatorship everywhere in the Soviet sphere, usually by salami tactics – outlawing anti-Communist opposition elements one slice at a time. A special case was Czechoslovakia, where the Communists abruptly ousted a coalition government and seized power in the *coup* of February 1948, a turning point in the escalation of Cold War tension between East and West.

The Communist revolutions thus carried out in Eastern Europe were highly artificial, imposed from above at Moscow's behest and conforming to the Soviet model not only politically but economically and culturally as well. 'National Communists' who wanted revolution but not Soviet dictation, and found themselves out of phase with post-revolutionary Russian imperialism, were purged and replaced by more pliant tools of Moscow. The outer empire of satellite countries was then geared into the Soviet sphere, economically by Comecon (Council of Mutual Economic Assistance, 1949) and militarily by the Warsaw Pact (1955).

The one striking exception to this pattern was Yugoslavia, where the Communist guerrillas of the Second World War – Josip Broz Tito's Partisans – came to power on their own. Tito established the most genuine and militant of the East European revolutionary regimes, only to break with the Soviet Union in 1948 when Stalin attempted to bring him to heel as he had the other Communists of the region. Tiny Albania came under Communist rule as a Yugoslav satellite, then broke with Belgrade and independently found protection, first under the Soviet wing and then with Communist China.

None of the countries of the outer empire (except Bulgaria) accepted Stalinist domination without restiveness and crises. Trouble tended to follow changes of leadership or reform efforts within the Soviet Union itself. Shortly after Stalin's death in 1953, East German workers vainly rose up against the puppet government – the 'German Democratic Republic' – implanted by the Soviet occupation. In response to Khrushchev's de-Stalinisation campaign, Poland defied Moscow and reinstated the purged National Communist leader Władysław Gomułka to curb the excesses of Communism against the Church, the peasants and small businesses; though

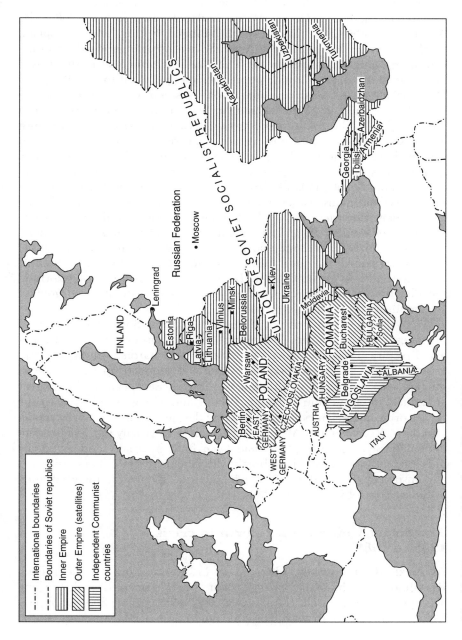

Map 12.1 Europe and the Soviet Union 1985

Gomułka subsequently pulled back from political reform, Poland remained the least Communised of the bloc countries. Hungary rebelled simultaneously, installed the reformist Communist Imre Nagy as leader, and attempted to quit the Warsaw Pact, only to be crushed by armed Soviet intervention. After the fall of Khrushchev in 1964, a reform movement gathered momentum in Czechoslovakia and took power early in 1968 under Alexander Dubček, to introduce the Prague Spring and its slogan, 'Socialism with a Human Face'. Again Soviet forces intervened, this time without meeting armed resistance. The Czech reformers were suppressed in favour of an abject hardline puppet regime, pursuant to the 'Brezhnev Doctrine' allowing no satellite country to fall away from Soviet-style 'socialism'. Romania under the megalomaniac dictator Nicolae Çeauşescu took a different path in the 1960s, manoeuvring between the feuding Communist giants Russia and China to assert its independence in foreign policy but without internal reform. Hardline Albania became ardently pro-Chinese, until the post-Mao Tse-tung reforms in China left it no sun to revolve around at all. Finally, Poland stirred once again in the late 1970s, with turmoil in its Communist leadership and the rise of the independent Solidarity trade union movement led by Lech Walesa. Under the threat of Soviet military intervention, Poland's Communist chief of the moment, General Wojciech Jaruzelski, declared martial law and put Solidarity down, but the country remained the most restive of the satellites. In the meantime, Hungary under its post-1956 chief János Kádár allowed gradual reform in the direction of intellectual freedom and market economics – 'goulash Communism', as it came to be known.

When the succession crisis of 1982 to 1985 in the Soviet Union opened the gates to deeper reform, Communist Eastern Europe presented a variegated picture. Pro-Soviet governments that were hardline internally were East Germany and Czechoslovakia, both still propped up by the Soviet military, plus Bulgaria, which alone of the East European satellites never attempted to stray from the fold. Poland and Hungary adhered to the Soviet orbit in foreign policy but already deviated from the Soviet model internally. Romania and Albania were Stalinist internally but independent diplomatically, and Yugoslavia had been both internally and externally independent ever since Tito's break with Stalin in 1948. These different circumstances governed the way each country responded to the weakening of Soviet control in the late 1980s.

The Soviet Union from reform to crisis, 1985 to 1989

As Alexis de Tocqueville observed in his classic work on the French Revolution, revolutionary change often begins when the old regime attempts to reform itself. So it was in the Soviet Union and its empire, when Gorbachev narrowly won the post of General Secretary of the

Communist Party of the Soviet Union in March 1985. Gorbachev knew that the system had to change: 'When I found myself at the helm of this state,' he recalled at the time of his resignation in December 1991,

> it already was clear that something was wrong in this country. . . . We were living much worse than people in the industrialised countries were living and we were increasingly lagging behind them. The reason was obvious even then. This country was suffocating in the shackles of the bureaucratic command system. Doomed to cater to ideology and . . . the onerous burden of the arms race, it found itself at the breaking point.

But his plans for reform were as yet vague, and only took shape step by step as his problems and challenges multiplied. The question remained how much reform was possible within the framework of the old system, and when cumulative reform might cause it to break down altogether. The ultimate outcome surprised Gorbachev as much as anyone.

Gorbachev's first steps were unremarkable: a resumption of Andropov's efforts to restore discipline and efficiency in the system, with campaigns against corruption and alcoholism and for economic 'acceleration'. At the same time he launched a sweeping renovation of the Soviet leadership; in his first year, he used his appointment authority to replace over 20 per cent of the 319 functionaries with seats on the party's Central Committee, and ousted all four of the Politburo members who had voted against him. One of the replacements he made proved to have fateful consequences: the appointment of the provincial party official Boris Yeltsin as boss of the city of Moscow, with the mission of cleaning up its notorious corruption.

The momentum of reform picked up in 1986 after the Chernobyl nuclear power plant disaster. Rejecting Soviet habits of secrecy and cover-up, Gorbachev proclaimed the principle of *glasnost* – openness or transparency – and appealed to the intelligentsia (a first for any Russian government) to back his reforms: 'Society is ripe for a changeover. . . . We have to make the process irreversible.' Censorship was eased, history and ideology were opened to controversy for the first time in decades, and the media came alive. 'I would equate the word restructuring with the word revolution,' Gorbachev declared. The popular reaction? 'We can breath now.'

In January 1987, after freeing Russia's best-known democratic dissident, the physicist Andrei Sakharov, from internal exile, Gorbachev began efforts to democratise the Communist Party organisation. He followed this with legislation to loosen central economic planning and allow small-scale private enterprise in the guise of 'cooperatives'. 'Informal organisations' sprang up all over the country to debate politics and press for further democratisation. But a reaction among political die-hard party officials led by Politburo member Yegor Ligachev was not long in coming. They targeted Yeltsin and blocked his logical promotion to the Politburo in June

1987, whereupon he denounced the whole leadership including Gorbachev for dragging their feet on reform. In response, Gorbachev humiliated Yeltsin and ousted him from his Moscow job, though he did not liquidate him or even arrest him in old Soviet style. Thus was born the personal feud between Yeltsin and Gorbachev that was to have a critical impact on the subsequent unfolding of reform in Russia.

Gorbachev and his supporters felt they had to tread carefully in dealing with the conservative party officialdom, for they recalled how the chiefs of the apparatus had been able to topple Khrushchev when his reforms went too far for their taste. The General Secretary decided to remake the base of his power, by shifting it from the party organisation to the regular structure of government that had been manipulated by the party ever since Lenin's time. To this end he executed a virtual *coup d'état*, the 'September Revolution' of 1988, shaking up the party leadership and removing even the Politburo members who had voted *for* him in 1985; downgrading the Secretariat that had controlled the party organisation and all key appointments (the *nomenklatura*); and instituting a new constitutional arrangement with himself as president and the promise of democratic elections. The elections – partially free though defective in many places – duly took place in March 1989 to choose a new Congress of People's Deputies of 2250 members, who in turn selected from among their own numbers a new Supreme Soviet of 542 that would really legislate.

In its political impact, the election of the new Congress was equivalent to the convocation of the Estates General at the outset of the French Revolution. For the first time in living memory, Soviet citizens were witness to free electoral campaigning and parliamentary debate. One revealing measure of the reality of reform was Yeltsin's political comeback as a Moscow deputy and leader of the rapidly crystallising opposition to Gorbachev from the democratic side. In the words of the American journalist Robert Kaiser, 'Gorbachev . . . had started a revolution he could not control'.

By 1989, undoing Stalinist totalitarianism and the command economy, Gorbachev was leading the Soviet Union back through its history to find new reference points in the earlier phases of the Revolution. He took the mixed economy of the 1920s as a model, though he clung to the 'socialist choice' of the October Revolution. In politics he called into question Lenin's principles of Communist Party dictatorship and centralism. By these steps Gorbachev was accomplishing the moderate revolutionary revival, in its Left variant, to be sure, but he was making a return to the Stalinist post-revolutionary dictatorship difficult if not impossible.

Revolutionary decolonisation, I: Eastern Europe, 1989

The most spectacular immediate consequence of Gorbachev's attempt to reform the Soviet system occurred in Moscow's outer empire. Over a span of barely six months, the system of Communist rule that the Soviets had maintained in Eastern Europe for more than forty years abruptly collapsed. In a chain reaction of popular protest and Communist surrender, Soviet-dominated governments gave way to democratic national movements in Poland, Hungary, East Germany and Czechoslovakia, while in Romania a violent uprising swept the Çeauşescu dictatorship away. As in Napoleon's realm, once the aura of superpower omnipotence had been dissipated, no force could keep the post-revolutionary empire together.

Reform in the Soviet Union had often been the signal for ferment in individual East European countries. This time, however, Soviet reform was far more profound, and the ferment seized the whole of Eastern Europe almost simultaneously. In loosening the heavy hand of dictatorship over Soviet society, Gorbachev not only opened the way for opposition movements in his own country, but also signalled his unwillingness to coerce the satellites any longer.

Democratisation in the Soviet Union divided and disoriented Soviet clients abroad. Governments that had already allowed some internal reform – Poland and Hungary – welcomed *perestroika* as vindication of their own policies. Hardline governments that had depended on the Soviet military presence – Czechoslovakia and East Germany – sided nervously with the Communist conservatives in Moscow. Independent but hardline Romania held out to the last. Docile Bulgaria fell into line pro forma.

Poland, the most populous of the satellite states, and the most obstreperous, was where Communist authority first began to sag. With its private business and agricultural sectors and the powerful Catholic Church, Poland had already departed further from the Soviet totalitarian model than any other East European country. A newer element of pluralism was the Solidarity labour movement, held down but not crushed by the martial law that President Jaruzelski imposed in 1981. Solidarity was encouraged by the winds of change out of Moscow to come into the open again, call a wave of strikes, and demand the country's democratisation. Jaruzelski's government yielded, realising that there was no longer a possibility of Soviet intervention, and early in 1989 it entered into a series of roundtable talks with the opposition. Out of these negotiations came an agreement in April 1989 to end the dictatorship of the Communist Party (the so-called Polish United Workers' Party), and to hold free elections for one-third of the lower house of Parliament and for all of a newly created upper house. Solidarity swept the field, winning all but one seat of those at stake. The Communists' front organisations, the Peasant Party and the Democratic Party, came to life and defected, and the Communist Party could no longer control a parliamentary majority. Thereupon, in August, Jaruzelski dropped his Communist prime minister and designated the Solidarity lawyer Tadeusz Mazowiecki to head Poland's first real coalition government since the Communist takeover in Stalin's time. The Communists had lost their will to rule, and the anti-Communist revolution prevailed without a shot being fired or a law broken.

Hungary, like Poland, ushered its Communist dictatorship out without any very revolutionary revolution. The key change was a shift of power in 1988 inside Hungary's counterpart Communist Party, the Hungarian Socialist Workers' Party, when reformers of the Gorbachev stripe ousted General Secretary Kádár and legalised political opposition. In 1989 the new leadership entered into a series of 'trilateral political coordinated talks' with the trade unions and the non-Communist parties, a process much like that in Poland. Concluding an agreement with the opposition in September 1989, the reform Communists committed themselves to 'a peaceful and gradual transition to democratic socialism' through 'a constitutional structure based on a multi-party system'. To make good their promise of democratic freedoms, the government lifted restrictions on foreign travel, with immediate repercussions in East Germany.

East Germany, the rump of a divided country symbolised by the Berlin Wall, experienced the most dramatic collapse of the old regime anywhere in Eastern Europe. This was truly a revolution though still a non-violent one. Here, not only was the hardline Communist regime at stake, but the very existence of this artificial state, created by the Soviets, which could only survive by literally walling its citizens off from escape to West Germany. Thus a critical breach was created when the reforming Hungarian government opened its borders, allowing East Germans who transited Czechoslovakia to flee in their thousands through Hungary to Austria and West Germany. Simultaneously, a new democratic opposition movement in East Germany, sheltered by the Lutheran Church, made bold to organise itself in September 1989 as New Forum, dedicated to 'the quest for justice, democracy, peace, and the protection of our natural world'.

Into this uneasy situation a catalyst was introduced in the person of Gorbachev himself, when he came to East Berlin in October 1989 for the fortieth anniversary of the German Democratic Republic. Rousing huge crowds to clamour for reform, much as he had done in China in May in the run-up to the Tienanmen massacre, Gorbachev made it clear to the hardline East German government of Erich Honecker that they could not count on Soviet force to keep them in power. Confronted by the opposition's plans for a huge reform demonstration in the city of Leipzig, security chief Egon Krenz obtained Gorbachev's permission to countermand Honecker's orders to put down the protesters by force, and the opposition swelled unchecked. This was the crucial moment for the Revolution, like the fall of the Bastille in France in 1789, when the old regime loses its nerve and the populace loses its fear. At that point, power, which is at bottom psychological, ceases to exist.

After another month of escalating popular protest, mass flight through Hungary and fruitless leadership shake-ups, including the ousting of Honecker, the East German government obtained Gorbachev's assent to ease travel restrictions. On 9 November the East German Politburo voted accordingly, but rumours spread of a more sweeping decision to allow free access to West Berlin, and the border guards yielded to the crowds at the Wall. Thus was this infamous barrier breached by popular revolutionary action. From that point on, the East German regime lost all control; there was nothing left to do but surrender the party dictatorship and allow a coalition government under reform Communist leadership. They put Honecker under house arrest, reorganised the Socialist Unity Party as the Party of Democratic Socialism, and promised free elections for the coming year. This was like the Polish and Hungarian outcomes, but a very temporary one, as it turned out, for East Germany.

After the crisis of East German Communism and the opening of the Berlin Wall, the days of the equally hardline Communist regime in Czechoslovakia were predictably numbered. As in Poland and Hungary, protest demonstrations encouraged by reform in the Soviet Union had escalated throughout 1989, and they leapt out of control after the opening of the Berlin Wall and the fall of Honecker in East Germany. On 17 November, ignoring Moscow's instructions to the contrary, the Czech Communist authorities cracked down violently on a student demonstration in Prague. This proved to be the trigger for a nationwide wave of defiance and strikes, coordinated by anti-Communist dissidents organised as Civic Forum, with the playwright Vaclav Havel at its head. The authority of the isolated hardline government evaporated in this 'Velvet Revolution', and on 10 December a coalition cabinet was formed under the former Communist minister Marian Čalfa, who quit the party in order to accept this new democratic role. The hardline Communist president, Gustav Husak, resigned, and the National Assembly, heretofore a Communist puppet, joined the revolution. It resurrected Dubček to be its chairman, and elected Havel as the new president of the republic. The Communist Party surrendered its privileged role and its Marxist–Leninist ideology. Thus, aimed at a Soviet-created regime that had lost all belief in itself, Czechoslovakia's revolution proved to be the easiest, quickest and most complete of any in Eastern Europe.

Events took a very different course for the independent-minded but hardline Communist government of Romania. Here the old regime did not crack until late in 1989, but then it went fast and violently. Trouble began early in December with protests among the Hungarian minority in western Romania, setting off the familiar dialectic of popular demonstrations and police atrocities. The opposition movement rapidly turned into a real revolution with the defection of the army on 22 December. As the military put down armed resistance on the part of the security police, President Ceauşescu and his wife fled Bucharest, but were captured and executed on 25 December. Romania's dictator and his die-hard supporters, accustomed to ruling without dependence on the Soviet Union, did not lack the will to resist the Revolution, but only the means. Hence their quick but violent overthrow. A self-proclaimed 'Council of National Salvation', led by the reform Communist Ion Iliescu, then took charge with promises of ultimate democratisation.

Bulgaria's outcome was similar to Romania's, though the path it took was much quieter. Bending to the winds of change from Moscow and the rest of Eastern Europe, the Bulgarian Communists simply deposed their Soviet puppet leader Todor Zhivkov, renamed their party 'Socialist', and took their chances – successfully at first – in electoral politics.

Revolutionary decolonisation in Eastern Europe in 1989 was remarkable in several ways. The Soviet imperial power, itself undergoing a critical transformation and weakening of its system of rule, was both unwilling and unable to assert its control over the outer empire as it had in the past. This was an acid test of the Gorbachev regime's commitment to reform. Soviet restraint made possible the extraordinary ease and peacefulness of the 1989 Revolution in most places. Former minions of the Soviet Union, no matter whether hardline or reformist, had little stomach for forcibly holding out on their own against the urge among their peoples to throw off Communist domination. Even more clearly than the ruling officialdom of, say, pre-1789 France or pre-1917 Russia, the East European Communists ceased to believe in themselves. This made it impossible for the Soviet system of control to survive in a reformed mode; it could only be maintained by force or swept away.

Paradoxically, the overthrow of Communist regimes came most smoothly in the countries that had been subservient to the Soviet Union, while it proved to be disruptive and unstable in the more independent Communist countries. Even more distinctly than in the Soviet Union, change in Eastern Europe flowed through the channels offered by the dummy constitutions, parliaments and collaborationist parties that Communist rule had maintained in these countries. Much of the impetus for reform came from critics who surfaced within the various Communist parties, or from anti-Communist dissidents who had survived in the underground, or from the Protestant and Catholic churches (not the Orthodox) which, though often curtailed, had never been suppressed. All these circumstances made the revolution of decolonisation in most of Eastern Europe a decidedly unrevolutionary process in the way it came about. It had a more disturbing impact back in the old imperial centre of Moscow.

The Soviet Union between reform and counter-reform, 1989 to 1991

Simultaneously with decolonisation in Eastern Europe, reform in the Soviet Union went out of control. Attempting to democratise, the Gorbachev government lost its ability to manage the hitherto planned economy and the restiveness of the Soviet national minorities. The events in Eastern Europe in 1989 abruptly sharpened these difficulties, politically by shocking Russian nationalist sensitivities and goading the Soviet minorities on, and economically by disrupting the integrated trade relations between the Soviet Union and its former satellites. The question arose for the

Soviet Union itself as to whether the Communist system was reformable, or whether efforts to overcome its faults would necessarily lead to its complete breakdown.

The Congress of People's Deputies of 1989 opened a Pandora's Box of challenges to Gorbachev's policies. Reformers rallied around Yeltsin to urge faster democratisation, while conservatives protested the lapse of national discipline (though ironically, in openly opposing Gorbachev, they inadvertently contributed to the cause of political pluralism). In these debates, the usual terms for the political spectrum were reversed: the Communist officialdom were the traditionalists, hence considered Right, while the democratic critics of socialism were the radicals, hence thought of as Left.

At the beginning of 1990 Gorbachev forged ahead in the democratic direction, surrendering the Communist Party's political monopoly as a constitutional principle, and holding free elections for the governments of the fifteen union republics. Democrats and minority nationalists prevailed almost everywhere. Yeltsin became head of state in the Russian Republic (as chairman of its Supreme Soviet), with an across-the-board anti-Gorbachev programme – anti-Communist in politics, anti-socialist in economics, and anti-centralist in nationality matters. At the same time, to secure his power base in the Union government against the Communist Party conservatives, Gorbachev had the Union Supreme Soviet elect him to a newly empowered presidency (as distinct from the old figurehead office), but he did not venture to ask for a popular electoral mandate. At the Twenty-eighth Congress of the Communist Party in July 1990 he was able to cow the conservative delegates into further dismantling the powers of the party's Politburo and Secretariat; nonetheless, the radical reformers under Yeltsin's leadership demonstratively quit the party.

Political reform was not good for the Soviet economy, as post-Communist governments discovered as well. In democratising the government, Gorbachev sacrificed the old mechanism of central economic planning and trouble-shooting by the Communist Party organisation, without getting effective market mechanisms of supply and demand and competition into place. At the same time he could not resist populist demands for wage increases. Worsening deficits, already serious when Gorbachev took office, were covered by printing rubles, and controlled prices only invited consumers to clean out the shops while an 'inflationary overhang' of unspent money threatened the economy. There was an eerie parallel here with the fall of the Tsarist regime which, like Andropov and Gorbachev, tried to curb drinking during the First World War, lost the vodka revenues, made up its deficit with the printing press, and suffered a fatally destabilising inflation.

The gathering economic crisis prompted Gorbachev's own State Committee on Economic Reform to seek a radical solution. But, with an eye on the free-market experiments just then being undertaken by the new post-Communist governments in Eastern Europe, reform thinking went further than intended. Economists newly steeped in Anglo-American economic theory drew up a 'Five Hundred Days Plan' of radical reform, to introduce the market and privatise state-owned enterprises: 'No one is to direct or give orders to anyone else', the plan asserted. The proposal was quite utopian, particularly as an emergency measure under Soviet conditions, and Gorbachev rejected it. Yeltsin, on the other hand, endorsed it and made it the basis of his programme after the collapse of the Union government. The plan represented a fundamental paradigm shift in Russian economic thinking, towards the Western classical model of free-market capitalism. Meanwhile, without waiting for legal changes, many state managers *de facto* privatised their own enterprises.

After his rejection of the Five Hundred Days Plan, but still under attack by the Communist conservatives as well as the reformers, Gorbachev reversed his field and retreated from reform. Shrugging off his own supporters' warnings about a return to dictatorship, he reshuffled the government and appointed conservatives as vice-president, prime minister and minister of internal affairs (i.e. police). But the conservatives were not appeased. Then, in the spring of 1991, Gorbachev reversed himself again, backed away from the use of force against the democratic opposition, warned of the conservative threat, and tried to conciliate Yeltsin and the democrats as well as the now virtually independent leaders of the non-Russian republics. This did not work either; Yeltsin got himself popularly elected as president of the Russian Republic, called for sovereignty for all the republics including his own, and consolidated a rival government right alongside the Union government in Moscow. Gorbachev nevertheless browbeat the Communist Central Committee into adopting a new programme that abandoned Marxist–Leninist doctrine, party discipline and the idea of the dictatorship of the proletariat. He prepared a new Union Treaty giving the republics the sovereign rights they demanded. All this was too much for the Communist conservatives, and they prepared to strike.

Early in the morning of 19 August 1991, a self-proclaimed 'State Committee on the Emergency Situation', including the very same men whom Gorbachev had just brought to the top, ordered martial law in Moscow and put the vacationing president under house arrest. The *coup* was woefully ill prepared, however, and it failed even to suppress Yeltsin's Russian government; the headquarters of the Russian Supreme Soviet, the White House, became the dramatic centre of popular resistance, galvanised by Yeltsin's bold appearance on the tank to defy the plotters. Elsewhere in the country, local authority took a wait-and-see stance; as in so many revolutions, control of the capital city would decide the outcome.

In critical revolutionary situations like Moscow in August 1991, everything depends on the mood and resolve of the armed forces. In this case the command wavered, and the plotters lost their nerve; the expected assault on the White House never came. On the morning of 21 August the troops pulled out of Moscow and the *coup* leaders gave up; Gorbachev was freed to return to the capital, while his enemies were put under arrest. Ostensibly, Gorbachev was back in power, but the events of the *coup* had shattered the psychological base of his authority. Yeltsin subjected Gorbachev to a public humiliation – revenge for 1987 – and proceeded to sabotage the Union president's efforts to save his office. Well before the end of the Soviet Union, Gorbachev's rule was reduced to a mere fiction.

Revolutionary decolonisation, II: The breakup of the Soviet Union

Most spectacular of all the elements of Communism's collapse, and most important in its impact on world politics, was the dissolution of the Soviet Union following the failed conservative *coup* of August 1991. The reasons for the cataclysm lay deep in the ethnic fault lines of Soviet society, and of the Russian Empire before that, but political reform under Gorbachev brought them visibly to the surface. The Soviet breakup may not have been as inevitable as the evaporation of Communist power in Eastern Europe, but its results were equally irreversible. Ethnic solidarities and animosities proved to be the most powerful of all forces driving the post-Communist revolutions.

There was ample twentieth-century precedent for the breakup of the Soviet Empire, including the abandonment of their overseas empires by Britain and France and the dismantling of the contiguous but multinational empires of the Austrian Habsburgs and the Ottoman Turks, not to mention temporary decolonisation in the Russian Empire after 1917. Post-Communist decolonisation in the Soviet Union was unusual, however, in taking place without the defeat of the colonial power by outside enemies, and almost without violence in the relations between the Union government and its rebelling subjects. (Ethnic violence within the various Soviet successor states was another matter.)

Trouble began as soon as Gorbachev opened up free political discussion and electoral campaigning between 1988 and 1989. So-called popular fronts sprang up to advance the local nationalist cause, and in many areas they defeated official Communist candidates in the 1989 elections. The local elections of March 1990 allowed the separatists to take control in the Baltics, Armenia, Georgia and the western Ukraine; they immediately proclaimed their 'sovereignty' and disputed the applicability of federal laws. All this occurred, interestingly, within the republic boundaries established by the Soviet regime, as the dummy federalism of the old Soviet Union came to life.

Violence during this time of nationalist upsurge was only sporadic. Most serious was armed conflict between Armenia and Azerbaidzhan over the status of the Armenian minority in Azerbaidzhan and the Armenian-speaking enclave of Nagorno-Karabakh. A crackdown by the central authorities on Georgian nationalist demonstrators in Tbilisi in April 1989 poisoned nationality relations everywhere, and tarnished the reformist image of the Gorbachev regime. Bloody attacks by security police on the nationalists in Lithuania and Latvia in January 1991 shocked the world. But even during Gorbachev's brief turn back towards the conservatives, Moscow showed no systematic will or ability to suppress separatism by force, just as it had failed to do in Eastern Europe in 1989.

Separatism in the non-Russian republics was powerfully abetted by the government of the Russian Republic after Yeltsin took control of it in 1990. Yeltsin joined the other republics in claiming sovereignty for Russia against the Union government, an odd demand considering that the Soviet Union was really Russia writ large: Russia could hardly be independent against itself. The real issue was that the Union government represented Russian domination over the non-Russians, whereas sovereignty for the Russian Republic was an endorsement of sovereignty for all the others as well, in other words, decolonisation. Behind this division, in turn, was the rivalry between the two governments in Moscow, Union and Russian, driven by the personal feud between their respective leaders.

Gorbachev's Union Treaty was about to be signed when the *coup* plotters struck in August, citing the disintegration of the Union as their most serious concern. But the *coup* and its failure put an end to effective Union authority over the republics, Russia included. Yeltsin actually took it upon himself to ban the Communist Party on Russian territory. Gorbachev struggled for a time with various schemes to salvage some role for the Union, though by now he had lost control of tax revenues and could only support Union functions – including the military – by printing more money. The denouement came with ridiculous ease: Yeltsin, President Leonid Kravchuk of Ukraine and President Stanislas Shushkevich of Belarus, meeting secretly at the government hunting camp of Belovezhsk in Belarus on 8 December 1991, proclaimed the liquidation of the USSR and its replacement by a nebulous 'Commonwealth of Independent States'. This was the real *coup*. Gorbachev was left with no choice but to abdicate his empty presidency, which he did on 25 December, and the Soviet Union ceased to exist. All the former Soviet republics were cut loose to fend for themselves, economically as well as diplomatically, whether they had fought for this new freedom or, in the case of the Central Asian republics, accepted it reluctantly.

Post-Communist Russia

The crisis of 1991 was not the end of Russia's post-Communist transformation, but only the mid-point. With the fall of Gorbachev and the breakup of the Soviet Union, the experiment in a Left variant of the moderate revolutionary revival had failed, and a more disruptive, Right variant ensued under Yeltsin. Emerging from the August *coup* with an aura of charismatic legitimacy, Yeltsin had virtually unlimited power to determine Russia's subsequent development. His decisions were mainly shaped by the anti-Communist, anti-socialist and anti-Union positions that he had embraced in his duel with Gorbachev.

Yeltsin took the step of abolishing the USSR in December without any legal authority or consultation with his Russian legislators, among whom this abrupt act of decolonisation did not rest easy. He and his prime minister, the free-market economic theorist Yegor Gaidar, then launched the programme of privatising state-owned enterprises, and simultaneously decreed the end of most price controls, unleashing galloping inflation. These steps gave the Supreme Soviet second thoughts about Yeltsin. Under their new chairman, Ruslan Khasbulatov, who had actually been hand-picked by Yeltsin, the Russian legislators rebelled against the Right variant of post-revolutionry reform, in a struggle that came to a head in the spring of 1993. The legislators tried to impeach the president, but Yeltsin defied the move, won a referendum of popular approval, and in September ordered the Supreme Soviet to be dissolved, an extra-constitutional move under the law at that time. When the legislators barricaded themselves in the White House and drew the support of Communist and nationalist rioters, Yeltsin accused them of attempting an uprising, and ordered an assault with tanks to liquidate parliamentary resistance. Thus, at the same locale as the August 1991 confrontation, the sides were reversed, but this time victory was on the side of the attackers.

From this moment on, guided as he was by a sense of the presidency as above politics like the Tsar in the semi-constitutional monarchy between 1905 and 1917, Yeltsin ruled essentially by decree. Ignoring the noisy parliamentary opposition, he stubbornly pursued the theory of free-market economics, even though inflation, underemployment and non-payment of wages impoverished the mass of Russians everywhere outside of Moscow itself. Crime and corruption escalated, and a new oligarchy of financial barons, accumulating wealth from privatised natural resources, governmental largess and sheer speculation, took control of the key economic positions. This was Russia's post-Communist outcome, until the financial crisis of 1998 reversed the political pendulum and turned the country back in the direction, perhaps, of a compromise between the Right – Yeltsinite – and Left – Gorbachevian – variants of the post-revolutionary settlement.

In most of the other CIS states political and economic circumstances turned out no better than in Russia. In the Muslim republics of Central Asia, the end of the Soviet Union left the former Communist bosses in power and paradoxically diminished the prospects for democracy. The Baltic States, by contrast, firmly embraced democracy, though it was constricted in Estonia and Latvia by a reluctance to give full civil rights to their large Russian-speaking minorities. Ukraine mirrored Russia in its political tensions and economic troubles, while Belarus, weak in its sense of national identity, sought reunification with Russia, and the newly independent countries of Transcaucasia were torn apart by civil and ethnic strife. Economically, excluding the more Western-oriented Baltics, the whole of the CIS sank along with Russia.

Meanwhile, the CIS functioned less and less as an entity. By the mid-1990s the decolonisation of Russia's inner empire had become as irreversible as the loss of Soviet control over Eastern Europe. Russia had not only lost the superpower status enjoyed by the Soviet Union, but had virtually ceased to be a major player on the world scene.

Eastern Europe after Communism

In most cases the East European countries managed their paths out of Communism far better than Russia or the other Soviet successor states. They implemented democratic government more consistently, reformed their economies with less disruption, and handled their ethnic problems reasonably. The sad exception was Yugoslavia, lapsing into a vicious civil war and new authoritarianisms.

As in its challenge to Communist rule, Poland led the region in the pace and smoothness of democratisation and economic reform. Hungary and Czechoslovakia were close behind, though Czechoslovakia was pre-occupied by the tension between the Czech and Slovak portions of the country that led in January 1993 to the peaceful division of the country between those two ethnic elements. In Romania, Bulgaria and Albania, adjustment to the fall of Communist power was slower and more difficult. East Germany, created by Soviet occupation, lost its *raison d'être* when the Soviet Union abandoned its outer empire. Gorbachev acceded to the East German clamour for a merger of the two Germanys, and by the treaty of reunification of September 1990 East Germany was formally absorbed into the Federal Republic.

Yugoslavia was the great tragedy of post-Communist Eastern Europe, the more so because it was the country that had enjoyed the greatest degree of reform and independence from Soviet domination almost from the inception of Communist rule there. If decolonisation affected Yugoslavia, it was in Belgrade's relations with the six 'republics' and two 'autonomous regions' that Tito had set up to reflect the country's ethnic diversity. The individual republics were more interested in national self-assertion than in a reformed federation, and the country inexorably dissolved into internecine war, quelled only by Western intervention.

Throughout, in Eastern Europe as well as in the former Soviet republics, the empty democratic forms that the Communist governments had maintained for propaganda purposes took on surprising importance in shaping the course of revolutionary change and the political character of the outcome. Paper constitutions became the framework for democratic reform. Communist parliaments, with or without renovation of their personnel, repudiated the old and backed the new. Puppet non-Communist parties that had been retained in most East European countries swung at critical times to back anti-Communist reformers. Artificial federal systems became the basis for national independence movements without modifying their provincial boundaries.

Political forces instrumental in toppling Communist Party rule included in the first instance oppositional elements within those parties themselves. It appears that many East European Communists, left to themselves without Soviet dictation, were not unhappy to be rid of Soviet-style totalitarianism. To this force were added non-Communist dissidents who had survived earlier repression, youth elements too young to have been cowed by the totalitarian past, and west of the cultural divide, the churches. In most parts of the region, following the Revolution, ex-Communists remained legal and active in the democratic framework, and even won elections.

All these circumstances contributed to making the anti-Communist revolutions quite unrevolutionary in form, however revolutionary their consequences. For Eastern Europe it was a massive reflex of decolonisation when the opportunity presented itself. Back in the Soviet Union, Eastern Europe's defiant example helped destabilise Gorbachev's attempt to reform the Old Order, by radicalising both the reformers and their conservative opposite numbers.

In terms of the geopolitical map of Europe, the decolonisation of the Soviet bloc created a huge power vacuum. The Russian successor government had neither the resources nor the psychological attractiveness to maintain any influence in the region, which was driven towards the West in every way – politically, economically, strategically – by its reaction against the experience of Soviet Communist imperialism. In sum, the strategic consequences of the anti-Communist overturns in Eastern Europe and the Soviet Union amounted to a geopolitical disaster for Russia unmatched for any country not crushed in a war, and a total realignment, formal or otherwise, of the entire region lying between Russia and its traditional Western enemies.

All revolutions bequeath great changes in the fabric of their respective societies, but no revolution alters everything. Measured against the ultimate results of the classic revolutions of history, the anti-Communist overturns in the Soviet Union and Eastern Europe changed their respective countries dramatically, as revolutions go, leaving of course those deep cultural continuities that shape a nation's behaviour and destiny whatever surface upheavals may pass by.

The anti-Communist revolutions were more than anything else a triumph of ethnic identity, for better or worse. Even Russia became a more purely ethnic state once the union republics were let go, though significant (and often troublesome) ethnic minorities remained within the Russian Federation. Democracy and capitalism were embraced above all for the negative reason that they were not Soviet. Little wonder that years of difficulty faced the countries of the region as they tried to assimilate what their revolutions had accomplished.

Chronology

(In Russia/Soviet Union unless otherwise noted)

1905		Russian Revolution of 1905; semi-constitutional monarchy.
1917		February Revolution; fall of Tsar Nicholas II; Provisional Government.
		October Revolution; Soviet republic,
1918	March	Treaty of Brest-Litovsk.
	November	Armistice; Poland and Baltic States independent.
		Russian civil war and 'War Communism'.
1921–28		New Economic Policy (NEP).
1922		USSR formed (implemented 1924).
1928–29		Stalin dictator; 'revolution from above'.
1936–38		Purges.
1939	August	German–Soviet Non-aggression Pact.
1939–45		Second World War; Soviet annexation of eastern Poland, south-east Finland, Baltic States and Moldavia, 1939–40; German invasion of USSR, June 1941; German surrender, May 1945.
1945–47		Communist takeovers in Eastern Europe.
1948	February	Communist *coup* in Czechoslovakia.
	June	Soviet–Yugoslav break.
1949		'German Democratic Republic' established.
1953	March	Death of Stalin.
	June	East German uprising.
1955		Warsaw Pact.
1956	February	'De-Stalinisation' under Khrushchev.
	October	Poland: Gomułka restored.
	October–November	Hungarian Revolution, Soviet intervention.
1961	August	Berlin Wall.
1964	October	Fall of Khrushchev, Brezhnev General Secretary.
1968	August	Prague Spring in Czechoslovakia, Soviet intervention.

1979–80		Poland: Solidarity trade union movement; martial law (December 1980).
1982	November	Death of Brezhnev; Andropov General Secretary.
1984	February	Death of Andropov; Chernenko General Secretary.
1985	March	Death of Chernenko; Gorbachev General Secretary, begins *perestroika*.
1986	April	Chernobyl disaster; Gorbachev begins *glasnost*.
1987	January	Gorbachev begins democratisation of Communist Party.
1988	April	Soviet withdrawal from Afghanistan.
	September	'September Revolution'; Gorbachev defeats Communist conservatives.
1989	March	Election of Congress of People's Deputies.
	April	Tbilisi massacre.
	May	Poland: Roundtable agreement on free elections, Solidarity wins (June).
	August	Mazowiecki (Solidarity) prime minister of Poland.
	September	Hungary: Trilateral agreement on democracy.
	October	East Germany: demonstrations allowed.
	November	Berlin Wall opened; reform government.
	November– December	Czechoslovakia: 'Velvet Revolution'.
	December	Romania: overthrow of Çeauşescu.
1990	February	Communist Party of the Soviet Union gives up monopoly.
	March	Gorbachev elected president by Supreme Soviet.
		Election of republic parliaments; 'Popular Front' victories.
	May	Yeltsin chairman of Supreme Soviet of Russia
	July	Twenty-eighth Party Congress; Politburo weakened, Yeltsin quits.
	August– September	500 Days Economic Reform Plan.
	September	Germany reunified.
	December	Gorbachev appoints conservatives.
1991	January	Vilnius massacre.
	March	Democracy demonstration; Gorbachev rejects repression.
	April	Agreement on new Union Treaty.

	June	Yeltsin elected president of Russian Federation. Yugoslav wars of secession begin.
	July	Last Central Committee plenum, new democratic programme.
	August	Failed hardline *coup*.
	December	Soviet Union dissolved, Commonwealth of Independent States proclaimed; Gorbachev resigns.
1992	January	Yeltsin decontrols prices, starts privatisation.
1993	January	Czechoslovakia divided.
	September– October	Yeltsin dissolves Russian Parliament, suppresses resistance.

Further reading

Ivo Banac (ed.), *Eastern Europe in Revolution*, Ithaca and London, 1992.

Michael Cox (ed.), *Rethinking the Soviet Collapse: Sovietology, the Death of Communism and the New Russia*, London and New York, 1998.

Ralf Dahrendorf, *Reflections on the Revolution in Europe*, London, 1990.

Robert V. Daniels, *A Documentary History of Communism* (3rd edn) (2 vols), Hanover, NH, and London, 1993.

Robert V. Daniels, *The End of the Communist Revolution*, London and New York, 1993.

Timothy Garton Ash, *The Magic Lantern*, New York, 1990.

Jerry Hough, *Democratization and Revolution in the USSR, 1985–91*, Washington, DC, 1997.

H. Lyman Letgers (ed.), *Eastern Europe: Transformation and Revolution, 1945–1991*, Lexington, MA, and Toronto, 1992.

Raymond Pearson, *The Rise and Fall of the Soviet Empire*, New York, 1998.

Gale Stokes, *The Walls Came Tumbling Down: The Collapse of Communism in Eastern Europe*, New York and Oxford, 1993.

Stephen White, *Gorbachev and After*, Cambridge and New York, 1991.

Index

HOW HAVE FOUR CENTURIES OF REVOLUTIONS DEFINED THE SHAPE OF MODERN EUROPE?

Revolutions and the Revolutionary Tradition presents eight European case studies including the English revolution of 1649, the French Revolution and the recent revolutions within the Soviet Union and Eastern Europe (1989–1991) and examines them not only in their specific political, economic and social contexts but also as part of the wider European revolutionary tradition. A chapter on the American Revolution is also included as a revolution which grew out of European expansion and European political culture.

Revolutions and the Revolutionary Tradition brings together a prestigious group of leading historians, who make a major contribution to the controversial debate on the role of revolution in the development of European history. *Revolutions and the Revolutionary Tradition* is a truly comparative book which includes discussion on each of the following key themes:

• *the causes of revolution, including the importance of political, social and economic factors*
• *the effects of political and philosophical ideas or ideology on revolution*
• *the form and process of a revolution, including the importance of violence and popular support*
• *the outcome of revolution, both short-term and long-term*
• *the way revolution is viewed in history particularly since the collapse of Communism in Europe*

As well as providing new historical perspectives on the concept of revolution, this book also provides a comparative survey of all the major revolutions in the West over the past 400 years. *Revolutions and the Revolutionary Tradition* will be essential reading for students and scholars alike.

David Parker is Senior Lecturer in Modern History at the University of Leeds

Contributors: Colin Bonwick, John Breuilly, Robert V. Daniels, Dick Geary, Roger Griffin, Ann Hughes, Gwynne Lewis, Maureen Perrie, W. A. Speck, Marjolein 't Hart, C. J. Wrigley

HISTORY/POLITICAL PHILOSOPHY

ROUTLEDGE
Taylor & Francis Group

11 New Fetter Lane
London EC4P 4EE
29 West 35th Street
New York NY 10001
www.routledge.com
Printed in Great Britain

ISBN 0-415-17295-0

9 780415 172950

Cover illustrations: (top front) The Parisian market, women marching to Versailles, 5 Oct. 1789 (Second march of the Sansculottes), 'A Versailles! A Versailles!' (bottom front) Revolution 1848/49. 'Erection of barricades May 1849.' (back cover) Boston, 16 December 1773, 'Boston Tea party'. ©AKG Photo
Cover design: Leigh Hurlock